NEGOTIATING CONFLICT IN LEBANON

Bordering Practices in a Divided Beirut

MOHAMAD HAFEDA

I.B. TAURIS
LONDON · NEW YORK

To the two poles of the journey: Marya and Karim, and my grandmother Fayza.

CONTENTS

4   INTRODUCTION:
Bordering Practices

ADMINISTRATION
36   Bordering Practice 01: Hiding
The Chosen Two

SURVEILLANCE
102   Bordering Practice 02: Crossing
At Her Balcony

SOUND
158   Bordering Practice 03: Translating
*This is How Stories of Conflict Circulate
and Resonate*

DISPLACEMENT
208   Bordering Practice 04: Matching
The Twin Sisters are 'About to' Swap Houses

258   EPILOGUE:
Temporal Bordering Practices of Resistance

266   ENDNOTES

273   BIBLIOGRAPHY

278   LIST OF FIGURES

280   LIST OF INTERVIEWS

281   ACKNOWLEDGEMENTS

284   INDEX

Introduction:
Bordering Practices

Fig.01
Demarcation line: Mazraa Main Road.

On 23 January 2007 Beirut woke up to the eruption of sectarian violence. On that day a general strike was implemented in Lebanon by the 8 March bloc with the aim of bringing down the government of the 14 March bloc, these having been the two rival political blocs in the country since 2005. Young men took control of the streets, changing the material arrangement of political and social life: they blocked roads with burning tyres and sand from construction sites, and they created human barriers to sever main roads and to prevent pedestrians from passing to get to their jobs. The events led to confrontations and violent clashes between supporters of the rival blocs on the streets of Beirut, and to the emergence of demarcation lines cutting across neighbourhoods. One of the major demarcation lines was the Mazraa Main Road separating Tarik Al Jdide from Mazraa area.

A couple of days after the Lebanese army had cleared the roadblocks, I followed the traces of the burning tyres on the streets and pavements. I was looking to learn about and piece together the new political and sectarian map of power and segregation drawn by the remaining black fumes. It was a task that proved to be difficult, primarily because of the intricacy and intertwining of the demarcation lines created by the mix of communities and political parties in the city, but also due to the fear I felt while wandering the streets with my camera among groups of angry men.

However, the key questions this event raised for me, especially after the material evidence of violence had been cleared away – the evidence that I had been attempting to follow – were: What is a border made of, and where, how, and when is it created? Can it disappear and, if so, what happens afterwards? With these questions in mind, I started to consider how borders transform, and are transformed by, the lives of residents and city spaces. Not able to quite grasp the fluctuating border, I embarked on the current site-specific practice-led research project that I now present.

Fig.02 (Here and Overleaf)
Photographs taken from residents' interior spaces, asking them about the trace
left of violent clashes and physical borders, *The Trace Series*, 2010-present.

INTRODUCTION

Negotiating Conflict in Lebanon: Bordering Practices in a Divided Beirut offers an alternative way of thinking about borders. It moves away from considering borders simply as artefacts that produce physical division in the form of walls and fences, and towards an understanding of how borders are produced as forms of material and creative processes and practices embedded in the every-day life of city dwellers.

In what follows, I will examine bordering practices in the context of Beirut's political–sectarian conflict. This involves studying the impact of existing borders on residents' lives. I explore the spatial practices produced by borders – practices that are used by residents to negotiate the borders – and I discuss the borders that residents construct as passive and active modes of resistance. At the heart of this book is the idea that bordering practices are specific kinds of spatial practice. These practices are played out through processes of negotiation and narration, and they amount to political strategies and tactics that relate to everyday life (and to research and writing on everyday life and on critical spatial practice).[1] My focus is on the immateriality, spatiality, and temporality of these bordering practices in the everyday spaces of the contested city of Beirut.

My project engaged actively in sites of civil conflict by working with residents of the city. This involved negotiating the political constraints that affect urban space and the spaces of residents within the city. The research methods and media used to conduct the project, and the representations produced out of the research, relate to the political conditions of the border under investigation. Consequently, the book proposes a method of negotiating, one that considers how artistic research can itself be considered as a form of critical spatial prac-tice and, in particular, a bordering practice. This enables the rethinking of border positions, including those between disciplines – such as between practice and theory, art and social science – and between spatial conditions – such as between private and public, interior and exterior. Ultimately, as I will argue, this rethinking potentially leads to the transformation of certain border positions, such as the divisive positions of dominant narratives.

Thus, *Negotiating Conflict in Lebanon* aims to extend the definition of bordering practice from the sociological use of the term,[2] to include the bordering practices of research and art. It focuses on the capacity of artistic research processes to propose spatial alternatives to borders and to critically reflect upon their own bordering activities.

The particular modes of bordering practices that I explore are:

> those produced by conflict mechanisms, negotiated and narrated by residents, such as the demarcation lines and security checkpoints that emerged in Beirut in 2005;

those negotiated and narrated through my engagement with residents of Beirut, such as the taking of photographs of surveillance from two women's balconies and the recording of political sounds from taxi drivers' cars;

and those negotiated and narrated through the art installations I produced in response to my investigations of Beirut's bordering practices.

The book is structured into four projects, and these constitute the borders of its four chapters: *Administration*, *Surveillance*, *Sound*, and *Displacement*. Each chapter identifies strategic divisions and their associated border conditions as practised by political parties; then it investigates residents' spatial practices and how they exist as responses and negotiations to the strategic divisions; and, finally, it considers how these practices transform borders into multiple shifting practices and representations that divide *and* connect through acts of negotiation and narration. In particular, I look at the following practices of bordering: in *The Chosen Two*, *hiding* behind the border of administration between an elected district's representative and his fictional television character; in *At Her Balcony*, *crossing* the border of surveillance between two women at their balconies; in *This is How Stories of Conflict Circulate and Resonate*, *translating* the border of sound between riding in a taxi and walking journeys; and in *The Twin Sisters are 'About to' Swap Houses*, *matching* the border of displacement between twin sisters and their husbands.

BORDERING AS A POLITICAL–SECTARIAN PRACTICE

Civil unrest in Lebanon resurfaced after the assassination of former prime minister, Rafic Hariri, on 14 February 2005. The assassination led to the withdrawal of Syrian troops from Lebanon in May 2005, thirty years after their arrival in the country. These events polarized the country and resulted in the formation of two main political blocs: the pro-Syrian 8 March bloc, which was allied with Iran, and the 14 March bloc, which accused the Syrian regime of carrying out the assassination and was allied with Saudi Arabia and the West.[3] The names of the two blocs reflect the split in space, communities and dates, since they refer to the two demonstrations that took place within the space of a week in adjacent public plazas in Beirut Central District.[4] The events took on a sectarian dimension because of the political schism between Sunnis and Shiites, the former supporting the Mustaqbal movement, the party created by Hariri, and the latter being supporting Hezbollah, which was allied with the Syrians; Christians were also divided between political alliances with one or other of the two Muslim parties.[5]

The spatial manifestation of the 2007 sectarian violence (mentioned at the beginning of this introduction) came after a long period of political turmoil between

Fig.03
Collage of the gradual intensification and transformation
of bordering practices, 2005-8.

the parties. Exacerbated by the Israeli war on Lebanon (2006) that deepened the internal political divisions in the country due to conflicting assessment of the causes and aftermath of the war, the sectarian conflict in Lebanon has gradually transformed from demonstrations (2005) and long sit-ins (2006–2008) to street fights, demarcation lines (2007), street bombings, assassinations, and armed clashes known as the May 7 events (2008). After the government's decision to remove the group's telephone network, Hezbollah and their allies took to the streets of Beirut on 7 May and fought with other armed groups from the 14 March bloc; within a few hours, Hezbollah declared control over the city (Fig. 03).

Yet the reason for referring to the event on *23 January 2007*, out of many other possible events in an investigation into borders, is that it is illustrative. It provides a material example against which to position a discussion of the immateriality of borders, in relation to spatial practices and the emotional and social experience of residents who encounter these borders. Moreover, this date marked a particular spatial pattern of the sectarian manifestation of the political conflict in the streets; it revived memories of civil war clashes and the subsequent creation of borders (demarcation lines) that divided both Lebanon and Beirut along the Green Line from 1975 to 1990 into a predominantly Muslim west and a Christian east, with further sectarian, political and class divisions on either side of the line (Fig. 04). Revealing the sectarian demography of the city, that event indicated that segregation of different communities would increase in the following period as fears increased about a new sectarian war appearing on the horizon.

I refer to the ongoing Lebanese conflict as political–sectarian in order to propose that the dialectic of politics and religion produces social life. The political–sectarian bordering practice across the history of Lebanon is evident through the recurrence of conflict and the persistence of sectarianism, yet with every new cycle of violence, new lines of geographic and political divisions and alliances, as well as new spatial practices, emerge. Ussama Makdisi defines sectarianism (*Taifiyya*) in the Lebanese context as a modern invention that deploys religious politics for political and social purposes.[6] For Makdisi, sectarianism has been institutionalized in the Lebanese political system since the rise of the republic in 1943, when European powers and local elites divided authority and official positions according to religious affiliation and among the various sects.[7] He explains how the politics of sectarianism was adopted by militias during the 1975–90 civil war, loosening social ties and leading to the territorialization of the different groups' sectarian identities in urban space, which continues to be evident in present times.[8] It is this spatiality of sectarianism and its practices in urban space in the current conflict that I explore in this book.

When I began my research, my aim was to investigate the impact of the political situation on residents' spatial practices and everyday life, and to examine the interplay between material and immaterial borders. I asked: What bordering practices of the political–sectarian conflict exist in urban space? And: How do the bordering practices of art and research operate in urban space in their attempt to negotiate, document, transform and narrate the conflict mechanisms

Fig.04
Map of the civil war division across the Green Line.

and borders? Residents directed me to invisible borders that even I, a resident of Beirut for 30 years, had never noticed in local neighbourhoods, despite the visibility and boldness of the spatiality of the conflict and the borders it has made manifest in urban space.

When W.A., for example, looked at the pine tree outside her living space, she re-called the rocket-propelled grenade fired from the adjacent neighbourhood that had passed through the tree and her line of sight. A.A. told me she had removed her husband's surname, and hence any clue about his sectarian background and political affiliation, from the intercom at the building entrance to prevent any possible harassment. I.A. looked at the television monitor in her shop and talked to me about the censorship imposed by the satellite provider who had removed a particular TV channel due to the provider's opposition to its political affilia-tions. I saw how H.S.'s balcony was being used to hang political banners across the street by the dominant political party in her area; she was contemplating freeing the balcony balustrade to disrupt this tradition and improve her own visual horizon, which was impeded by the banner. In the course of my research, S.H. stopped visiting her sister in the adjacent neighbourhood, fearing that her daughter might be harassed by the militia members who patrol the streets. These practices deployed and experienced by residents in different neighbourhoods of the city are manifestations of how political–sectarian borderings impose constraints on their mobility, their social interactions with family and friends, their decisions about where to live, and their future plans (Fig. 02). These invoke violent memories inscribed in present time–space, anxiety, myth and censorship.

My work with these residents highlighted central themes that provide insights into current bordering practices in contemporary Beirut, especially those related to specific borders connected with administration, surveillance, sound, and displacement. The border conditions I study in this book vary in the tactics and strategies utilized to negotiate urban space and to construct a border that ranges from the material to the immaterial.

The immaterial borders of administration, for example, manage the everyday life of residents and materially shape the urban space through forms of representation and procedure. The borders of administration are contested and manifest a discrepancy between the reality of an urban space and its past and present representation. These borders are implemented by state institutions and challenged by the actions of political parties and the lived experience of residents. They are everywhere and nowhere, and they provide the urban framework in which everyday bordering practices operate.

In addition, I discuss the expansion of the borders of surveillance in city spaces. Surveillance is the political observation of individuals by the members of political parties. Its apparatuses are materially fixed in urban nodes for direct control, and its gaze crosses the private spaces and lives of residents through a reach that is both immaterial and emotional. These borders result in residents' self-surveillance of their own daily practices.

Equally effective is the way in which sound produces borders. Sound is mobile and short-lived, and it travels invisibly across divided sectarian geographies. Sound and sonic practices, such as political–sectarian songs, speeches and fireworks, are employed as confrontational immaterial borders in Beirut to embed specific sonic content in the ears of others. Sound is also used by political parties' members and supporters at times of retreat and reduced tension, when it becomes a substitute for violent encounters and the physical occupation of space.

Displacement, in the current Lebanese conflict context, can be defined as the voluntary movement of residents from one area to another in order to match their political affiliation with where they live. This self-displacement takes place within family social structures and real estate routes. If compared to the visibility of forced displacement of refugees, for example, the movement of self-displacement is invisible at an urban scale. Notwithstanding its invisibility, however, it is a bordering practice 'suggested' or indirectly forced by political leaders onto residents who perform it, and it is one that confirms the ultimate state of division of people and geography.

BORDERING AS A CRITICAL AND SPATIAL PRACTICE

The subject of borders within the city of Beirut requires a close investigation into the current spatial practices of its dwellers, specifically defined as residents, politicians and political parties/militias. These are the border practitioners I study in this research. The list could be expanded to include the army and the private sector and I will refer to other groups as well when required. These border practitioners are involved in shaping everyday life at times of conflict with varying power positions, and they engage in bordering practices in different capacities and modes of participation in the city of Beirut. For these people, borders are tools for configuring urban spaces along political and religious lines and for segregating and differentiating different uses of space. But borders are also the site of counter practices – tactical and/or critical – through which residents resist and negotiate political strategies of conflict as part of everyday life.

In their work on various practices that relate to power, Henri Lefebvre and Michel de Certeau consider spatial practices to be closely tied to the production of everyday life and lived experience. De Certeau describes a distinction between spatial practices in terms of strategy and tactics produced respectively by those in power and those who occupy positions of resistance,[9] while Lefebvre contrasts the practices of those in power with the passivity of users' practices – a passivity that can sometimes give way to dramatic subversion of the power relationship.[10] Other types of practice, termed by Jane Rendell as critical spatial practices, offer critiques of a society's mode of practice. Critical spatial practices explore the border as a potential space between theory and practice, between art and architecture, and between public and private. Such practices take the form of everyday tactics, as well as site-specific art and design projects that are both spatial and critical in their aim for social and political change.[11] For Rendell, critical spatial practices aim to reflect on the spatial conditions, situations and experiences through which they are produced, and to offer alternatives to the existing political situations and modes of binary thinking.[12]

The bordering practices that this project investigates and produces do not all belong to the same category. I define bordering practices as practices that construct material and immaterial borders as part of the socio-spatial interaction between individuals in time, as well as those practices that negotiate the splits created by existing borders by crossing and transforming them. This lends a more conceptual dimension to the notion of bordering practices; hence, while some bordering practices intend division and segregation, others seek to work across borders, to critique them, and to change them – or what I term critical bordering practice. Thus, critical bordering practice addresses the condition of borders, is critical of them, and aims to transform certain border positions. Specifically, I explore the possibilities that, in times of conflict, the critical bordering practices of research and art can operate as sites of resistance in everyday life by negotiating the bordering practices of political conflict. My project involved producing artwork as just such a critical bordering practice.

Throughout my research I have been gathering and documenting a 'List of Bordering Practices'. These bordering practices vary in the ways in which they occupy spaces – their locations, durations, materials and uses, and in the specifics of their practitioners. Some are located in fixed urban nodes – for example, the positioning of posters, monuments and street-corner gatherings; some involve transportable objects – for example, wearable accessories and gadgets, and aural and mobile practices such as fireworks, songs and political speeches in cars; and some are located on temporary demarcation lines that separate areas – for example, barricades of street objects, tyres and sand hills.

These bordering practices emerged gradually in Beirut and each political event associated with them gave rise to a practice that in turn suggested another prac-tice, and so on. Responses to political and violent acts – whether a politician's speech, a demonstration or a bomb – might include, for example, motorcycle convoys cruising the streets, flags being hung on balconies and windows to show affiliation, or people going into the streets at night to protect the neighbourhood. To take another example: men smoking the hubble-bubble (*arguilé*), in men-only cafés or outside shops, is a common activity in the country; in the current conflict, this activity has been utilized to self-secure neighbourhoods from possible 'invasions' by outsiders or to monitor the street against the setting up of explosives at night.[13] The spatial practice of smoking *arguilé* on the street has been displaced from the social context that produced it; instead, it is used as a bordering practice for a different political purpose in the conflict. Such security practices were suggested by the leaders of political parties, who capitalized on civilians' fear and their desire to participate in protecting their neighbourhoods; later, these practices were formalized or legitimized. In the absence of state protection, the security of neighbourhoods justified civilians being armed for self-protection; this, in turn, confirmed the use of arms in the public space and in some places the practice was a camouflage for military training by armed groups.[14]

De Certeau makes a distinction between spatial practice as a tactic and strategy, and their association with space and place, that can help explore further the spatiality of bordering practices mentioned above and their political dimension. Spatial practice as a tactic is the domain of users who do not have a '"proper" spatial or institutional localization';[15] spatial practice as a strategy is the domain of those of 'will and power'[16] who own a '"proper" place or institution'[17] from which they operate. De Certeau argues that tactics 'constantly manipulate events in order to turn them into "opportunities"',[18] and that these tactics of consumption 'in which the weak make use of the strong, ... lend a political dimension to everyday practices'.[19] He also differentiates between space and place: 'space is a practiced place',[20] is fluid, and is an 'intersection of mobile elements' set in time;[21] whereas place 'delimits a field',[22] is static like geometry, and is a fixed urban location as well as institutions and disciplines.[23] De Certeau argues that tactics as practices transform '"places" into "spaces"', commenting that 'a tactic insinuates itself into the other's place, fragmentarily, without taking it over in its entirety, without being able to keep it at a distance'.[24] In relation to borders and the formation of the other, he proposes that space produces tactics and forms the 'other', yet without creating a fixed boundary or a border, and without domination of either of the actors involved.[25] In this respect, the power of a tactic as a bordering practice is in occupying and manipulating a space without fixation and while transcending the limits of both places and spaces.

De Certeau's theory allows us to highlight two categories of bordering practices: tactical bordering practices that are interested in 'space' occupation/manipulation and transportable (transient and ephemeral) borderings, and as such have a critical capacity for change; and strategic bordering practices that are interested in 'place' acquisition and fixed borders, and as such institutionalize the border into a fixed political logic that replaces the process of negotiation.

A different way of considering how to negotiate between borders and bordering and their material and immaterial interplays is offered by Lefebvre's theory of space, as outlined in the *Production of Space*. Lefebvre proposes a twofold spatial triad to explain space as a 'social product',[26] consisting of 'spatial practices', 'representations of space' and 'representational spaces',[27] which are linked to the 'perceived', 'conceived' and the 'lived'.[28] In this triad, 'spatial practices' mainly concern the material production of life in the form that subjects or individuals 'perceive' as a physical spatiality.[29] 'Representations of space' are conceptions and imaginations in the form of maps, documents and information, which are 'conceived' by, for example, planners, institutions and 'social engineers';[30] for Lefebvre, this is the 'dominant space in any society'.[31] 'Representational spaces' or 'spaces of representation' are spaces that are associated with 'images and symbols',[32] such as monuments and buildings, and they are forms not used to describe the spaces themselves, but which are inscribed materially and experienced by users. 'Representations of space' stand, for example, against the spaces of power and state: they are passively 'lived' by subjects and provide the space of resistance.[33]

Lefebvre's definition of space is fluid and dialectally encompasses many 'spaces' – representational, imagined, mental, immaterial, social and physical. His dynamic definition of space helps to understand borders as practices diffused in space, at times material, at others immaterial. The distinction between border and bordering practice is a direct correlation between Lefebvre's representations of space (border) – the imagined and conceived – and spaces of representation (bordering practices) – the lived and resisted.

In the context of this research, spatial practices, and the process of their gradual transformation into border/ing practices, take place over time. Time's relation to space can be usefully considered according to Edward Soja's 'triple dialectic' of the socio-spatio-temporal that he employs to think about and interpret space.[34] The process of border production, which is part of the production of social space, involves time. This temporal aspect is twofold: it indicates time as the gradual intensification of violence and the duration of the time it takes to build a border, or the quality these borders may have as they move, transform, or

LIST OF BORDERING PRACTICES

Territorial / Marking

Hanging political posters on buildings

Hanging political banners in the street

Commercial billboards and advertising campaigns

Displaying politicians' photographs

Painting buildings and shops façades in a party's political colour

Roundabout statues from posters and found material

Opening up political party offices

Control of cable broadcasting

Neighbourhood Security / Surveillance

Men gathering on street corners

Smoking *arguilé* on street corners

Gathering around fire on street corners

Watching out for suspicious behaviour

Installing surveillance cameras

Prohibiting photography in specific areas

Opening *arguilé* café as surveillance front

Hiring private security companies

Access and Mobility Control

Checkpoints

Military tanks/vehicles

Human barriers

Burning wheels

Barricades (trash bins, sand bags, barbed wire, etc.)

Aural / Mobile

Motorcycle convoys with political flags

Vehicles playing loud political and sectarian sonic material

Fireworks following a speech of a politician

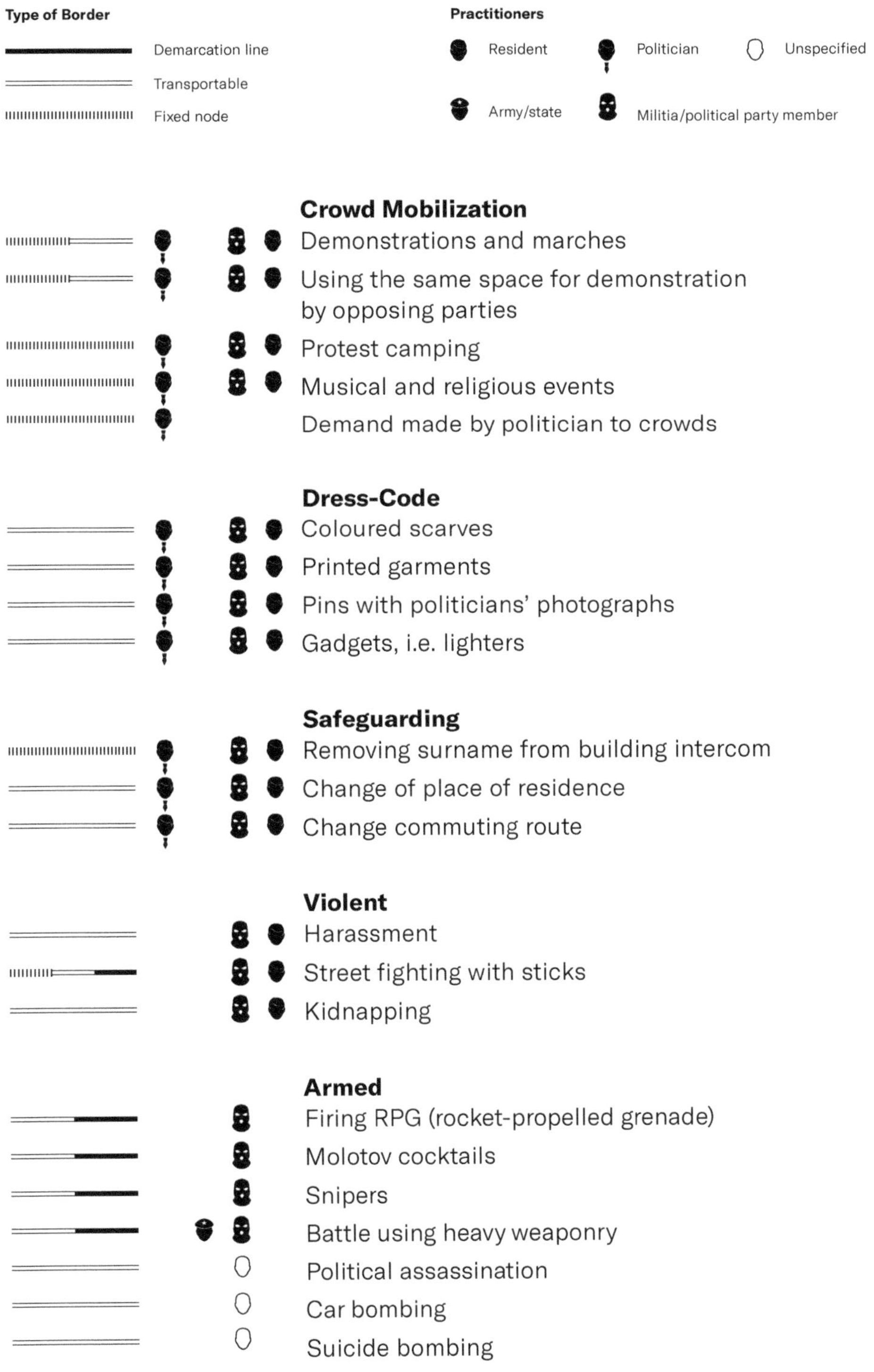

Type of Border

━━━━━━━━━ Demarcation line

═══════ Transportable

||||||||||||||||||||||||| Fixed node

Practitioners

⬤ Resident

⬤ Politician

◯ Unspecified

⬤ Army/state

⬤ Militia/political party member

Crowd Mobilization

Demonstrations and marches

Using the same space for demonstration by opposing parties

Protest camping

Musical and religious events

Demand made by politician to crowds

Dress-Code

Coloured scarves

Printed garments

Pins with politicians' photographs

Gadgets, i.e. lighters

Safeguarding

Removing surname from building intercom

Change of place of residence

Change commuting route

Violent

Harassment

Street fighting with sticks

Kidnapping

Armed

Firing RPG (rocket-propelled grenade)

Molotov cocktails

Snipers

Battle using heavy weaponry

Political assassination

Car bombing

Suicide bombing

disappear over time. And it also involves diachronicity, that is, how time can be employed as an element of confrontation and occupation in the bordering practices associated with conflict, such as practices of recurring and being on hold for a long period of time.

The list of bordering practices that I documented highlights how different communities of interest are formed, whether through direct or indirect involvement, among residents, politicians, militia members and the army. It also indicates how they shift and negotiate their positions according to specific situations. The shifting of positions by individuals/groups is a tradition in Lebanese life, particularly because of the way political parties shift between being militias on the streets to returning to state and government positions. It is notable that most militia leaders who fought in the civil war are present and represented in state institutions, as, for example, members of parliament, speaker of the house, and ministers, while the militia members are integrated into the police forces.[35] Thus, the notion of operating from someone else's position, such as a resident becoming a militia member, is formalized as a cultural and social tradition by those holding positions of power.

It is the negotiation of positions, and of spatial practices as tactic and strategy, material and immaterial, within the space of the other, that I explore as bordering practice. To consider borders as spatial practices and critical spatial practices and as part of everyday life helps generate a deeper understanding of the making and using of borders that socially and physically divide people while simultaneously connecting them.

FROM BORDER TO BORDERING PRACTICES

There is currently a proliferation of the logic of border, war and division, and the practices of bordering, in the domain of social life not only in Beirut but also in many of the world's cities. Racial segregation in the US, the rise of exclusionary politics and discrimination against minority groups and 'others' in Europe, and religious sectarian tensions in Africa, the Middle East and South Asia are evidence that borders and bordering practices are found well beyond Lebanon. The changing aspects of borders have been well expressed by Etienne Balibar who describes their vacillation in terms of layout and function, noting that borders 'stopped marking the limits where politics end ... but have indeed become ... the space of the political itself'.[36]

It is the thinking of two sides, according to Noel Parker and Nick Vaughan-Williams, that structures Western political and social thought and underpins the notion of borders. They suggest that borders need to be considered in relation to epistemology, ontology, and spatial-temporality and, in so doing, they 'begin thinking of [the border] in terms of a series of *practices*'.[37] Alexander C. Diener and Joshua Hagen suggest that the changing 'nature of borders and practices of territoriality' in modern times asks us to consider the 'alternative dimensions of boundaries, bounded space, and the process of "bordering" in the contemporary world'.[38] Hence scholars in the field of borders have marked the shift from the border as a physical entity located on international boundaries and other traditional border-control sites such as ports and airports,[39] to the bordering practice of different materiality and locations dispersed in real and cyberspace across nation-states. This shift is related to the wider development of technology and the sophistication of modes of control and governance.[40]

Within political and judicial borders, and not separated from them, this research on bordering turns towards the human subject, and to the invisible borders of the coordinates of the subject who is exposed to the politics of borders. These coordinates are 'the body, the self, the person, identity and subjectivity', [41] which Steve Pile and Nigel Thrift consider as malleable interconnected boundaries. The spatial dimension of the subject's coordinates can be explained through their social formation, particularly in their relation with 'the other'.[42] The distinction or limit between the self and 'the other' creates spatial categories, such as interior/exterior divisions, and influences socio-spatial thoughts about divides and oppositions.[43]

Notions of identity formation and subjectivity, in relation to differences and the other, are important in discussing bordering practices, as these notions structure material and immaterial (and emotional) borders through human interaction and activities. Of particular relevance to Lebanon is the subjectivism of borders, especially since the borders/boundaries are 'arbitrary constructions' that relate to the identity of the different contested political and sectarian communities, and thus to the individual's experience and relationship with the particular border.[44] It is necessary to consider how the processes of border relations – on an emotional level – are situated with respect to everyday life and spatial practices. In addition, it is important to consider the political affiliation, the social, cultural, and religious differences, and the geographic location of city dwellers as they engage in the spatial practice of their everyday lives in cities of conflict.

NEGOTIATING AND NARRATING AS FORMS OF BORDERING PRACTICE

Negotiating and narrating are the two main forms of current bordering practice in Beirut on account of their relational and immaterial aspects in the making and crossing of borders.

'Negotiation' can be defined as 'an act of dealing with another person',[45] without a pre-agreement to discuss or to start a negotiation and without necessarily reaching an agreement or a conclusion on conflict issues. Negotiating, as I understand it in my research, is a continuous process; as such, it is a bordering practice that deals with the contested space between opposites and where the condition of division is lived and is not necessarily demarcated by walls. Negotiating can be a mode of resistance and a coping mechanism for residents who wish to deal and engage with situations that attempt to dehumanize them; negotiating allows them to respond in an active way rather than as passive receivers who accept marginalization. The opposite of the process of negotiation is the physical border and segregation.

Negotiating, among residents and other bordering practitioners in situations of conflict, brings the relational aspect to the forefront of bordering practices. The concept of relational aesthetics, according to Nicholas Bourriaud, puts less value on the product of art and more on the process, particularly on art practices that emerged in the 1990s as a response to the spread of urbanization, the increased mobility of individuals and their speed of life, and the need for a new economy of the arts.[46] For Bourriaud, the relational seeks to achieve social relations and exchange; it is an alternative to the commodity exchange of the capitalist economy.[47] I employ the term 'relational' to consider bordering practices in situations of conflict to focus less on the physical border as that which demarcates, and more on processes that infiltrate spaces of social life through forms of exchange and communication, whether as dialogues or confrontations, and where negotiating and narrating are part of the relational process.

The process of narrating in this research relates to the role of the stories of conflict that people tell and exchange. In addition, there are the narratives that are produced out of the research itself – these take the form of artworks and gallery installations. In all these narratives, the focus is on the interrelated processes of narrative and material reality – or everyday life.

To explore the role of narratives in the practice of borders, it is useful to consider Susan Friedman's view that narrative is spatial. Narrative's spatiality is discussed by Friedman through her mapping of the imagined boundary of identity; she maintains that this imagined boundary of identity is closely tied to different modes of narrative, whether through the stories that people tell about themselves or 'the intertextual narratives of resistance and domination' which they pass on across generations.[48] Teresa Caldeira, on the other hand, looks at narration and violence in relation to the building of physical borders. Noting that narratives are 'expressive' and 'spatially productive', she describes how stories of crime and fear of crime are contagious and shape urban space and the practices of people; for example, they result in the social and spatial segregation of walls, fences, and gates.[49]

Caldeira specifically draws on de Certeau's notion of spatial stories that 'go ahead of social practices in order to open a field for them'[50]. For de Certeau, space intervenes in the production of narratives, just as narrative produces space. This happens first at the level of language and then through physical practices/activities. For de Certeau, spatial narratives have the capacity of both 'setting and transgressing limits'[51] that are of social and cultural specificity. The spatial quality of narrative in transforming limits – creating 'transportable limits'[52], as de Certeau puts it – is of importance in this book in general, and particularly for understanding and describing art and design practice as a bordering practice of displacing and transforming borders, and of transporting limits from one context, the urban space, into another, the gallery space.

The negotiation between the fictional and factual in the structure of narratives gives narrative a crucial role, particularly in sites of conflict where the issue of truth as an 'ideological product'[53] is, according to Keith Jenkins, always contested between opposing groups and 'acts as [a] censor' that 'draws the line'[54] of opposition. Jenkins maintains that the issue of truth in the historical narrative of past events has been, and continues to be, contested.[55] This is very much the case in this research and in the way I refer to the artworks' narratives and representations to reflect on and highlight the role of the real and imagined in historical and political narratives and their interplay in producing 'real' or everyday life.

In this respect, the general (political) narrative that this book puts forward challenges the constitution of the political–sectarian narrative in Lebanon by dealing with it as a construct, and as a bordering practice, negotiated and contested between different opposing practitioners and shifting through time. The book's narrative and approach differ from those more common in Western geopolitical ideology that usually constructs the Arab world, and Lebanon in particular, as primordial tribal societies divided along sharp religious and sectarian lines. These normative Western ways of representing Beirut, and the Middle East in general, seek to reinforce discriminatory narratives about Arabs and Muslims in the West. The narratives enhance cultural divisions through media representations and are employed as part of larger military strategies. Hence my work aims to study the implication of these political strategies and to produce new representations and narratives that expose the politics of production of dominant narratives.

Consequently, I argue that narrative has spatial qualities, particularly in the way that narrating might be used in relation to conflict and as a bordering practice – in one sense it is linguistic, and in another it is materialized in space and through acts of spatial division and connection. Through modes of negotiating the political borders with the residents and the different modes of narrating their experiences of those borders, the research constructs new narratives and representations in the form of artworks and gallery art installations that transform the immaterial borders in Beirut into a series of bordering practices to be negotiated by viewers'/users' experiences.

BORDERING PRACTICE AS A METHOD

I began this site-specific research project at the end of 2009 and carried it out over the following four years through site visits, conversations, interviews and research exercises in different media such as photography, drawing and video,

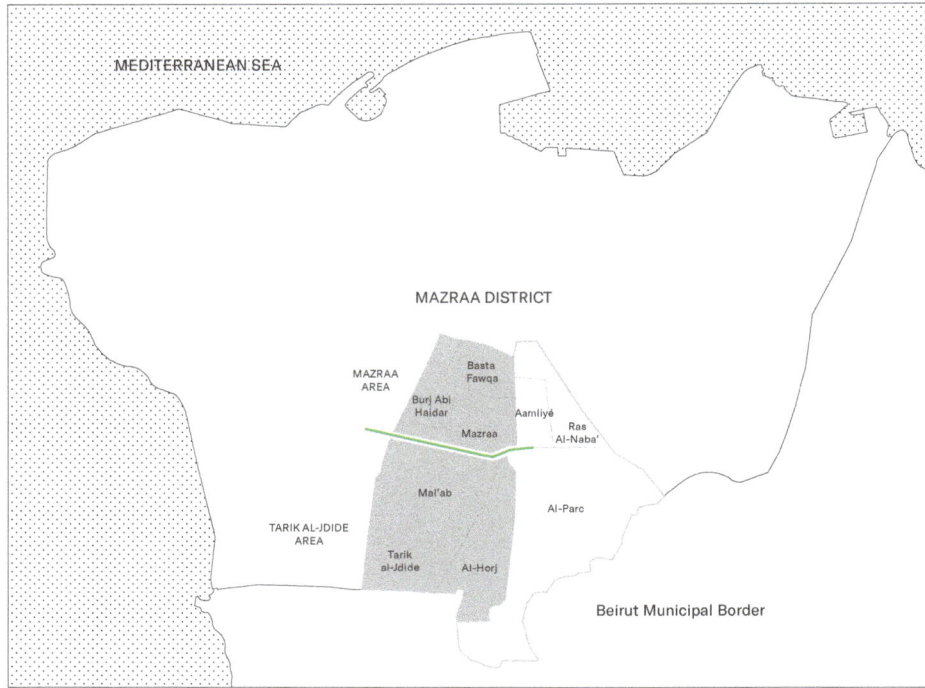

Fig.05
Map of the administrative border of Mazraa district and Municipal Beirut.

concluding it in 2013. In that time, I worked with the residents of two adjacent areas within the Mazraa district (*hayy*) in Beirut (Fig. 05). These areas have witnessed demarcation lines on the Mazraa Main Road (Corniche Mazraa): the road, which separates the administrative borders of the district into north and south, was one of the main demarcation lines that emerged in Beirut after 2005. The south of the Mazraa district is an area known informally by residents as the 'Tarik al-Jdide' area; administratively, it includes the three sectors (*manatiq*) of Mal'ab, Tarik al-Jdide and Al-Horj. The area has a Muslim Sunni majority and is under the political power of the Sunni Mustaqbal movement. The north of the district is the 'Mazraa' area and includes the administrative sectors of Mazraa, Burj Abi Haidar and Basta Fawqa. This area has a mix of Sunni and Shiite residents, as well as a Christian Orthodox minority, and is under the political power of the Shiite Amal movement and Hezbollah. The two areas are examples of how the political–sectarian conflict in the country is played out at a close proximity within Beirut's municipal borders across the Mazraa Main Road.

My choice of the site of Mazraa district and the selected method of working closely with residents in their interior spaces is related to my deep knowledge of the site and my personal connection to its residents. I am originally from the Mazraa district: I lived my entire childhood and part of my adult life in the Tarik al-Jdide area, and I still vote there. My research aim was to explore the particular practices and the conditions at the site and the general political situation in the country. I defined two groups of residents to work with, in and off the geographic site of research of the Mazraa district. I assembled a network of people, including family members, friends and colleagues, and they introduced me in turn to the first and second group of residents and other site-users in designated areas that fell within my research interest, as well as to specific streets, buildings, shops or spaces associated with particular professions and political affiliations. Overall, by the end of the research there were around 80 people in total contributing to the project. This allowed me access to many different sites through Beirut and Mazraa and secure movement in and within city spaces. In other words, I navigated my project through the safe interiors of the social network I had set up and the domestic spaces associated with those people. However, this method assumed a relationship of trust with the residents I was working with, and it did not exclude confrontations and sensitivities that were part of the interior experience of the subjects I engaged with. These tensions relating to interior space will be developed and shown at different instances in the chapters which follow.

Out of this wider group, I selected four pairs of narratives of residents whose stories are defined in relation to the temporary lines of demarcation that emerged for a few days in 2007 and 2008 on the Mazraa Main Road that separates the two areas (Fig. 06). The four narratives (constituting the book's four chapters) are themselves forms of border-crossing that negotiate the physical line of division between both areas, through the geographic location of the residents across the road, and the specific immaterial bordering practice presented by each narrative.

I devised a research method that would respond to the conditions of borders and the challenges of conducting research in areas of conflict, particularly within the political constraints in urban sites on residents' and researchers' practices. Due to the continuous political unrest in Beirut and the associated security measures in place, photography and documentation were problematic: they were monitored in most public spaces by security operatives, militia members, military officers, and even ordinary residents. However, the level of daily censorship has varied since 2005, according to the intensity of the security situation and level of threat. Adopting a 'tactical' approach that corresponds to the 'strategic' practices of security, my chosen research method accessed the neighbourhood through the private interior of residents and of their spaces – their houses, balconies, shops, and cars. This approach was not merely practical, given the context of the political and social divisions in Lebanon; it also took into account the different ways in which people build knowledge about space, since their different social, political, professional, and geographical standing shapes how they relate to conflict. The role of the participants was to direct and frame what I, as the researcher, was allowed to perceive of urban space: it was their own divisions and differences that influenced the production of knowledge out of the conflicted condition.

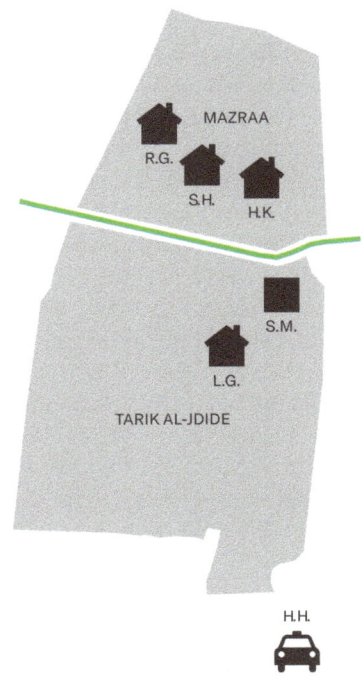

Fig.06
Map of the geographic location of residents involved in the research project.

I adopted ethnographic research methods through field notes, documentation and interviews on-site over lengthy time periods. Steve Pile and Nigel Thrift write about 'the politics of positions' that considers both the researcher and the subjects researched when writing about others. They note the existence of a political and theoretical desire to think of difference and subjectivity, especially in postcolonial and feminist writings, 'as a qualitative multiplicity [that] can provide new, empowered speaking positions'.[56] Hal Foster, drawing on the field of anthropology, considers how the position of the artist in specific sites requires an 'othering of the self'; he argues that anthropology is based on alterity, in that it studies the sites of 'other' people.[57] I applied this 'othering' in my method, particularly by implicating myself and my activities in the urban site, and as part of the artwork I produced; at the same time, I separated my position from that of the participants in order to indicate the many positions operating in the urban site.

To that end, I questioned the research ethics of dealing with participants and I employed censorship (borders) as a conceptual and structural language in setting up the relationship with the participants. First, I established a position of temporary trust between the participants and myself, explaining to them the intention behind my questions and documentation carried out with them in their spaces. Second, I responded to censorship by protecting my participants' identities using visual practices that make the omissions obvious – for example, by using visual deletions and cuts, and by refraining from filming the whole body. More importantly, I protected the participants' identity in accordance with the ethical procedures required in academic institutions. In addition, the research questions put to the participants were linked to the border under investigation and the form of media I used to document it; for example, I asked taxi drivers what they listened to in their cars, which was linked to the use of sound recordings to consider questions relating to the audio environment.

This censorship method with the residents was a bordering practice I developed that positioned my research and myself in between many places – whether between private and public, such as the residents' interior spaces and the public space outdoors, or between different media, such as video, audio recording and photography, and other representations, such as sound, image, text and language. My art practice re-worked the visual techniques of censorship to mark borders, and censorship was used deliberately to politically charge the artwork I produced. In all these negotiations that responded to censorship and research ethics, I situated art practices at the core of border studies. The artworks I produced using this method are the result of these ethical negotiations with the residents and point to the ways in which political, institutional and emotional borders unfold in the sites.

The four projects in this book were conducted through practice-led methods that are propositional in constructing new sites in 'post-war' Lebanon from 2005 onwards. The documentation practices of audio and video recording that I developed to record the details of sites and the spatial and border practices of their residents allowed me to pursue the immaterial borders conditioned by politics; these immaterial borders inspired the formulation of representational techniques and spaces that were constructed as gallery installations. The four new bordering practices I constructed – *hiding* (administration), *crossing* (surveillance), *translating* (sound), and *matching* (displacement) – aimed to work against divides and to intervene in the space between. Each practice explored the borders between oppositions, whether to suggest situations that resist and transform borders and/or to propose divisions as living conditions in everyday spaces. These works were critical bordering practices in that they created their own places between disciplines, spaces, representations and media, and they transformed the conditions of the borders as well as the materiality between the borders of two sites, such as the urban space under research and the gallery space under construction.

This is evident in the bordering practice of *hiding* behind the border of administration, through the mukhtar's (an elected district's representative) use of official documents as answers to my questions when I interviewed him. This proposition was to consider how the administrative practices seek to 'hide' borders, either intentionally for political reasons or unintentionally because of the inadequacy

of the representational techniques followed in political representation and procedures. The juxtaposition of the actual mukhtar and a fictional mukhtar from
a television series in one space, as part of an art gallery installation of video,
audio and textual material, aimed to expose the discrepancy, and the imaginary,
in the workings of representation in administrative procedures and narratives.

Another bordering practice was the *crossing* of surveillance borders with the
two women at their balconies: this was a visual and a physical activity that
used photography and video recording. This activity of crossing geographical,
emotional and political distances allowed me to expand and comprehend the
neighbourhood panorama scene in a video and a multimedia installation that
had been restricted due to surveillance.

My bordering practice of *translating* the immateriality of sound borders involved
recordings from the space of taxi drivers and a walking journey. This translation
was a material process between sound and image, and a linguistic process between Arabic and English. The narratives of the film and the audio-visual piece
produced out of the process examine how the content of current sonic material,
such as political events and news broadcasts, is similar to that of the past civil
war. The process of translating removed these sounds from their original spatial
and temporal context and collapsed time–space distances between them.

Finally, the bordering practice of *matching* lines of displacement between twin
sisters involved finding spatial moments of twinning while they narrated a journey drawn on a map and tracked it on the city skyline across a visual horizon
using a video camera. The narrative of the video installation constructed out of
the footage obtained from the sisters aims to match divided geographies and to
mobilize and visualize the sisters' invisible self-displacement in comparison with
the visibility of forced displacements, such as those of refugees.

Hence, the critical bordering practice I conducted through my research method
was concerned not only with the conditions of borders and the practices that
produce them, but also with the practices that researchers and artists employ to
study borders. I consider these research and artistic practices to be inseparable
from the politics of the borders that are being investigated, and so I argue that
the narratives produced are forms of bordering practice in their own right.

A NOTE ON THE BORDERING PRACTICES THAT FOLLOW

In the following chapters I present the four projects that comprise this book.
Each chapter presents a narrative of a bordering practice and each bordering
practice charts my negotiation between the bordering practices of political–
sectarian conflict and the artworks I produced. There are three stages in each
narrative. I begin by naming the border condition to be explored; this is followed
by the research project's title that negotiates that particular border; I present

the proposed new bordering practice that comes out of the research and the art installation.

Each of my encounters with the residents begins with the question I asked them about the border condition of the particular site they occupied. These questions are accompanied by a map locating the residents' site(s) and a short text introducing the project and my activities at the site. The chapters employ the research projects with the residents to open up wider theoretical and cultural discussions around bordering practices in Beirut. The particular proposition of the four new bordering practices of the gallery art installations is discussed at the end of the chapters.

The four projects transform the border practices they encounter both materially and immaterially, as well as practically and theoretically. This book considers how these practices transform borders into multiple shifting practices and representations that divide *and* connect through acts of negotiation and narration. To do this, it explores the spatial alternatives to borders that have been at the heart of a politically dominant, sectarian and divisive narrative about Beirut. But, as I argue in this book, this narrative, like all narratives, has been constructed – my aim here is to contribute to the production of new narratives. Above all, *Negotiating Conflict in Lebanon* is intended as a negotiation and destabilization of existing border positions in Beirut's political–sectarian conflict – in doing that, a new narrative about Beirut and its borders might be told.

Bordering
Practice 01

HIDING

ADMINISTRATION

The Chosen Two

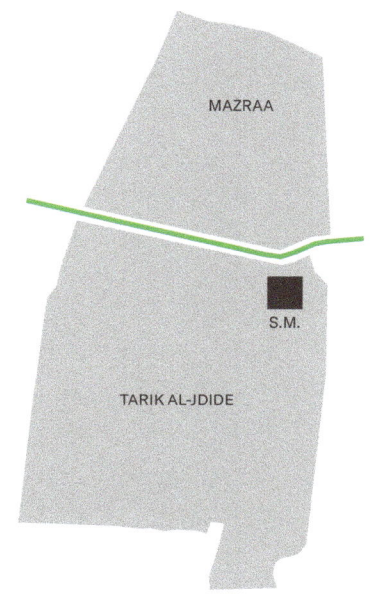

MAZRAA

S.M.

TARIK AL-JDIDE

Fig.07
Map of the geographic location of S.M. office.

Where is the administrative border?

I interviewed the oldest mukhtar for the Mazraa district
in his office off the Mazraa Main Road in Tarik al-Jdide.
His name is Salim al-Madhoun and he has been a mukhtar
since 1980 and during the period of the civil war. He is
an elected administrator for the district and one of 15
mukhtars, 14 of whom (including himself) are Sunni
Muslims and the remaining one an Orthodox Christian. I
asked the mukhtar about the administration and history of
the district, and what he thought of the fictional mukhtar
character played in a Lebanese TV series from the 1970s
and 1980s, *E'Dinyeh Heik*. To answer each of my questions,
the mukhtar referred to official documents that he has
in his office. In this chapter the actual and present-day
mukhtar is paired with the fictional and former mukhtar
to create a dialogue and a comparison across time that
allows for a questioning of the mukhtar as a role model and
a consideration of administrative, political, historic, and
cultural representations of mukhtars in relation to 'real' life.

Q. Mukhtar, why do some people love schism, cherish corruption, and spread hatred amongst people?

س. مختار، من هو المختار؟

Q. Mukhtar, why do people say that you should only befriend those you have had a fight with before?

س. مختار، أين تقع باعتقادك حدود المنطقة؟

Q. Mukhtar, why are some people pure hearted, while others do, God forbid, bear grudges and are disloyal?

س. مختار، من هي العائلات التي سكنت المنطقة؟ هل تغيرت؟

Q. Mukhtar, why is fate inevitable no matter how hard we try to avoid it?

س. مختار، هل من يسكن بالمنطقة هو نفسه من يقترع فيها؟

Q. Mukhtar, why do some people see themselves as a 'somebody,' when in people's eyes each of them is a 'nobody'?

س. مختار، هل قسّم الطريق الرئيسي المنطقة قسمين؟

Q. Mukhtar, they say an innocent kiss is the sign of love; what is the secret of this kiss?

س. مختار، هل كنت تشاهد مسلسل الدنيا هيك؟

Fig.08 (Here and Overleaf)
Text and stills from *The Chosen Two*, 2012-14.

س. مختار، ليش في ناس بحبّو الفتنة و ناس بحبّو الفساد وبيرموا شرورهن بين العباد؟

Q. Mukhtar, who is the mukhtar?

س. مختار، ليش بيقولوا لا تاخذ صاحب إلا بعد خناقه؟

Q. Mukhtar, where do you think are the borders of the area?

س. مختار، ليش في قلوب غامرها الصفا و قلوب، والعياذ بالله، بتحقد وما بتحفظ وفا؟

Q. Mukhtar, who are the families that lived in the area? Have they changed?

س. مختار، ليش القسمة والنصيب بيغلبوا الانسان وبجيبوه للطابق مهما عنّد وشد وقد؟

Q. Mukhtar, are those who reside in the area the same as those who vote in it?

س. مختار، ليش كل واحد هو بنظره شي وبنظر الناس ما شي، بكذّب الناس وبصدق حالو؟

Q. Mukhtar, did the main road divide the area into two sides?

س. مختار، بيقولوا البوسة البريئة عنوان المحبة، فشو سر هالبوسة؟

Q. Mukhtar, did you use to watch the TV series *E'Dinyeh Heik*?

INTRODUCTION

The Chosen Two is an enquiry into the bordering practice of administration. It is based on my own critical bordering practice: a research project and an associated gallery installation that articulate a definition of the borders – material and immaterial – negotiated partly by administrative and political representation and procedures, and partly by the lived experiences and practices of residents of the district. The chapter considers the administrative border(s) of the Mazraa district, as well as the history of those border(s) and of the district. The research into administration and history aims to explore the role of representation in the narrative and procedures of both, in order to reveal the bordering practice between the 'real' and the 'represented', and between fact and fiction, as well as to examine their reciprocity in producing the reality of everyday life. This bordering practice of representation is also located between the political representational processes of voting and the spatial representational techniques of mapping, with the aims of contributing to the discourse around representation, architecture/urbanism and politics, and of drawing out the distinction of the meanings of the term 'representation'.

This inquiry into administrative borders aims to understand the official (formal) aspects of the site's border(s) within which I present the other immaterial bordering that this book investigates. The chapter also provides a context for the following three chapters by offering a historical reading of the urban development of the Mazraa district. It examines how the borders of the Mazraa and Tarik al-Jdide areas have evolved in relation to the evolution of the Mazraa district and Beirut in general. I explore the constitution of the population of the district, investigating who lives and has lived there, whether and how the demographics of the district have changed in the past and present, and how elections for the mukhtars and other officials take place. Some of these questions about the district have well-defined answers in legislative and administrative documents, such as the municipal map of Beirut's districts and sector divisions, the electoral map of the mukhtars and the municipalities, and the district's personal logbooks that are used for the official identification of residents and for voting. Yet the chapter reveals the contested nature of these documents by examining the discrepancy between, on the one hand, this administrative and documentary representation of urban space and, on the other, the district's 'real' social, spatial and political conditions.

What is interesting about this early stage of my research project on divisions and the immateriality of bordering is that when one works directly with the mukhtars and the administrative representation, the Mazraa district appears as a unitary whole: a district (*hayy*) comprising a cluster of nine adjacent sectors (*manatiq*) (the official terms used by the municipality) with 15 mukhtars, in office locations spread across these sectors. Throughout the chapters of the book, the Mazraa and Tarik al-Jdide areas are presented in outline, as facing each other across the main road. Similarly, the site of the Mazraa district has been presented and drawn as one island within another island – the Mazraa district within Beirut's municipal border.

In this chapter, however, I question this representation of the administrative bor-der, and its validity and accuracy in portraying the site, by tracing other borders that emerge from my inquiry into the administrative border, none of which is easily drawn on a simple outline map. These are the borders of inheritance, and the electoral, demographic, numeric, urban and cultural borders that I examine. Wherever possible, I will present the administrative maps and documents for these six kinds of border, while allowing a discussion of what they represent to reveal further types of border that emerge from the investigation. Thus, the chapter and the associated gallery installation aim to reveal the immateriality of administrative representations and procedures, by following both the definite and the indefinite borders that go beyond the official documents, and by propos-ing instead a bordering practice of *hiding*. This proposition considers how the administrative practices seek to 'hide' borders, either intentionally for political reasons or unintentionally because of the inadequacy of the representational techniques themselves. My critical spatial practice as artist-researcher becomes, therefore, one of revealing immaterial borders, and I apply a bordering practice of *hiding* in the representational techniques I use and in the construction of the gallery's spatial experience.

My historical investigation outlines an official narrative of the country that divides the history of the republic into periods before and after the civil war: pre-war (1943–75), civil war (1975–90), and post-war (1990 to the present). The post-war period includes the years since 2005, which this book marks as a new date for the recurrence of political conflict in Lebanon and perhaps as the beginning of a new period in the war series. The recurrence of troubles since 2005 means that the historical breaks ('pre-war', 'civil war' and 'post-war') presented by the official narrative need to be questioned and replaced by a more continuous timeline. While practices connected to political–sectarian conflict continue across these periods – albeit in different forms and intensities – the official historical narrative is selective in what it mentions or remembers from the past, and it is keen to keep these periodic divisions distinct rather than overlapping. This is an important point to consider when addressing the aims of this chapter – namely, to explore carefully the discrepancies involved in the different forms of representation that produce life, which include, in addition to political and administrative representations, historical writing as another layer representing present and past events.

I present here the concepts relevant to the theoretical structure of *The Chosen Two* research project/installation and the writing of this chapter under the titles: 'Representation', 'The mukhtar', and 'Q&A format'.

THE CHOSEN TWO: REPRESENTATION

Representation is defined by W.J.T. Mitchell as 'things that "stand for" or "take the place of" something else'[1]. Mitchell explores how various forms of the arts, such as literature, painting and film, can be considered as forms of language and, therefore, as forms of representation open to semiotic readings; he also includes politics as a form of representation and as one of the things that, like language, 'stand for' something else in life:

> Since antiquity ... representation has been the foundational concept in aesthetics (the general theory of the arts) and semiotics (the general theory of signs). In the modern era (i.e., in the last three hundred years) it has also become a crucial concept in political theory, forming the cornerstone of representational theories of sovereignty, legislative authority, and relations of individuals to the state.[2]

Mitchell argues that artistic/semiotic and political representation share similarities; even though one might appear to belong to the realm of fantasy and the other to reality, the link between them is unavoidable.[3] He adds that the power of representation lies in its ability to go beyond the thing that 'it stands for' by having a life of its own that is uncontrollable and unpredictable and has many readings and impacts on real life. Mitchell argues for a reciprocity between representation and life: what people make, say, and write is not only a representation of life but is also a thing that has its own life, and that turns back to life and intervenes in it:

> Representation is that by which we make our will known and, simultaneously, that which alienates our will from ourselves in both the aesthetic and political spheres ... Every representation exacts some cost, in the form of lost immediacy, presence, or truth, in the form of a gap between intention and realization, original and copy.[4]

The 'real' and the 'represented' are continuously negotiated in and through administrative representation, which in turn exacts some cost and discrepancies in its operation and in what it stands for or represents.

The association between the political and cultural/artistic representation that Mitchell draws upon provides the theoretical framework for the dialogue that I construct in this research project between the actual mukhtar and the fictional mukhtar. The fictional is brought into this chapter to draw attention to the role of the imaginary (the fabricated) in the working of the different processes of representation, whether cultural, political, administrative or historic. In this respect, the imaginary is inherent in the processes of political and administrative representation. This is not to say that nothing exists, or that (as postmodernists maintain) there is no reality outside representation and the imaginary. Rather, it is to decode and understand the procedures of political and administrative representation and their bordering practice and negotiation in relation to real life.

It is helpful here to link questions concerning representation back to philosopher Henri Lefebvre's theory of the production of space and his distinction between 'representations of space' and 'spaces of representation'.[5] Lefebvre shows that the negotiation between the different forms of representation produces the space and practices of borders. In particular, there is a negotiation between what the official administrative documents present of borders – which are 'representations of space' – and how these borders are lived out as ambiguous and contested 'spaces of representation' through the bordering practices of everyday life.[6]

It is important to note that I use 'representation' as a term to describe forms of administrative and political process: the former concerns state institutions, while the latter concerns political life in the country, including the practices of political parties that may also exist outside state administration yet are powerful enough to shape political life. These types of representation are spatial practices in constant negotiation with each other, and, despite being associated with particular conceptual representations of space, they are also in search of 'spaces of representation'.

The different forms of representation that produce everyday life get played out often through different forms of narrative that include, but are not limited to, textual material, documents, maps and told stories. Narration is a form that exists between 'representations of space' and 'spaces of representation', and it allows a negotiation between these two terms – it is, therefore, a key aspect of bordering practice.

The imaginary (fictional) is part of narrative structure in general.[7] In this respect, the imaginary is part of the historical narrative as well as the administrative narrative that is practised by officials, such as the mukhtar, and it is also an indispensable part of everyday life.

THE CHOSEN TWO: THE MUKHTAR

In order to construct its argument concerning past and present, and the slippage between different modes of representation – whether administrative, political, historical or cultural – *The Chosen Two* stages a dialogue between two mukhtars. One is Mukhtar Salim al-Madhoun, who has held the position since 1980, and who himself comes from the Mazraa district; the other is a mukhtar character played by Mohamad Shamil in *E'Dinyeh Heik*, a comedy series aired on national Lebanese television in the 1970s and 1980s. My research and project create a contrast between a man who performs the administrative role of a mukhtar in his daily life, and an actor who also performs as a mukhtar, but in a fictionalized and idealized version of this role as constructed through *E'Dinyeh Heik*.

My research involved a series of meetings, comprising formal and informal interviews, conducted with a number of the mukhtars of the Mazraa district (in addition to al-Madhoun himself), who work in offices across its northern and southern sides. These meetings took place throughout my site-specific research period from the end of 2009 to the end of 2012. However, this chapter focuses on the last meeting in the series, which was conducted and video-recorded in January 2012 with al-Madhoun at his office in Tarik al-Jdide. The material al-Madhoun provided, his personal engagement and his knowledge of his field and role were incredibly rich compared to the other mukhtars I interviewed, and they greatly informed my understanding of the mukhtar's role within the context of the Mazraa district in particular and Beirut in general. Most importantly, al-Madhoun's use of documents to answer each of my questions, and his correction of my questions themselves, inspired both the conceptual structure of this chapter and the art installation I produced in response to this research. My interaction with him made me reconsider my understanding of the power and narrative forms of the political administration and its documents.

My interest in learning about the history of the district and its administrative procedures led me to look in detail at the role of the mukhtar. The term *mukhtar* in Arabic means 'the chosen'. He or she is elected as an administrator by residents in their local district or village to represent their district at state level. The mukhtar's role is to mediate between residents and the state, especially in relation to legal and administrative issues. The mukhtar is the lowest rank in state administration and, as most mukhtars live and work in the districts where they are elected, he or she is the closest link to the residents of their local area. I come to consider the mukhtars as a potential 'official and formal' witness, viewing from within their offices both the district as an outside space as well as the internal politics of their office place and its administrative concepts, procedures, facts and figures. Mukhtars are the perfect participants in my site-specific research project because they are the link between historical enquiry and the administration of borders.

In the television programme *E'Dinyeh Heik*, the mukhtar is portrayed as a neutral and wise man who solves people's problems and never takes sides. However *E'Dinyeh Heik* masks political and sectarian divisions in the country, as well as the particular form of conflict that was taking place in Lebanon at the time the show was produced and broadcast. The imaginary dialogue I have staged between these two mukhtars marks a meeting point in the 30-year period that separates them, between the civil war that took place from 1975 to 1990 and the continued political unrest since 2005. In that dialogue, the past and the present are played out in relation to the fictional and the actual. The comparison between the two mukhtars, and the distance and difference in time and in modes of representation that separate them, allow us to question both models (representatives) with regard to what a mukhtar is or ought to be, and to question the political life of both periods, without favouring or romanticizing the past. This process of comparison is a key aspect of what I am calling bordering practice, which operates between present and past and between different modes of representation.

THE CHOSEN TWO: Q&A FORMAT

Each episode of *E'Dinyeh Heik* discusses an issue in life or a problem that has occurred between residents in the neighbourhood, and ends with a question that one of the residents asks the mukhtar concerning this discussion. The mukhtar always answers these questions in the manner of a sage, and his voice ends each episode with '*e'dinyeh heik*', which translates into English as 'that's life'. The mukhtar's answer seems to work as a way of normalizing things; it stops further difficult questioning, and it brings in humour as a way of accepting one's situation in life and of avoiding the discovery of an answer that really addresses the question or makes sense of the dispute or issue under discussion.

In response to this format used by *E'Dinyeh Heik*, my own project, *The Chosen Two,* adopts the question-and-answer (Q&A) formula with the mukhtar al-Madhoun. By the end of the interview session with him, al-Madhoun has referred to material evidence contained in eight different documents, in addition to providing personal stories and interpretations. The documents shown to me by al-Madhoun, in support of his answers to my questions, are representations used by the administration to manage the district. He referred to them as a historian would refer to facts in writing his version of history. These administrative documents include facts that, arranged together, make up the official historical narrative of the district.

The mode of narration adopted by the mukhtar – his reference to documents – suggested that his narrative was objective, that what he was telling me was the 'truth', based on the 'official' information contained in these documents about the district, and that these documents could 'speak for themselves'.[8] This is not to criticize the mukhtar al-Madhoun, but rather to reveal the type of historical narrative that administrative documents offer, and the extent to which administrative representation relates to actual life.

Something of the truth does reside in the mukhtar documents, as they are documents that exist and were produced by the administrative institutions that relate to his profession. But the issue of truth as a contested site between opposing groups has shaped the discipline of historiography and the philosophy of history.[9] It is also a pivotal term in the Lebanese conflict and in the writing of the histories of that conflict: what is 'true' is contested among the different political parties, each trying to write their own version of that history/truth. A good example is the ongoing disagreement in Lebanon over the writing of a single history book to be used as part of the school curriculum covering the

Fig.09
Diagram of the conceptual planning of *The Chosen Two*.

period after independence in 1943 and including the civil war. The book currently used in schools does not include the civil war as part of Lebanon's history. As the Lebanese architect and scholar, Maha Yahya, has commented:

> It's almost as if we wanted to apply to history the amnesty laws that we applied immediately after the civil war, and said 'Nobody is to blame, everybody is equally not responsible for what happened'.[10]

Therefore, it is worth considering how administrative representations compare with post-structuralist historiography, which regards the idea of objective narratives and historical truth as constructions emerging from sites of contestation.

The Q&A format I adopted in this research project is a bordering practice negotiated through narration. It aims to examine the borders that exist between questioning and answering, and between the one who asks – the resident or in this case the researcher – and the one who answers and who holds authority. It aims to exercise/practise historical inquiry in an active way. The questions I asked were intended to operate directly: they were demands for information about the site's present and past and about the administrative procedures themselves, but they also had a more indirect, reflexive and critical intention. My questions were also directed at the form of democracy itself, and at the 'question' as a form of address to authority.

For the writing of this chapter, I present al-Madhoun's answers to my questions, translated from Arabic into written English, along with my photographic record of the documents and material evidence he presented to me in answer to my questions. The process resulted in the six kinds of border that emerged from my research. However, I will also refer to the answers of the other mukhtars – namely Nqoula Razzouq, Ghareib Hassan and Nizar Syoufi – whom I introduce where relevant in the later sections of this chapter. These other mukhtars are important to my inquiry concerning the district's past and present borders both because of their administrative position as mukhtars and because of their experiences and opinions as residents of the district.

In the following six sections, I present the particular borders of administration and their different representational forms, as well as the role of the mukhtar as a border practitioner – that is, as one who practises borders. In addition, I consider the role of the Q&A as a bordering practice and a form of negotiation that takes place through narration. The Q&A allows different ways of revealing the evidence hidden in administrative procedures and revealing the borders between the real and the represented. I end the chapter by discussing the gallery installation that puts into play the concepts and terms discussed throughout the chapter in a spatial experience. The installation is presented through a bordering practice of *hiding*.

INHERITANCE BORDER

Mukhtar, who is the mukhtar?

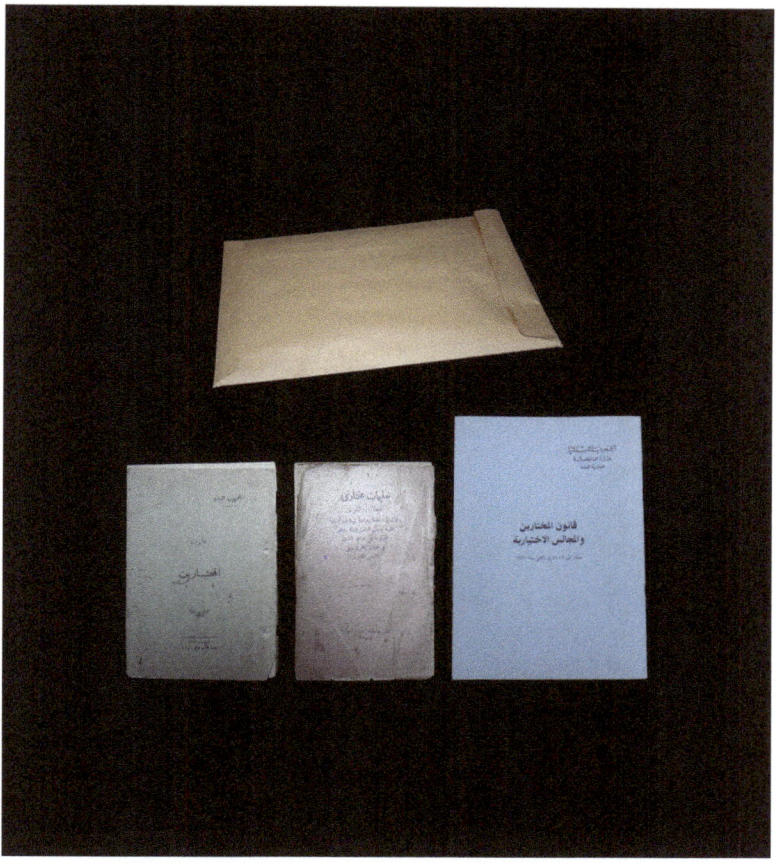

Fig.10 (Top)
Document 1: Envelope.

Fig.11 (Bottom, left to right)
Material Evidence 1: Three booklets referring to the mukhtar's
law by the Ottoman, French, and Lebanese authorities.

Q. For how many years have you been the mukhtar?

A. I was assigned mukhtar for the Mazraa district by a governmental/state decree issued in August 1980, following the death of my grandfather who was a mukhtar himself; his name was also Salim al-Madhoun. We have assumed this profession [mehne'] generation after generation in my family since 1946, before I was born. From 1980 till now I've been a mukhtar along with other elected mukhtars for this district.

Q. Who is the mukhtar? What is the definition of his profession?

A. I wish you wouldn't use the word profession; it's not a profession. The word mukhtar connotes an administrative activity. It began under Ottoman rule and continued during the French mandate, and later it was adopted by the Lebanese republic. The word mukhtar is defined by law – it's better to read it out of the book than trying to define it myself:

'Any residential area where the number of residents exceeds 50 should be administered by a mukhtar with the help of an elected mukhtar council.'

[The mukhtar stands up to get an envelope from a cabinet containing three different legislative documents – in Ottoman, French and Lebanese – that govern the mukhtar's administrative activities. He opens the first one.]

'The law of the mukhtar' – I might be the only one to have the Ottoman law.

Q. Which year is that document [the Ottoman law]. Does it have a date?

A. It has no date, but I estimate it's before 1914 [the end of Ottoman rule].

The French law was issued in 1928, as it shows on the document cover. These documents are from the time of my grandfather; they are heritage.

The Lebanese law was passed or formulated in 1947 and it has been applied ever since with many amendments that don't cover properly all the mukhtar's duties and status.

[The mukhtar reads out again the definition as stated in the Lebanese law – the same definition as the one mentioned above – in addition to articles that define the relationship between the mukhtar and the council as well as the process of election/voting by local residents.]

The Lebanese administration starts with the mukhtar; they don't mention parliament members or ministers. The law specifies that the mukhtar is to manage or administer an area with the support of a council ... the electoral process takes place directly in local areas; this is how he is elected. He is an elected administrator.

Q. What do you call it if it's not a profession?

A. It is not a profession. Usually you get paid for the profession you do, whereas the mukhtar doesn't receive a salary – instead he receives fees or charges [*rossoum*] for the services and certificates he provides.

[He opens the Lebanese law booklet and reads out the following passage:]

'The mukhtar: Practice of his Duty', you asked me what it is if it's not a profession.

Article number 14 from the law says: 'The mukhtar needs to take an oath before assuming his responsibilities. He should repeat the following:

'I swear in the name of holy God that I will fulfil the duties assigned to me with all truthfulness and faithfulness.'

The law doesn't mention the term profession; instead it is called duty or responsibility.

Only two people take an oath in the Lebanese state before assuming office: the president of the Republic and the mukhtar.

Q. Have you taken this oath?

A. Yes, of course.

Based on the fact that the mukhtar is not an employee of the government, we can consider him an employee of the residents of the district he is in charge of. He doesn't get a salary from the Lebanese government. If he was an employee, he should have a salary. For example, a parliament member gets paid 14 million a month for his duties. So the activity of the mukhtar is not paid and he doesn't get any benefits or pension from the Lebanese government. In addition, Article number 17 says: the duties or work of the mukhtar are free of charge. This Article concerns the relationship of the mukhtar with the state, but his relationship with the residents... [He continues reading the law]:

'They can charge fees for the services and certificates they provide to residents.'

Unfortunately, up till now the government since 1947 didn't fix these fees.

While in the French mandate period they defined the fees for the mukhtar.

[He flips over the page and starts reading out the French law.]

They call it the mukhtar's income and not charges or fees ... 'he gets paid six golden korsh for every certificate he produces'.

During the Ottoman period the mukhtars had to share their fees with the government, they would collect taxes for the government and take a small percentage in return.

Later, after independence, the Lebanese Republic didn't define the fees and that is the reason why this field of work is still chaotic to this day.

The mukhtars represent a certain residential district of the governmental administration and represent the administration – the Lebanese authority in their district. They act as mediators.

My question – *Who is the mukhtar?* – was really a double question. I wished to know about the mukhtar's duties, but I was also inquiring into the characteristics of the man who holds this elected administrative position with regard to the political–sectarian division that exists in the country. I was keen to understand how mukhtars deal with these divisions and how much they participate in them.

The simple question I asked the mukhtar about his current duties triggered information from him contained in his answer concerning the political inheritance of this position from previous ruling regimes that preceded the establishment of the Lebanese republic in 1943: the Ottoman Empire (1523–1914) followed by the French mandate in the Middle East (1920–43). The mukhtar referred to three documents to answer and define his current duties: the Ottoman law (the date was not shown on the document), the French law (1928), and the Lebanese mukhtar's law that was passed in 1947 (Fig. 11).

The country has been a democratic republic since it gained independence from the French mandate in 1943, and it adopts a 'confessional system' that is, as defined by Hassan Krayem, 'based on a formula allocating political and administrative functions to major sects'.[11] Currently the confessional (religious/sectarian) system distributes the governing authority with parity between Christians and Muslims in a way that, according to Krayem, aims to give 'confessional balance and confessional representation'.[12] The parity is a political distribution and not based on actual numbers of each religious community, and it comprises a structural system whereby the president must always be a Maronite Christian, the prime minister a Sunni Muslim, and the speaker of the house a Shiite Muslim.[13] This parity between Muslims and Christians includes the 18 sects that make up the population and, as Krayem observes, this parity 'may also be observed in the system of distribution of seats in Parliament and in Grade One posts, and their equivalent in public services jobs'.[14] The representation of the 18 sects in the political system appears to offer an 'equal' representation and participation for each sect. However, it is this same confessional system that is part of the continual troubles for the country. According to Krayem, commenting on the years since 1943:

> democracy was deficient as a system because equal opportunities for citizens as well as political accountability and political responsibility of officials and institutions were lacking ... Such a system [confessional system] has historical roots but it was the National Pact in 1943 that rigidly institutionalized it.[15]

It is worth noting that a Lebanese citizen is represented and officially exists in political life only through his/her sect; one cannot vote or take an administrative position outside religion.

Fig.12
Mukhtar Nizar Syoufi office, 2010.

Fig.13
Mukhtar Salim al-Madhoun office, 2012.

The mukhtar's answer concerning his profession not only illustrated the extent of political inheritance from the French and Ottoman rule but also revealed another layer or mechanism of inheritance in that system – the family.[16] When mukhtar al-Madhoun first began his job, he was assigned, but not elected, to the Mazraa district by governmental legislation or decree in August 1980. He was to replace his grandfather, Salim al-Madhoun, who had been the area's mukhtar from 1947 until his death in 1980. During the civil war, the country was divided, so no municipal and mukhtar elections were held. Not until 1998, eight years after the end of the war, did the country hold its first municipal and mukhtar elections since 1963.[17]

The mukhtar explained to me that there was family pressure on him to continue the legacy of the mukhtar status in the al-Madhoun family. Even though the mukhtar might be the smallest administrative position in the state's electoral procedures, and perhaps the lowest in rank, the social background of the mukhtar and his family's ties with the community play an important role in his election. The services the mukhtars provide for the community also play an important role in maintaining this status.[18] These local ties give the mukhtar a role in social and political life, especially at times of parliamentary and presidential elections in Lebanon. Particularly before the civil war, mukhtars were instrumental in promoting certain candidates and in helping to build a popular mass for political leaders.[19]

Political inheritance – that is, in general, the inheritance of a political position from father to son or from brother to brother, among other examples such as from husband to wife or father to daughter – is a common practice in the history of the country.[20] Lebanese politicians (such as leaders of political groups, ministers and parliamentarians) often come from prominent political families where they inherit their political leadership status (*za'ama*) from their predecessors. Samir Khalaf argues that 'kinship, fealty and religion' are the ties and loyalties inherent in the Lebanese political system. The family, rather than the individual, is the basic social unit in Lebanese society, which, as Khalaf shows, influences the political

Fig.14
Mukhtar Ghareib Hassan office, 2010.

Fig.15
Mukhtar Nqoula Razzouq office, 2011.

system: 'Not only is the family an agency of political socialization and tutelage; it is also an avenue for political power and a means for perpetuating leadership.'[21] The fealty tie is the personal relationship and loyalty between a *za'im*, or political leader, and his followers. According to Khalaf, there are three types of *za'im* that reflect the changes in Lebanese society and the political history of the country: 'the feudal, the administrative and the urban za'im'. Khalaf notes that the role of religion in political life goes back to the collapse of feudalism, when people found sentiment in religion to 'sustain identity and communal solidarity'. The first signs of the confessional system becoming institutionalized occurred in 1861 at the time of Mutasarrifiya, when the Ottomans granted a limited autonomy to Mount Lebanon (the Mutasarrifiya limit) within the Ottoman Empire and divided the governance between Christians and Muslims in an administrative council under the governorship of a non-Arab Ottoman Christian.[22]

The Mazraa district has a total of 15 mukhtars (currently 14 Sunni Muslim and one Orthodox Christian) and I interviewed five of them at their offices across the northern and southern sides of the Mazraa district. It became obvious during my visits that the mukhtars in Tarik al-Jdide – a predominantly Sunni Muslim area currently under the Sunni political power of the Mustaqbal movement – are also from the Sunni community, and that they display in their offices, among their family photographs, religious signs, slogans and photographs of the political leaders (all Mustaqbal figures). Mukhtar al-Madhoun, however, whose office is also in the Tarik al-Jdide area, had no sectarian or political signs in his office apart from Islamic calligraphy on his desk and on the wall behind him (Fig. 12–15).

In the Mazraa area, which is currently a mixed area of Sunni, Shiite and Christian communities and is under the political power of the Shiite Amal movement, the two mukhtars I met with – a Sunni Muslim and the only Orthodox Christian mukhtar – both had a framed photograph of the state's president on the wall behind their desks, similar to those found in governmental offices in Lebanon. There was no evidence of their sectarian backgrounds in their offices. When I asked one of them about the absence of sectarian and political signs, he replied that his loyalty as an official should be to the country's president. Soon after, he revealed that in the Barbour neighbourhood where his office is located, 'we' – the Sunnis – cannot display sectarian affiliation in 'our' offices (or shops), whereas 'they' – the Shiites – can. His answer implies the political hegemony of the Amal party in the northern part of the Mazraa district and the impact this has on residents' practices and freedom in the spaces they occupy. More importantly, his answer shows the tensions (perhaps borders) that exist when officials hold sectarian sympathies often not in line with the places where they live and work, and which can clash with their roles as 'representatives' of those places and people.

Krayem compares the 1998 municipal and mukhtar elections –the first to be held since the civil war – with those held before the war. He records that only two elections were held before the war, in 1952 and 1963, and that there was no regular basis to them.[23] In the 1950s and 1960s, the electoral procedure was dominated by family ties, which played a significant role in the absence of political groups' development programmes and visions. By 1998, and as a result of the war, the role of families in local communities had deteriorated in the face of political–sectarian groups who had taken control of residential areas and political life.[24] However, even in the 1950s and 1960s, sectarianism was central to the electoral process and formed the basis on which residents voted.[25]

Professionalism, neutrality and working for the benefit of residents, whatever their religious and political background, are at issue when discussing the role of administrators such as the mukhtars, especially in state institutions where people identify with their sectarian group, and where sectarianism is perpetuated by the political and legal setup and passed down (inherited) from one generation to the next. This is a condition that can be traced back to the formation of Lebanon, and to the role of the political elite at that time, and it is embedded in current social and cultural structures.

The mukhtar still plays a role in the electoral process for parliamentary candidates, but this role is not as influential as it once was. The shrinking of the social and political role of the mukhtar, as pointed out by al-Madhoun, is due to the development of other administrative positions in the state, such as the municipal council and ministries that have taken over some of the mukhtar's duties.

When we inherit something, such as a social status or a subject position in relation to an authority, we do not always question or reject what we have inherited. 'Who is the mukhtar?' is a question directed to us – as residents – about what we expect from the mukhtar as a figure and a role that we have inherited and for which we voluntarily cast our vote.

ELECTORAL BORDER

Mukhtar, where do you think the area's border is?

Fig.16 (Top)
Document 2: Beirut city guide.

Fig.17 (Bottom)
Material Evidence 2: Map of municipal Beirut.

A. It is not what I think; it is the geography of the place, an administrative border.

Administratively Beirut has a map; and this map defines the geography of cadastral zones.

[He takes out a booklet from his drawer, with a fold-out map of Beirut inside it, and he reads from the map.]

The geography of cadastral zones: Mazraa first of all is a cadastral zone. It is defined on its south by Chayah and Ghbayreh, on its west by Mousaytbeh, on its north by al-Bashora, on its east by Achrafieh and Furn al-Chibak.

Q. Do you know when these limits were drawn?

A. I think in the Ottomans' time.

Q. You mean the limits of areas inside or within Beirut?

A. And Beirut was only what we today know as the centre, downtown, with a wall surrounding it and everything else was considered outside Beirut – the suburbs. It is called Mazraa ['the farm']. Yesterday I was checking a book that I don't have here: the plots of Mazraa were vast, and these were divided by roads and urban planning into smaller properties, and plots of 1000m^2, 700m^2 and 500m^2 were sold.

Q. That's why it's named Mazraa ['the farm']?

A. Yes, it is used to be farms.

My grandfather on my mother's side, from the Saab family – God bless his soul – bought a plot in the Mazraa that had cows. They used to grow plants and raise animals/livestock on their lands.

Q. How did it expand and grow?

The expansion happened after the properties were divided into small plots of land; people were able to buy land and build houses. And due to the administrative division of roads, the state also appropriated land for free. With smaller plots connected by roads, people were able to reach their properties more easily. The borders of the plots were delineated by cactus trees. I'm not sure if you know what a cactus looks like ...

Q. What year are you talking about?

A. 1920s and before.

Q. So you heard about these stories from your family members?

A. Yes, from family but also from maps that I have. I wasn't born back then; I heard from my grandfathers. In addition, I have the French maps from the 1920s and 1930s and recent maps that show how the land was divided into smaller plots, reduced from $10,000m^2$ to smaller plots.

Although the question I asked – *Where is the area's border?* – apparently refers to the material specifics of a border, I also intended it in an abstract sense. I was interested in finding out what type of border a mukhtar might refer to when asked. The mukhtar answered by defining the current administrative border of the Mazraa district; this is the border which relates to the limits of his duties and to his electoral constituency. The map consulted by the mukhtar to answer my question and define the border is from the *Guide de la Ville de Beyrouth* (Beirut city guide) (Fig. 17), a document published by the municipality of Beirut. According-ing to the document, the municipality of Beirut is administratively divided into 12 districts (*hayy*), each of which is subdivided into numbered sectors (*manatiq*), numbering 60 in total. The Mazraa district is one of the 12 and is divided into nine sectors, named and numbered as follows: Burj Abi Haidar (50), Basta Fawqa (51), Ras el-Naba' (52), Mazraa (53), Mal'ab (55), Tarik al-Jdide (56), al-Horj (57), al-Parc (58), and Aamilye' (59).[26]

Interestingly, the name of the sectors on the map and the borders that corre-spond to each are not necessarily the same as the terms that residents use when talking about their neighbourhoods. Many of the streets are known not by their official names but by common ones given by residents, with people often referring to an area by the name of a landmark such as a mosque or a well-known coffee shop. For example, residents of Beirut and the media use the name 'Tarik al-Jdide' to indicate not only the precise Tarik al-Jdide sector (56) but also the southern part of the Mazraa Main Road within the Mazraa administrative district in general. 'Mazraa', on the other hand, is the name used by residents to denote the northern side of the main road within the Mazraa district, specifically the area around Mazraa sector (53), and not the larger administrative Mazraa district that comprises the nine sectors.[27] This discrepancy between, on the one hand, the definition and names of the administrative borders of sectors on paper, and, on the other, the everyday names used by residents, relates in part to how residents ethnographically navigate the city. In addition, it relates to the lack of a culture of maps in the country. Many people have not been exposed to the map of the city as a public document, not even for finding directions. This is in part due to the weak role of the state and public institutions that usually produce and distribute these types of maps for administrative organizational reasons.

The division of the city's districts is a similar concept to the dividing of the country into six Mohafazat (districts), each made out of Aqdeya (Qada is a sub-district). Beirut is both a Mohafaza and a Qada. However, Beirut's 12 dis-tricts are further assembled in three ways that follow three different electoral procedures according to political and administrative categories: the municipality and mukhtar elections that relate to local governance and municipal services, and the parliamentary elections that relate to the national legislature.[28] Although each election has its own specificity and role, the law and the electoral districting of each reflect and belong to the same confessional Lebanese electoral system that 'has always been based on a unicameral majority system; that is, winner takes all'.[29] While the parliamentary system is based on sectarian quotas by law (as I explain below), the municipalities and mukhtars are not. Nevertheless, the electoral procedure of the municipalities and mukhtars and its results show how the voting is sectarian, and in many districts the results are similar to those of the parliamentary elections.[30]

Paul Salem, a member of the National Commission for Electoral Law Reform in Lebanon, discusses how districting has been deployed throughout the history of elections in Lebanon for temporary electoral ends, and that no long-term reforms have been made to the electoral law:

> The main changes that had affected [parliamentary] election laws in the eighty years of electoral life in Lebanon [since the Lebanese constitution in 1926] had been limited to making districts smaller or larger... Post-war elections, of which there have been four so far (1992, 1996, 2000, and 2005), left much to be desired. The election laws that were adopted in each round were patchwork laws in which different districting was adopted in different regions, and which were designed to promote certain electoral outcomes that were favourable to the government of the time and the Syrian regime which dominated politics between 1990 and early 2005.[31]

If we take Beirut's administrative border as a whole, this municipal limit of Beirut is concerned with the election of the municipality's members (Fig. 18). Residents of Beirut from the 12 districts elect the 24 members of the municipal council of the city. Municipal election law does not specify any sectarian quotas, and candidates who receive the highest numbers of votes win. But the custom is to have an equal number of 12 Christians and 12 Muslims, which usually happens through electoral alliances: eight Sunni, three Shiite, one Druze, three Maronite, three Greek Orthodox, one Catholic, three Armenian, one Protestant and one other Christian.[32]

The electoral borders of the mukhtars are the same as those of the districts they govern (Fig. 19). Registered residents of each of the 12 districts elect their own set of mukhtars. Currently, Beirut has 106 mukhtars in total. As with the municipal elections, the mukhtar electoral law does not specify any sectarian quotas. Nevertheless, of the Mazraa district's 15 mukhtars, there is (as al-Madhoun explained) a custom to have 14 Sunni and one Greek Orthodox; this sectarian distribution relates to the sectarian background of the 'official' number of residents registered in the district.[33] Previously, from 1947 (the year the Mukhtar Law was issued in the republic) until the first election after the civil war in 1998, the number of mukhtars for the Mazraa district was seven: six Sunni and one Greek Orthodox. The number has changed since the civil war, as a result of changes

 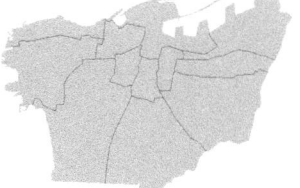 

Fig.18
Beirut municipal limit.

Fig.19
Beirut's districts.

Fig.20
Beirut's parliamentary
electoral division.

to the electoral system after the Taif agreement that ended the civil war in 1989 between the Lebanese political parties and brokered in Saudi Arabia with Arab and international support.[34]

The parliamentary electoral map and the administrative districting of Lebanon in general, and of Beirut in particular, have always been subjects of heated debate, and they are essential factors in any political deal regarding which electoral law to adopt and how to divide and combine the city's districts. The electoral map and division of districts in Beirut have been drawn differently at various electoral rounds, which are supposed to be held on a regular four-year basis. Beirut itself is sometimes considered as one electoral zone, while at other times it is divided into three zones, and there have been talks about dividing it again into two zones,[35] such as at the 2018 elections (Fig. 20).

The specificity of the electoral map of Beirut at the time of any given election, municipal (including mukhtars) or parliamentary, needs to be understood alongside another movement, which takes place on the ground, either to support or to challenge the administrative borders shown on the electoral map. This is the movement of the alliances among the numerous political parties. Bassel Salloukh has commented: 'Interethnic coalitions, vote pooling and bargaining have structured the results of these elections, as have the electoral laws demarcating the boundaries of the electoral districts'; and he notes how the cross-confessional alliances have emptied the electoral procedure of its democratic political life and have instead served the interests of client-focused confessional candidates rather than national ones.[36] A case in point was the round of mukhtar elections in 2010: the only elected Christian mukhtar for the Mazraa district was Nqoula Razzouq, and he had to seek support from the Sunni Mustaqbal list from the 14 March political bloc.[37] This is due to the small number of Christians registered to vote in the district in comparison with the number of registered Sunnis; hence, in order to win, he had to obtain Sunni votes. Moreover, in the 2010 mukhtar elections, the main competing parties – the Shiite Hezbollah and the Sunni Mustaqbal – were allies on the same list in Beirut. Rola Mouawad suggests that this alliance was formed to avoid tension and to control the outcome of the election in advance.[38]

A particularly important feature within the administrative and electoral borders that I have described, and in addition to the alliances movement, is that the political parties' personnel exist in urban space, in buildings, on the streets and at security checkpoints. This presence creates a political territorialization of the districts and sectors in Beirut, which clearly relates to the elections as part of a logistical plan to gain formal political power in the city on the part of the different political groups. But the presence of the political parties in the sectors is not simply for electoral reasons, since the electoral representation in the administration is not necessarily a reflection of the actual political power and presence in the city's sectors. Neither is it the only way to exercise political power in the country. For example, in the northern part of the Mazraa district, in the Mazraa sector and the area around it, the political power on the ground is mainly exercised by the Shiite Amal movement, whereas the political representation in parliament and the municipality is predominantly held by the Sunni Mustaqbal. This illustrates how the administrative political representation at parliamentary and administrative levels does not necessarily correspond to the actual political presence or power on the ground. Political parties work by claiming administrative political representation in state institutions and at a municipal level, while simultaneously and continually negotiating the districts' urban borders.

The current political–sectarian conflict validates these bordering practices – practices that challenge these administrative borders, so making them popular. It is specifically during elections that people become aware of the administrative borders and the city's map, as these borders operate through election procedures to preserve and reassert the sectarian identity of Beirut's inhabitants.

DEMOGRAPHIC BORDER

Mukhtar, who are the families that live in the area? Have they changed?

Fig. 21 (Top)
Document 3: Lebanon 2010, guide to municipalities and mukhtars.

Fig. 22 (Bottom)
Material Evidence 3: no information used.

A. Residents of the Mazraa area have changed many times. First of all, the Mazraa area was not all inhabited or populated at the same time. The area initially extended from Mar Mikhaël church and Raas Al Nabeh to the Damascus road; these are the areas that were inhabited first, these were the centre of the Mazraa area.

Q. Who are the families that reside there?

A. There are Christian and Muslim families.

[He lists family names]

The Nahra family, Tadrous, Rozoq, Razzouq, Al Majdalani [all Christians]; also, other families resided in the area, such as the Sabra family, Saab, Al Ousta, Al Arayssi [all Muslims]. These are the old families who bought properties and settled there.

Q. The Mazraa was of Christian majority, is that correct?

A. Christian majority, no – the centre of the Mazraa was where the Sunni residents clustered at the northern border of the area [around the Christian area] in Al-Bashora closer to Beirut downtown, what we call today Al Basta Al Fawqa.

Q. But since 2005, has there been an internal immigration? We hear that people prefer to live in areas of the same sect, such as Shiites leaving Tarik al-Jdide, and the same is happening in Mazraa.

A. We didn't hear about anyone selling or buying property.

No one moved. Neighbourhoods with a majority of Sunni residents now have more Shiites. It's not true that they left these areas; they live in all places.

The demographic changes are not due to sectarian reasons; rather, they are for economic ones.

Nowadays, if someone has a house, he will sell it to buy a few houses for his children in cheaper areas outside Beirut.

Q. So you are saying it's a normal phenomenon due to economic reasons.

A. It's a normal trend resulting from hatred in families. The father dies and the sons fight over inheritance and the women force their husbands to sell and there is someone who is interested in buying.

Q. You mean there is an interest from the other sect to buy?

A. We are telling Dar El Fatwa, Lebanon's highest Sunni authority, to pay attention to its 'group' and to provide houses for them; the Christian Orthodox Church is doing the same for its people.

When people in Beirut learnt about my current research subject, they immediately asked why I was interested in the Mazraa district in particular. As I explained in the Introduction to this book, since 2005 the area has come to be known for the recurring practices of border demarcations along Shiite/Sunni divides, along the main road separating its northern and southern sides. I had always thought that it was common knowledge that the Mazraa district is a great example of the so-called 'coexistence' of different sects in one district: a small example (a prototype perhaps) offered on behalf of the country. But I have discovered that even people in Beirut, especially the young (post-war) generation, are unaware that the Mazraa has a history where Christians and Muslims lived side by side until the civil war.

The Mazraa sector (not the district as a whole) is where Christians were once the dominant population; since the beginning of the civil war in 1975, however, they live there in small numbers. Some of the streets are still named after the Christian families who used to live there – for example, Majdalani and Zreiq. Hoda Rizk has mapped the demographic changes caused by the civil war in the country, noting that in Beirut, for example, Greek Orthodox people from the Mazraa sector and Protestants from Mosaytbeh in west Beirut have moved to the Metn (Christian mountain), although they are still registered to vote in Mazraa. Similarly, Muslims who lived in Achrafieh, Rmeil and Saifi in the east of the city were displaced or moved to the west of the city during the civil war.[39]

Elected in 2010, Nqoula Razzouq is the only Christian mukhtar of the Mazraa district. He is from the Mazraa sector and his office is located a few metres behind his residence there. When I met him, he recalled from his youth a beautiful scene of old Mazraa, describing a series of yellow houses fenced with cactus trees – a description not dissimilar to the one given by mukhtar al-Madhoun. According to Razzouq's narrative, Christians who lived in Mazraa were from the middle class; neither rich nor poor, they were property-owning landlords. They lived a simple life that attracted people from outside Beirut to come to Mazraa and rent apartments. He distinguished the lifestyle in the area from that of the aristocratic 'velvet society' (as he termed it) of the Christians in the Achrafieh area to the east of the city. He added that there was now nothing left from that scene, except one old heritage house and street gutters, which he thought were from the time of the French.

In analysing the reasons behind population change in the area, mukhtar Razzouq explained that not all the Christian families left, and that some of the younger generation remain in the area. He added that, while there are fewer Christians in Mazraa, Sunni Muslims have increased in number in Tarik al-Jdide, and the Shiite population has increased in Beirut in general, having started to settle in Mazraa in the middle of the last century. He identified two political dates, 1958 and 1975, that he believed had influenced the presence of Christians in Mazraa. The year 1975 marked the beginning of the civil war in Lebanon that led to major demographic changes, with internal migration in the whole country across a clear geographical division between west and east Beirut, mainly between Christians and Muslims. But previously, in 1958, he discussed how political troubles between Christians and Muslims almost led to a civil war, and ended with the election of a new president.[40] Razzouq related this movement by Christian residents from Mazraa to the fear and insecurity that they felt in the presence of the Muslim communities amid the political tension of the time.

I wanted to learn more about the social dynamics and interactions between Christians and Muslims before the civil war in the district, and across the two areas of Tarik al-Jdide and Mazraa. Mukhtar Razzouq was careful in his answers when I asked him about the social interaction between Christians and Muslims; he talked about his friendships with Muslim families from the neighbouring Tarik al-Jdide, and he dismissed any notion of tension.

Usama al-Aref, in his book *Zakerat Al-Raml* (Memory of the Sand), an autobiography exploring the author's memories of Tarik al-Jdide, writes about the tension between Christians and Muslims as they were expressed through the practices of childhood. He notes that the two communities were reluctant to mix with each other. This was reflected in the practices of one group of children who used to sneak a look across the Mazraa road from the top of the sandhill of Tarik al-Jdide at children playing on the opposite side, without inviting or engaging with them; instead they would sporadically throw stones at them across the road.[41] Al-Aref recalls that in the 1930s the fear of the other was promoted and supported by the dominant religious institutions in each community, such as faith schools. It was not until the end of the 1950s and early 1960s that Muslims from Tarik al-Jdide and elsewhere began to cross the road to live with the Christians in Mazraa. The country was evolving economically and culturally at this time and, according to Samir Kassir, this prosperity was coupled with more interaction between Christians and Muslims in the city.[42] By the mid-1970s, the Mazraa sector had been transformed from a predominantly Christian space into a mixed space comprising a Sunni and Shiite majority and a Christian minority; this transformation occurred most notably at the outbreak of the civil war.

Frank Mermier has discussed the 'real and imaginary' city of Beirut in relation to the common representation of the city as a Sunni and Greek Orthodox place, and how its current population, which now includes other sects, has been a threat to the original residents of the city:

> the common representation of Beirut urban life considers the Sunnis and the Greek Orthodox as two groups which are the only truly urban communities under a so-called 'right to the city' linked to their urban historical antecedents. Maronites, Druze and Shi'i are linked to spaces of reference other than the city, such as the mountains for the first two, and the south and the Bekaa regions for the Shi'i.[43]

According to Mermier, the urbanization of the Shiites happened after independence; in moving into Beirut at that time, they resided mainly in the southern suburb of the city, but also in various other neighbourhoods, such as in the Mazraa district.[44] By 1973–4, just before the outbreak of the civil war, the Shiites constituted 20.3 per cent of the population within Beirut's municipal border.[45] This number has since grown, partly due to the displacement of the Shiite community by the Israeli occupation of the south of Lebanon from 1978 to 2000 and their series of wars and invasions in the years 1978, 1982, 1996 and 2006.[46]

Al-Madhoun related demographic changes to economic factors and to the high prices of property in Beirut, which has caused 'Beirutis' to sell their properties and buy and live outside the city in the suburbs to secure houses for their children in more affordable areas. The issues around the population shifts were also pointed out to me by mukhtar Ghareib Hassan, whose office is in Mazraa.[47] When I met him in January 2010, he mentioned that by the end of 2009 nine Sunni families had sold their houses in the building where his office is based and nine Shiite families had moved in. Demographic changes along Sunni–Shiite lines in Beirut are not mapped, nor are they the subject of political debates in the media. The current debate concerning property in the media is mainly related to Arab investors from the Gulf and Lebanese Shiite investors buying properties from Christians in Kiserwan and from Druze in the Chouf Mountain[48] (which I discuss in Bordering Practice 4 on Displacement). However, residents talk about changes in the city with great anxiety, hinting at a political plan behind these population movements; this is particularly the case among the Sunni community who fear the expansion of the Shiite population in Beirut and their buying of properties and land.[49]

It is interesting to note that, to answer my question concerning demographic change, the Greek Orthodox mukhtar referred to the period before the civil war, when the Christians had a strong presence in Mazraa and were threatened by incoming Muslims in general, whereas the Sunni mukhtar focused on the present time of the current Sunni presence in Mazraa being threatened by Shiite expansion and/or dominance. Between the two mukhtars, and the political events with which each was concerned, lies the period of the civil war and its aftermath – these 15 years remain an important gap in time, during which the confessional power-sharing system persisted, but the political equation in the country changed. The mukhtars expressed different opinions; an absent voice was that of a Shiite mukhtar, as it is this sect which is officially and administratively unrepresented within the Mazraa district, despite the local political power and presence of the Shiite Amal movement and Hezbollah.

NUMERIC BORDER

Mukhtar, are those who reside in the area the same as those who vote in it?

Fig.23 (Top)
Document 4: personal registry logbooks.

Fig.24 (Bottom)
Material Evidence 4: written information on the edges of the books.

Q. Nowadays Mazraa residents are from different sects? What is the distribution or number of residents by sect?

A. Sure, the Sunni sect is the highest percentage at 80 per cent; the Shiite and Greek Orthodox are of equal percentages.

Q. Ten per cent Shiite and 10 per cent Orthodox?

A. No, there are other sects in the Mazraa, 18 sects; all of them constitute 20 per cent.

[He shows me two piles of documents for residents who are registered to vote in the Mazraa: males and females, and their sect. He demonstrates and compares numbers between the logbooks that are for the Sunni residents – nine in total – with one for the Shiite and Orthodox residents and another for the other sects. He asks me to calculate the percentages myself, and I see that the Shiite and Orthodox are less than 10 per cent each. He then says: 'I said both are 10 per cent, but I guess they are less.' He adds: 'Pack the papers on top of each other and you do the calculation.']

Q. Is the mukhtar election based on a sectarian quota system? Is it similar to the parliamentary election?

A. No, there is no sectarian distribution in this field of work. It is based on numbers of votes.

Q. So is there an official law that defines and specifies the number of Sunni and Christian mukhtars?

A. No, but we [Sunnis] being the major sect in the Mazraa prefer to have one Orthodox Christian mukhtar among the 15 mukhtars for the district, because this is an old custom that we are committed to continuing [the number of mukhtars in total per district is based on the number of the population of that district]. In the past two electoral rounds – 1998 and 2004 – the Orthodox candidate had no luck because Greek Orthodox residents could not agree on one candidate. In the 2010 electoral round, we insisted that only one Orthodox should run in the election, to avoid the division and the low number of votes. And this is exactly what happened – he got a similar number of votes to us, around 16,000.

Q. You mean mukhtar Razzouq.

A. Yes, Tony Razzouq [his real name is Nqoula Razzouq].

Q. Are the documents in the cabinet for residents who live in the area?

A. No, they are for the residents who vote in the Mazraa. You are asking me about residents who vote.

Q. Okay then, current residents are different from those who vote.

Those residents who do not vote – do they refer to you for their official procedures/paperwork?

A. If the procedure needs a mukhtar, they can refer to the mukhtar of their place of residence as well as the mukhtar of their original place of birth [Kayd].

Q. Is it possible to know the sect of residents living in a certain neighbourhood?

A. That is what we and the government do not agree on. Not all of those who live here are registered with us and we are constantly being asked to identify all of them in official procedures, but we don't know anything about newcomers.

Q. Since you are originally from the Mazraa and you live and work here, from your own observation, to what extent does the percentage of current residents match the percentage of those who officially vote in the Mazraa?

A. It does not match at all; I would say 50 per cent.

Q. Do you think that the Mazraa's current residents of non-Sunni sects should have their own mukhtar from the same sect, for example the Shiites?

A. Not necessarily; the Shiites are not a majority in the Mazraa.

Q. You previously said that there is a custom to have one Greek Orthodox mukhtar.

A. I said the custom before the end of the civil war was seven mukhtars: six Sunni and one Orthodox [since then this number has gone up to 15 mukhtars in total]. And we kept this practice which we consider heritage. Shiite residents are new to the Mazraa; they are not from the original residents. Our Shiite brothers are less than 10 per cent and if they were able to have [elected] their own mukhtar, they would have already done that – sorry for saying that. First of all, the Shiites are Muslims and we have the same holy book, but the Orthodox are Christians and I do not understand and so I am not able to deal with procedures that relate to their religion. Whereas I'm able to do that for the Shiites as they are Muslims.

The answer I received to the question concerning the numbers and percentages of the sectarian background of the population in the Mazraa revealed the discrepancy between the numbers in official records and the reality on the ground. The mukhtar gave percentages of people from each sect in the Mazraa district, both from before the civil war and more recently. The numbers he gave were based on the personal registry logbook that he used to answer my question. The logbook contains personal information of residents registered in the district and their families, including name, sex, religion, sect, and registry number. These numbers and percentages are used for electoral purposes, whether parliamentary or municipal. But the place where someone is registered and votes (in other words, their place of origin) is not necessarily the same as their place of residence. The country has witnessed many demographic changes, especially due to internal migration from villages to cities as a result of economic hardship or the civil war; Beirut, in particular, has a high population density of people from all over the country. People who are originally from the Mazraa and registered there, for example, could now be living outside Beirut in the suburbs. Similarly, some of the current residents of the Mazraa might come from southern Lebanon and go back to their place of birth to vote in elections.[50]

Krayem relates the main deficiency in the current municipal and mukhtar electoral law to the fact that voting is based on the place of origin of voters and not on their place of residence.[51] This creates municipalities that do not represent their residents, especially in Beirut city. This issue of local representation is central to the notion and practice of citizenship, particularly at the level of the municipality and districts.

The demographic changes and perseverance of the political representation system create a clash in the relationship between places and their residents, and between the 'legal' and the 'real' cities.[52] According to Mermier:

> The current electoral system, which maintains the political and symbolic link to the locality of 'origin', keeps this 'communitarian' link alive while distorting it through a combination of demographic changes, which make such populations more or less homogeneous. This results in the discrepancy between the 'legal city' (with an absentee electorate) and the 'real city' (with an urban population composed largely of immigrants and war refugees).[53]

Prior to the civil war, the Christians feared that the collection of statistics would reveal that they were not a majority, and that this would entail a change in the distribution of political power; later, in the post-war era after the Taif agreement, the fear was of changing the parity between Muslims and Christians. In the present, fear of numbers is still valid, especially in the Christian community, which is said to have shrunk further due to emigration. This fear has also increased among Muslims, between the Sunni and Shiite populations, as new numbers might reveal one or other sect to be in the majority. Arda Arsenian Ekmekji, commenting on the anxiety among the Sunni and Shiite communities and how this has affected their relationship with the Christians, writes: 'It is even true that most Lebanese Muslims would feel safer with a Christian neighbor than with the "wrong" Muslim one.'[54]

Much criticism has been made of the Taif agreement for regenerating and further institutionalizing the confessional political system in the country.[55] Nevertheless, more recently there have been unofficial talks that call for a new agreement to reflect the actual sectarian distribution of the population. The rationale behind this is that the parity between Muslims and Christians is no longer valid, and that the division, rather than being between two major religions, should be among three sects: Christian, Sunni, and Shiite.[56] However, since no political party has proposed an alternative agreement or has officially voiced its opposition to the Taif, it remains unclear whether this new proposed equation could dictate the future political system in the country – or perhaps even trigger a new war.

Wendy Pullan, referring to a map produced through her architectural research, described the current sectarian distribution of residents in Beirut as 'dangerous'.[57] Her comments were based on what the map reveals about the high concentration of the Shiite community within the municipal borders of Beirut, and how, over time, this community has extended north from the southern suburb of Beirut. This situation contradicts the common official representation of Beirut as the 'Sunni Orthodox Christian' city, and it exposes the potential concern behind the use of numbers to state which sectarian community is in the majority. As I have explained above, the issue of numbers relates to the administrative and electoral representations in the city. The map that Pullan presented, and the personal registry logbook, shown me by the mukhtar, that documents the district's residents, reveal different and at times conflicting information. Taken together, they indicate the discrepancy that exists between different representations of the city. The concern is that an official document can distort and replace the situation on the ground, particularly if it is treated as the sole representative record of a place and its residents.

URBAN BORDER

Mukhtar, did the main road divide the area into two sides?

Fig.25 (Top)
Document 5: Tarik al-Jdide health and social guide.

Fig.26 (Bottom)
Material Evidence 5: tramway photograph.

A. The old train route used to connect the beginning of Tarik al-Jdide – behind my office – to downtown Beirut, then Jemayzeh. Here is a photo of the Beirut train, which you do not know. [He shows me a book that has a photograph of the Beirut train on its cover.]

The end of the train route indicates the limit of residents' habitation. The Mazraa used to end at the end of the train route.

Tarik al-Jdide is relatively new – it is from the 1940s and 1930s – compared to the Mazraa which was built in the 1910s and 1920s and maybe even earlier. During the Ottoman period the Mazraa was not very developed.

[Here the mukhtar tells me a story about his grandmother, who lived under Ottoman rule. She was born in 1886 and died aged 96, and she told how people of central Beirut used to consider those who left to live in the suburbs of Beirut, such as Mazraa, as emigrants who travelled far away.]

Beirut's urban growth started in the downtown commercial district.

As for the Tarik al-Jdide area, at the time of the French mandate, Greek Orthodox residents of the Mazraa say that they were given land in Tarik al-Jdide by the French. The land used to be measured with the belts that men used to wear around their robes. Plots of land around 10,000 m².

This land was previously Waqf Imam Ouzai. You know, each new state or regime considers the land of a previous state to be theirs, and the French distributed this land to Christians for free.

Q. Did Muslims reclaim their land from the Christians?

A. No, Christians sold them the land. I bought property for the Arab university from our Christian brothers in the Mazraa.

Q. Since 2005, there have been many changes in the city, new demographic distributions. You mentioned that during the Israeli invasion of 1982 the Mazraa district was divided into two areas, but also during the civil war there were clashes and divisions between Tarik al-Jdide and Mazraa?

A. I said once that they are following the same logic of the Israelis by dividing areas and disconnecting them.

We had a demarcation line that separated west Beirut from Achrafieh (east Beirut) during the civil war.

Q. So you don't consider Mazraa to have always been two areas, the Sunni Tarik al-Jdide and the Christian Mazraa, and now the Sunni and the Shiite areas?

A. No, there was no Tarik al-Jdide.

Q. But in the 50s?

A. Tarik al-Jdide land was owned by Christians and they sold their land to Muslims; then the Mazraa borders used to end where the Mazraa Main Road is today. It used to be full of cactus trees that marked the edge of the Mazraa. Beyond that was empty land. If someone wanted to kill a person, he would take him to the cactus field and no one would notice.

The main road was paved in the 50s, more precisely at the end of the 50s.

Q. Did it divide the area into two?

A. Why to divide it? I'm against this story. Anyway, the Sunnis were a majority in the Mazraa [the old borders] and remained a majority on the other side [the new Mazraa that includes Tarik al-Jdide]. The Sunni majority in Tarik al-Jdide is not originally from the Mazraa, they are from outside Beirut from Al Iqleem.

The original Mazraa Sunnis live in the northern side of the old Mazraa and not in Tarik al-Jdide.

You need to look at the other neighbourhoods in the Mazraa around the Christian zone – they are full of Sunni residents and they used to live together with the Christians.

There is nothing called separation or division – people mix and live together.

Q. Let's go back to the 2005 incidents or conflict.

A. What are these incidents?

Q. The assassination of Prime Minister Hariri.

> A. This is not an incident or conflict; the Hariri assassination has nothing to do with the Tarik al-Jdide situation. Tarik al-Jdide was under political custody at many times. The Palestinians during the civil war considered Tarik al-Jdide their security zone; it was their border. The Lebanese army in 1973 stood there [at the Mazraa Main Road] and wanted to enter Tarik al-Jdide and they could not. The Palestinians in recent incidents went to the streets and stood at the Mazraa Main Road. They consider it a primary defence line for their military that no one should go beyond, because if anyone crosses that line it means then they can access the neighbourhoods behind it. It is an exposed line.

Q. So it's a symbolic line?

> A. No, it's a strategic line, one that they can defend the whole area and have barricades on. It's a wide demarcation line, a logistical line that does not separate areas but rather protects them. It is a military separation.

> And for your information, it is not true that there are no Shiite residents in Tarik al-Jdide; there are plenty. The building on the opposite side from the building we are in is inhabited by Shiites and the one over there ... and the one behind ... They live together and they don't say anything. I'm the mukhtar and I know.

> In Afif Al Tybe commercial district, all the wholesale traders are from our Shiite brothers.

Q. So it is still a mixed area?

> A. People try to portray the area as a Sunni area but it's not. If Shiite residents want to make trouble, they very well can. They have property and own depots. Who knows what they are hiding there?

Fig.27
Map of Beirut by Julius Loytved, Danish Vice-Consul, 1876.

My conversation with the mukhtar became strained when I attempted to understand the kind of borders that exist between sects across the Mazraa. The intention of my initial question was to try to imagine, and perhaps visualize, the old geographic landscape and the urban scenery of the area before the main road was built between Mazraa and Tarik al-Jdide. Through my question I had hoped to examine whether the mukhtar thought that urban and architectural planning had helped to create or support social and political segregation and even violent demarcation, such as the clashes and demarcation lines experienced on the Mazraa Main Road and throughout the history of conflict in modern Beirut.

The Mazraa Main Road, or Corniche Mazraa, built in 1957–8, splits the Mazraa administrative district into a northern and a southern side and separates Mazraa from Tarik al-Jdide. This is mentioned in the municipal booklet referred to by the mukhtar. A series of maps produced in years that witnessed events of key importance in Lebanese history – for example: the 1870s, during the Ottoman rule; the 1920s, and the French declaration of Greater Lebanon with its present limits under the French mandate; the 1940s, and the independence of Lebanon from the French mandate; the 1950s and 1960s, during a period of development and prosperity for the Lebanese republic – illustrate the urban growth around the road.

An old map dated 1876 and presented to Sultan Abdul Hamid II by Julius Loytved, the Danish Vice-Consul,[58] includes a legend that names Beirut's 12 districts, of which some are known by different names today; notably, Mazraa (Farm)

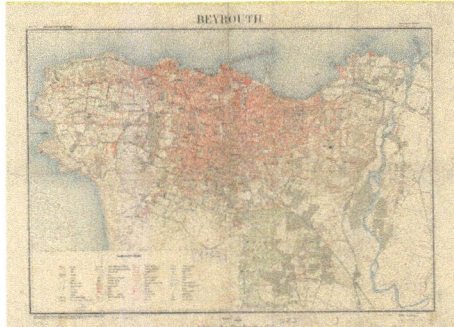

Fig.28
Map of Beirut, Bureau Topographique de L'Armée Française du Levant (A.F.L.),
1922.

district is named Mazraat el-Arab (Arab Farm). Mazraat el-Arab appears as a less developed area compared to the city centre (downtown) in the north of Beirut and its surrounding areas. There is no mention at all of Tarik al-Jdide in the map of 1876. Topographically, what is known today as Tarik al-Jdide looks like an empty sand hill to the southern side of Mazraat el-Arab on the outskirts of the city – it marks the limit of the map (Fig. 27).

A map dated 1919 mentions the name Mazraa instead of Mazraat el-Arab. In a more detailed map with a legend, dated February 1922,[59] the Mazraa roads, pavements, vegetation and built houses are visible. The area appears developed but still less dense than the city centre and the areas around it. The map names Rue d'Alsace Lorraine as a main road in Mazraa, with houses along its north and south sides. The road and the area appear to define the southern border of habitation and urban planning in Beirut. To the south is the hill; what later becomes known as Tarik al-Jdide appears almost deserted, apart from a few houses. The map shows the tramway route going all the way from the north of the city, through the city centre, and along Mazraa's east side, ending in Mazraa where dense habitation ceases. Towards its end, the tramway route extends into a main road with houses around it; the road continues further south of the city. Along its east side, the road defines Forêt des Pins (Pine Park) and cuts through Beirut's municipal border towards the south (Saida city). The end of the tramway route also connects to an unpaved (dotted) side road that goes around the hill's eastern and southern borders; the map does not name these roads (Fig. 28).

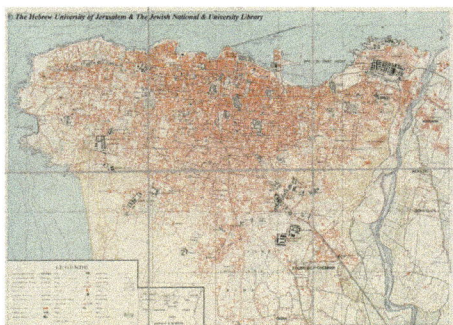
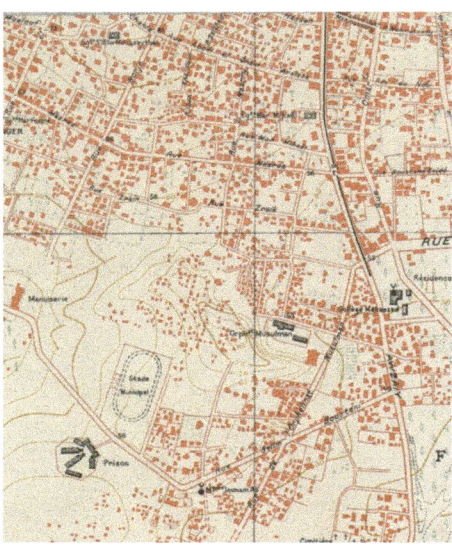

Fig.29
Map of Beirut, Bureau Topographique des Troupes Françaises du Levant
(T.F.L.), 1936.

Mukhtar al-Madhoun showed me a photograph taken in the 1920s of the old tramway, where the road ended right behind his office (Fig. 26).

In a map from 1936,[60] Mazraa has expanded along its southern side towards the beginning of the sand hill that will later be called Tarik al-Jdide. There is an increase in the number of houses scattered on top of the hill and down its eastern and southern sides. The map names the two roads east and south of the hill that were unpaved in the 1922 map. These are Rue de l'Orpheline Musulman and Rue Salim Bustani, the latter heading towards the Beirut prison. Around these roads and adjacent to Pine Park the habitation is denser. It is clear from this map that the urban development towards what is now known as Tarik al-Jdide began around the end of the tramway route parallel to Pine Park (Rue Awzaiy), and that it developed further around Rue de l'Orpheline Musulman and Rue Salim Bustani. The map does not name Tarik al-Jdide either as a road or as an area (Fig. 29).

In a 1941 map,[61] Mazraa looks even more developed and extended: there is a cluster of building plots surrounded by narrow roads, but no distinct urban division between its northern and southern sides, where the main road is currently located, apart from the natural division of the hill between the northern and southern sides. The location of the current main road can be traced on this map by following a road that is unnamed, narrow, short and less linear. It is interesting that in the maps from 1941 and 1936 Rue d'Alsace Lorraine is renamed Rue Mazraa, and Rue Mazraa appears as a major road in the Mazraa area, and that

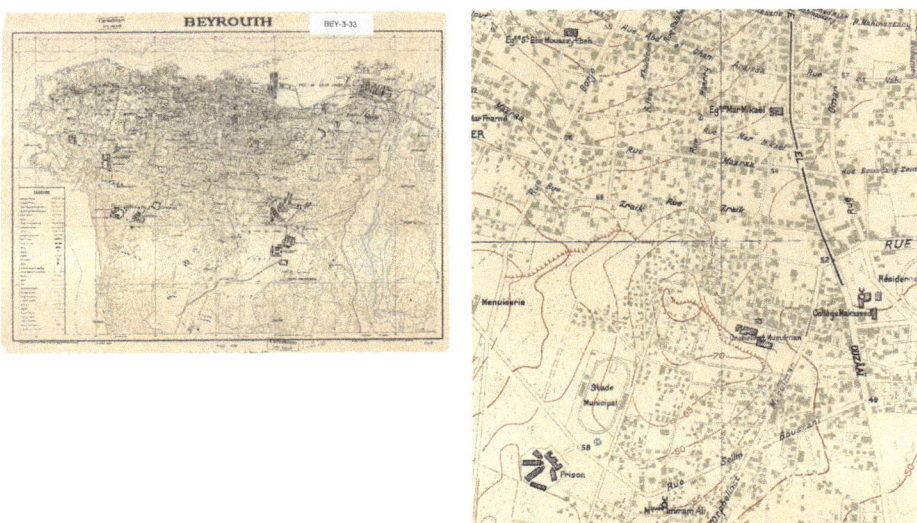

Fig.30
Map of Beirut, Annexe de l'Institut Geographique National au Levant, 1941.

on the map it looks wider than the other roads and is connected to the major road network in the city. The 1941 map also shows another important, albeit narrower, road on the southern side of Mazraa – closer to Tarik al-Jdide – which is named Rue Zraik. That this road is named on the 1941 map is an indication of the importance of Mazraa's southward urban growth to fill what was once empty land. Tarik al-Jdide still does not appear as a name on the map (Fig. 30).

A map from 1959[62] – a time of prosperity in the republic – shows the birth of the wide main road named Boulevard Mazraa or, as people call it today, Corniche Mazraa, as an extension to Rue Fouad in the east of the city; the latter first appeared as Rue du Parc, a main road in the 1922 map. Boulevard Mazraa splits the cluster of plots and introduces a divide not just in the area around it but also in the city of Beirut as a whole. It is part of a circular road that goes around Beirut from its southern to its eastern side along Beirut river, continuing north and west of the city along the coast. Boulevard Mazraa appears as if it defines the edge of the city, marking its southern urban border, whereas the other three borders are defined by water: the Mediterranean Sea on the west and north sides, and Beirut river on the east. The road leaves the southern part of Mazraa district on the other side of this belt; however, the map still does not name Tarik al-Jdide. The map also names only Rue de l'Orphelinat Musulman and Rue Selim Bustani as important roads in the area (but with different spellings from Rue de l'Orpheline Musulman and Rue Salim Bustani) (Fig. 31). The number of houses in Tarik al-Jdide increases over this period, and the area is developed with a school,

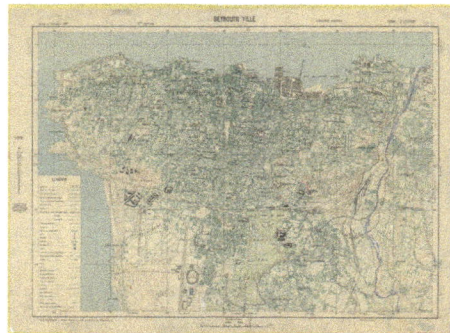

Fig.31
Map of Beirut, Service Geographique, 1959.

the Stade Municipal, and the Beirut prison (Prison de Sables). Even if the area has no name, it was called Tarik al-Jdide by those who lived there – such as mukhtar al-Madhoun and Usama al-Aref.

In an untitled map dated 1962, Beirut's major areas are clearly named and include, for the first time, Tarik al-Jdide (Tariq ej Jdide) to the south of Corniche Mazraa (Corniche el Mazraa); the Mazraa area (El Mazraa) is on the northern side of Corniche Mazraa.

In the map of the Beirut administrative division of districts and sectors issued by the municipality, and which the mukhtar presented, the east part of Rue Salim Bustani, which was unpaved in the map of 1922, has been renamed the Tarik al-Jdide road, or the New Road. The end of that road on its south side marks the limits of the Tarik al-Jdide sector (number 56 of the Mazraa district). However, I have no information on the exact date that the sector and the road were officially recognized and named.

The historical maps provide a certain narrative of the urban development of the area. The maps raise questions about what it means for a place to be recognized. Is it when it becomes politically important to name an area for those who make the map? What does it mean not to recognize an area as important enough to have a name, even if it is densely occupied and called something else by those who live there?

Reading the maps from the years 1876, 1922, 1936, 1941 and 1959 shows the direction of urban growth in Beirut: moving out from the city centre – located in the north by the sea – towards the south, east and west. The construction of Corniche Mazraa after Rue Mazraa (in time) and below it (in location) indicates the direction of the gradual expansion of Beirut and of Mazraa, as the new road becomes the centre of the Mazraa district. This urban development of Beirut also gave birth to the Tarik al-Jdide area that was developed to the east and south of the Mazraa district and expanded north to connect with the Mazraa area.

It might be possible to argue, then, that Rue Mazraa in the 1930s and 1940s was defined by the Christians living around it on both sides and as the centre of the Mazraa district, whereas, by 1958, Corniche Mazraa was defined as the district's centre and divided the Christian Mazraa (a mixed area today) from the Muslim Tarik al-Jdide. The main road was paved in 1958, which was also a year of revolution – a signal of civil war in the republic – and a date mentioned by mukhtar Razzouq as the starting point for the departure of the Christian Mazraa and the sharpening division of east and west Beirut. It is also worth reflecting that, in relation to my research project, the road operates as a border – as an edge, between one area and another, or as a division through an area, between one side and another. It is a subtle but complex difference, which perhaps depends on the kind of representations that lines make on maps, and on who draws them and for what purpose.

Mukhtar Nizar Syoufi, whose office is off the Mazraa Main Road on the Tarik al-Jdide side and who is a resident of Tarik al-Jdide, told me in an interview of the recurring history of violence of the whole area and the role played by the main road as a demarcation line, something he has witnessed from his shop since the 1980s. In response to my questions about how the road operates as a demarcation line, Syoufi related stories which depict the road and the sur-rounding neighbourhoods as a battleground where new political parties (militias) and alliances repeated events similar to those that occurred in the past. His stories refer to dates and times, moving from 1982 when the occupying Israeli army divided the area at the main road, to the civil war clashes in the 1980s, particularly in 1984 between many opposing parties struggling for control over west Beirut, including the Sunni Mourabitoun party from the Tarik al-Jdide side, the Shiite Amal movement from the Mazraa side, and the Druze Progressive So-cialist party.[63] He also told of the more recent incidents of 2007 and 2008, which took place between the Sunni Mustaqbal in Tarik al-Jdide and the Shiite Amal movement in the Mazraa. Syoufi's narratives present the negotiation between present and past, as he narrates the shifting demarcation lines on the streets of Beirut along different political alliances.

On 24 January 2007, after a day of rage in the country that I referred to at the start of this book, *An-Nahar* newspaper ran a piece entitled 'Violent clashes centred in Corniche Mazraa brought back the memory of civil war'.[64] On 23 January 2007, a general strike was called in Lebanon by the Shiite-affiliated 8 March bloc with the aim of bringing down the Sunni-affiliated 14 March bloc government. Their strategy was to block the country's main roads with human barriers, sand hills and burning tyres. Corniche Mazraa was one of these roads, and people in Beirut followed the events there with great apprehension, anxiously watching news on television screens as the strike turned into street clashes, with stones and sticks being thrown between supporters of the two opposing blocs living in the two adjacent areas. That day marked the spatiality of the sectarian dimension of the political conflict in the streets through the actual and symbolic role of the Mazraa as a border and place which engenders bordering practices, and the broadcast images brought back memories of the civil war and associated sectarian territories. The incident of 23 January 2007 demonstrated the symbolic role the road still holds for both sides as the line of Sunni–Shiite sensitivities, the clashes in 2007 being confined to a short, 200-metre stretch of the road, leaving the rest of it and the other geographic borders of Tarik al-Jdide and Mazraa almost untouched. My reading of this localization of clashes in 2007 is that it provided a small-scale testing ground or a show of power between the opposing groups for assessing potential scenarios in preparation for the next round of more elaborate and extensive clashes. The road is also, as al-Madhoun described, a strategic logistical line to protect the Sunni community behind it, including the Sunni Palestinians who live in the Shatila refugee camp on the south-west fringe of Tarik al-Jdide. Currently, the road and the two areas it divides continue to represent and symbolize the country's ongoing Sunni–Shiite tension.

CULTURAL BORDER

Mukhtar, did you used to watch the TV series *E'Dinyeh Heik*?

Fig.32 (Top)
Document 6: Beirut mukhtars' council guide.

Fig.33 (Bottom)
Material Evidence 6: photograph of Ibrahim al-Kaissi, the head
of the first mukhtars' council in Beirut.

A. This was not during your time; you probably heard about it. I know Mohamad Shamil, the main actor, and his entire crew.

Q. To what extent do you find his character similar to that of a real mukhtar?

A. No, it was a comic character; it doesn't reflect the real mukhtar.

Q. But it was an ideal character, too.

A. Not true at all. This is a comic character created by Mohamad Shamil. My grandfather was a mukhtar from 1946 till 1980. He could 'rap politicians over the knuckles', and everyone used to respect him. If the mukhtar didn't agree on a parliamentary candidate, this candidate wouldn't win.

E'Dinyeh Heik was a comic programme.

Q. But in the TV series people used to refer to him to solve their problems – he was the wise person.

A. But not in this comic sarcastic way. I still play that role; people trust and respect the mukhtar. He is known to be wise with his words and in his actions, and he is serious in his relationship with others. He makes jokes and he is fun, there is no harm in that.

There is a person I would have liked to introduce to you if he was still alive; I wish I could have. He was the president of the first mukhtars' council in Beirut, Ibrahim al-Kaissi. In 1948 they created the mukhtars' council and my grandfather was the treasurer.

[He gets a booklet out of his drawer to show me the photos of the mukhtar he has just mentioned.]

Q. Who is the oldest mukhtar in the Mazraa today?

[He shows me a series of the Mazraa mukhtars' photographs in the book he has.]

A. You can consider the sequence of these photographs to lead to the oldest.

Q. So you are the oldest.

E'Dinyeh Heik was produced by the Lebanese national television station TV Liban between 1973–4 and 1992–3,[65] so it began a couple of years before the outbreak of the civil war and lasted until a couple of years after it ended, with a few breaks in between. The series was written by Mohamad Shamil, who also played the role of the mukhtar, and it was directed by several people over the lifetime of the programme.[66] Before and during the civil war, TV Liban produced many local series that were characterized by reference-less, nameless and sect-less characters and site-less places. The names of the characters in these series carried no indication of their religious affiliations and the places bore no local reference to any area in the country. No males were named Mohamad or George, for example, and no females were Fatimah or Marie. Instead the characters were given modern and more neutral names, such as Samar or Sameer. The removal of religious references from the programmes could be interpreted as an attempt to create an ideal place with no religious differences, or as a strategy to address the range of different sectarian communities in the country without provoking sensitivities, or as a deliberate denial of religious background. However interpreted, these programmes hid the problems caused or provoked by religious difference through neutral cultural connotations. *E'Dinyeh Heik* belonged to this genre of programme.

It was shot in a studio set of apartment interiors, shops and a men's café. Similar to other television dramas of that period, *E'Dinyeh Heik* had a low budget. The mukhtar's office depicted in the episodes changed over time, but its main feature was a desk, with documents and a logbook on top of it, and sometimes with a map of the world behind it. The office feels empty, like a mock-up in a furniture gallery. The mukhtar's office in *E'Dinyeh Heik* differs from the offices of the current mukhtars I visited, in that the current ones usually contain religious material and/or the president's photograph, depending on each mukhtar's situation.

The issues or topics discussed in the episodes are Lebanese – socially and culturally – Shamil having drawn inspiration from his own family life in the area of Tarik al-Jdide, as his son Naji Shamil told me in an interview.[67] That Mohamad Shamil has lived in Tarik al-Jdide was not known to me when I decided to include *E'Dinyeh Heik* in my research. However, the social life and interaction between neighbours in Tarik al-Jdide had inspired his writing of the episodes. The show's narratives are simple, everyday stories that present a social critique, rather than a political one. According to the son, Shamil was interested in addressing social issues and personal relationships indirectly and through humour. He presented characters that represent the full spectrum of society, including, for example, the 'traditional' man, the jealous or evil person, the loving married couple, and their narrated stories begin with a problem in a neighbourhood and end with the mukhtar character negotiating and resolving this problem.[68] Thus, the programme uses narrative as a form of bordering practice, and capitalizes on the mukhtar character as someone who practises borders by negotiating.

I have watched around 40 out of the 120 episodes produced, and I could not tell

Fig.34
Stills from *E'Dinyeh Heik*.

from the topics discussed which episodes were shot before or during the civil war. For example, one of the episodes presents a song by a female character, Zmurod (played by actress and singer, Feryal Karim). In the episode, Zmurod moves on from the neighbourhood to pursue her dream of being a singer in one of the city's clubs; her song in *E'Dinyeh Heik* was about the war, yet there was no discussion of war during the episode.

When I discussed *E'Dinyeh Heik* with mukhtar Razzouq, he told me that he admired the fictional mukhtar; for him, putting the figure of the mukhtar on national television gave it status and charm. It is interesting to compare mukhtar Razzouq's view with that of mukhtar al-Madhoun, for whom *E'Dinyeh Heik* is a 'sarcastic representation' that does not reflect the reality of the mukhtar, particularly, perhaps, the 'reality' of the older mukhtar – it is notable that, when defending his point of view and that of the mukhtar's position, al-Madhoun referred to Ibrahim al-Kaissi, the head of the first mukhtars' council in 1947, and not to any current mukhtar (Fig. 33).

The representation of life and of characters such as the mukhtar in cultural forms such as television programmes can also intervene in life and influence our perception of what life is, which recalls Mitchell's argument about the reciprocity between representation and life.[69] The way the pre-war generation, who grew up before and during the civil war, perceive the mukhtar and their relationship to him is constructed partially through their encounter with the fictional mukhtar character on television and partially through their encounters with actual ones in the districts. Today's post-war generation have a far less developed social relationship to the mukhtar; for these people, the mukhtar is the person who signs papers that facilitate legal procedures.

The mukhtar stands, however, somewhere between the image constructed of him – represented through a television series like *E'Dinyeh Heik*, as well as through old narratives and even songs such as those sung by Fairuz, Lebanon's popular singer since the 1960s, and told in the theatrical works and films of the Rahbani brothers – and the daily interactions that occur with him or her in the local district. Located between these different modes of representation, the mukhtar's character and role have changed over time.

HIDING

THE MUKHTAR: A PRACTITIONER OF BORDERS

All the evidence I have presented above plays a role in representing a particular kind of border. Each of the six kinds of border relates to administrative functions. Some of them are well defined through maps, documents, and regulations, and when applied through practice partially shape the life of the district; these borders are also negotiated through the practices of political parties operating inside and outside the state's institutions and residents' lived experience. Other administrative borders are less definite: they might be unwritten (such as customs), yet they are still practised and create a challenge to the officially announced borders – they are discordant with what they apparently represent or stand for.

Thus, asking mukhtar al-Madhoun about the Mazraa district revealed the social, spatial and political discrepancy and tensions between the administrative representations of the district and the current urban life of the district. The questions and answers revealed the border between the 'real' and the 'represented' and the ways in which the reciprocity and discrepancy between both constitute a site of negotiation. This is particularly the case at times of political conflict, when political and administrative representations are contested, detached from and symbolic of what they 'stand for' or 'take the place of'. The Q&A process also showed the role that narrative can play in this negotiation of borders: it was a form of bordering practice that revealed the evidence hidden in administrative procedures.

The mukhtar as a negotiator is a motif for bordering practice in situations of conflict, akin to the *flâneur* who, as an urban stroller, operates as a motif of modernity. Mukhtar al-Madhoun seemed to support, perhaps even defend, the official system, particularly when the content of the documents suited both his political position as a resident of the district and, perhaps, his sectarian background. At first, he referred to the official documents in order to represent the district; later he referred to his experience and what he knew as a resident of the district in order variously to correct, add to, explain and interpret the administrative representation and give a fuller picture of the district. In this respect, there are at least two realities to the Mazraa district, the legal city versus the real city.[70] But, this discrepancy does not position representation as separate from the everyday and its practices; rather, it renders the reality of the present time/space as a stage, product, and perhaps also condition, of these political and administrative representations.

Administrative and actual lives are related: both are in a constant negotiation that forms the social, spatial, and political space of the district and, hence, its reality, including its spatial practices and lived experience. The border practised by the mukhtar is one negotiated between the overt codes of (to use Lefebvre's terms) 'representations of spaces', as collated in maps and other official documents, and the more clandestine and hidden 'spaces of representation' narrated by the mukhtar in his negotiation of legalized procedures through and with those he represents in his district, as well as in his way of answering my questions. The mukhtar practises the borders of administration by oscillating in response to a question between that which can be shown as evidence and that which emerges through narration.

While it is possible to document in writing the questions I asked the mukhtar and the answers he narrated as a form of bordering practice in its own right, and while I have been able to describe in writing the different aspects of the borders practised by the mukhtar, the installation, *The Chosen Two*, which I devised out of the research material I gathered, does something else – something less direct and that is able to focus on the implicit rather than the explicit issues my questions sought to address. *The Chosen Two* suggests that different kinds of answers are hidden inside the administrative documents, answers which point towards the role of administrative, political and cultural representation in constructing 'real' life. It draws attention to the tensions between the real and representational through the construction of a spatial experience around bordering practices, characterized here in 'hiding'.

The Chosen Two gallery installation consists of three related components and media, located in a rectangular room: video footage projected on to the back wall faces the viewer as s/he enters the room; an audio recording plays out into the room; and two parallel lines of text positioned at eye level (at a height of approximately 160 cm above floor level) are applied along the two opposite walls leading from the entrance to the projection.

The video projection begins with a still image, showing the outline of an anonymous man sitting behind his office desk. This visual footage is coupled with audio footage in which a question in Arabic is directed to the mukhtar; these are taken from the lines spoken by actors in *E'Dinyeh Heik*. Similar still images, each with a slightly different body position, appear six times, accompanied each time by a different question. At the end of each question, the footage changes from a full-screen still image to a smaller image with a strip cut off at either the right, left, or lower side of the screen. The cuts reveal an image of the mukhtar himself – the man I interviewed – and frame his body as he moves from the desk in his office to fetch a document from the place in the room where he stores it. The audio accompanying these cuts includes sounds of office furniture and of the mukhtar moving around his office.

Consecutively, the six documents collected by the mukhtar are gathered, each one appearing after a cut, and are positioned in a growing line-up at the bottom of the screen from left to right. Once the six documents complete a line, the questions play again in the gallery space, and the order of the documents on the screen flips from left to right, announcing the start of a new scene and a new reading. After each of the six questions is asked again, the footage changes and shows a horizontal strip at the bottom of the screen framing the mukhtar's hands on his desk as he opens each of the six documents. The six documents at the bottom of the screen are replaced one after another with another set of material evidence extracted and highlighted from the initial documents, hinting that further answers are contained in the documents. The new set of documents stays horizontally on the screen, positioned at eye level at the same height as the text printed on the adjacent walls in the gallery space. As soon as the video ends, it begins again with the still image of a man behind his office desk.

The audio of the six questions from the television series is heard in the space, transcribed in Arabic, and translated and transcribed into English. The questions are printed one after the other and line up in a sequence in gold-coloured vinyl on the white walls. The Arabic text is on the right-hand side wall – running from the entrance into the gallery – and the English text is on the left-hand side wall – running from the projection wall to the entrance. Below each of the questions taken from *E'Dinyeh Heik* is another question in a grey colour: one in Arabic below the gold English question, and one in English below the gold Arabic version. The grey questions appear as if they are the translation of the text above them; in fact, however, they are not direct translations – rather, these are the actual questions I asked the mukhtar in my question-and-answer session with him. Having two different questions in two languages, one above the other, draws attention to the gap between the Arabic and English languages and the space of discrepancy generated by the process termed by Walter Benjamin as the untranslatability and foreignness between languages; this process offers a space of possibilities generated out of difference.[71] This is another aspect of the practice of bordering cultures: the role of translating in negotiating the gap between narrators working in different languages. It is a theme I explore in detail in *Bordering Practice 03: Translating*; here, I wish to draw attention not only to the gap between languages but also to the gap between real and represented and the role narration plays in presenting evidence. I regard this as a form of

bordering practice, one which operates as a form of critical spatial practice in alerting the audience to how evidence is also a form of cultural construction.

The linguistic arrangement follows the direction of each language and creates a spatial flow for the audience to follow between Arabic and English: where the Arabic questions end on one wall, the English ones begin on the opposite wall, and vice versa. The video footage of the documents on the wall between the two languages follows that flow. The documents lined up in the projection, and the texts printed along the walls, create a horizon through the exhibition space, connecting questions with answers, and bringing evidence into line with representation.

The design and conceptual planning of the installation follow a language of *hiding*, one which attempts to highlight how representations which present one reality might be obscuring another. This is evident from the juxtaposition of different media and sources of material in the gallery space, such as video footage from an interview, sound extracts from the television programme, and written text from both interview and programme. The resultant space, constructed out of these different forms of representation and media, aims to produce the experience of hiding, thereby highlighting how layers of representation of conflict do not simply represent an existing condition but actually construct it. I sought to do this by separating the administrative procedures into different spatial layers, where the mukhtar's movement and his use of documents – what he does and what he says – point beyond the image's frame to places and times located outside his office.

The official political system in Lebanon appears to provide a model of ongoing contestation throughout the history of the country by continuing to formulate definite official representations, which are deliberately symbolic in being extremely detached from what they stand for or 'represent'. This is a logic that applies both to the country's historical narrative and to its administrative one. These definite modes of political, cultural, and historical representation order – although differently – the city's social and political space by producing other forms and practices that hide between these layers of representation, and between the present and the past; thus, it becomes a perfect space for maintaining conflict in response to the ambiguity that is offered.

What I have presented in this chapter maps the discrepancies of the representations of the borders of the Mazraa district, in order to examine and describe the space of the everyday: a space constructed and negotiated through a bordering practice that 'hides' between the layers of representation, between the various forms of administrative procedures – even when contested – and between the practices of residents and political parties which operate in and outside the limits of the administration.

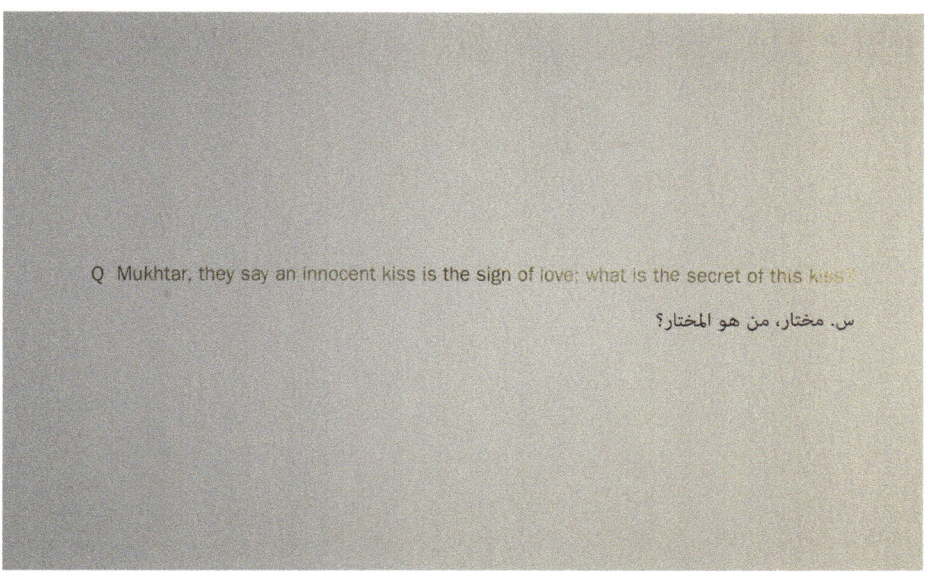

Q Mukhtar, they say an innocent kiss is the sign of love; what is the secret of this kiss?

س. مختار، من هو المختار؟

Fig.35 (Previous and Above)
The Chosen Two gallery installation at Exposure 2012 exhibition,
Beirut Art Center, Beirut, 2012.

Bordering
Practice 02

CROSSING

SURVEILLANCE

At Her Balcony

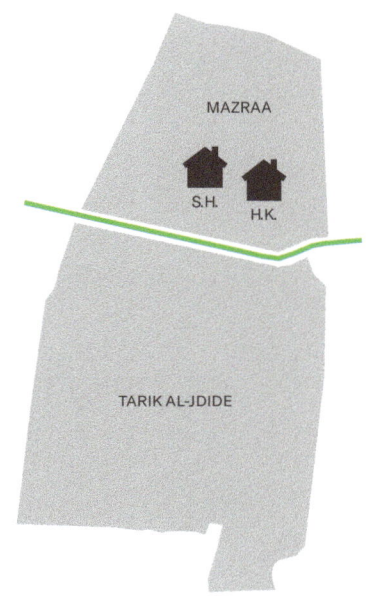

MAZRAA

S.H.

H.K.

TARIK AL-JDIDE

Fig.36
Map of the geographic location of S.H. and H.K residences.

Can I take a photograph from your balcony?

I selected two women, each of whom lived in an apartment with a balcony, in the same neighbourhood of Barbour (part of the Mazraa area) off the Mazraa Main Road. I asked them if I could take a photograph of the street from their balconies. The first woman, S.H., asked me to step back with my camera, not to turn left, and to stop photographing, as a hidden camera had been fixed somewhere on the opposite building by militia. The result of this was a single photograph. An hour later, and in an apartment building on an adjacent street, the second woman, H.K., eagerly led me to her balcony and removed the washing to show me the surveillance camera installed by the militia men on a tree opposite and very close by. Once she was sure the surveillance camera lens was pointing towards the street, she allowed me to take a photograph of it, though with caution. Ten days later, I took a car journey with a camouflaged video camera and recorded the crossing of the border of the Mazraa Main Road where the Lebanese army tank is positioned. The car and the video recording also passed by the two women's balconies and by the surveillance mechanisms S.H. and H.K. had pointed out to me and where the two photographs had been taken.

Fig.37
Photograph taken from S.H. balcony (above), and from
H.K. balcony (opposite), *At Her Balcony*, 2010.

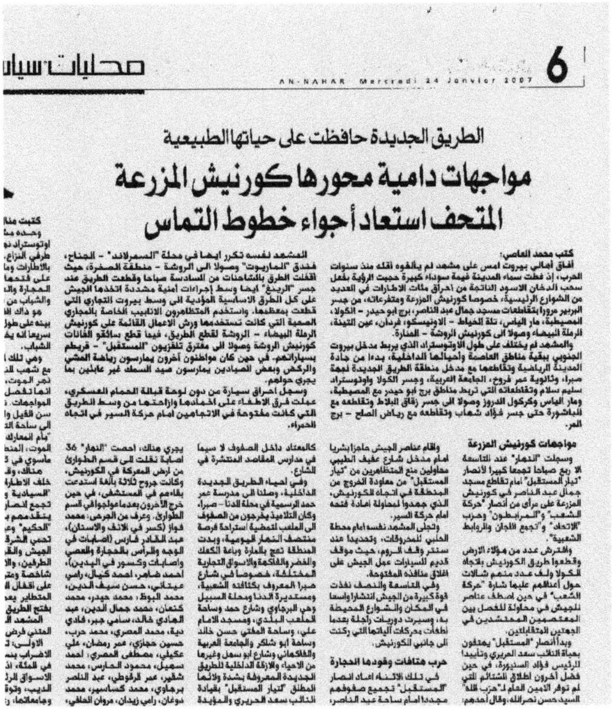

محليات سيا

AN-NAHAR Mercredi 24 Janvier 2007 6

الطريق الجديدة حافظت على حياتها الطبيعية

مواجهات دامية محورها كورنيش المزرعة المتحف استعاد أجواء خطوط التماس

كتب محمد العاصي:

أفاق أهالي بيروت امس على مشهد لم يألفوه أقله منذ سنوات الحرب، إذ غطت سماء المدينة غيمة سوداء كبيرة حجبت الرؤية بفعل سحب الدخان الاسود الناتجة من احراق مئات الاطارات في العديد من الشوارع الرئيسية، خصوصا كورنيش المزرعة ومتفرعاته، من جسر البربير مرورا بتقاطعات مسجد جمال عبد الناصر، برج ابو حيدر – الكولا، المصيطبة، مار الياس، تلة الخياط – الاونيسكو، فردان، عين التينة، الرملة البيضاء وصولا الى كورنيش الروشة – المنارة.

والمشهد لم يختلف على طول الاوتوستراد الذي يربط مدخل بيروت الجنوبي ببقية مناطق العاصمة وأحيائها الداخلية، بدءا من جادة المدينة الرياضية وتقاطعها مع مدخل منطقة الطريق الجديدة لجهة صبرا، وثانوية عمر فروخ، الجامعة العربية، وجسر الكولا واوتوستراد سليم سلام وتقاطعاته التي تربط مناطق برج ابو حيدر مع المصيطبة، ومار الياس وكركول الدروز وصولا الى جسر زقاق البلاط وتقاطعه مع الباشورة حتى جسر فؤاد شهاب وتقاطعه مع رياض الصلح – برج العر.

المشهد نفسه تكرر ايضا في محلة "السمرلاند" – الجناح، فندق "الماريوت" وصولا الى الروشة – منطقة الصخرة، حيث اقفلت الطرق بالشاحنات من السادسة صباحا وقطعت الطريق عند جسر "الرينغ" ايضا وسط إجراءات أمنية مشددة اتخذها الجيش على كل الطرق الاساسية المؤدية الى وسط بيروت التجاري التي قطعت بمعظمها. واستخدم المتظاهرون الانابيب الخاصة بالمجاري الصحية التي كانت تستخدمها ورش الاعمال القائمة على كورنيش الرملة البيضاء – الروشة لقطع الطريق، فيما قطع سائقو الفانات كورنيش الروشة وصولا الى مفترق تلفزيون "المستقبل" – قريطم بسياراتهم. في حين كان مواطنون آخرون يمارسون رياضة المشي والركض وبعض الصيادين يمارسون صيد السمك غير عابئين بما يجري حولهم.

وسجل احراق سيارة من دون لوحة قبالة الحمام العسكري، عملت فرق الاطفاء على اخمادها وازاحتها من وسط الطريق التي كانت مفتوحة في الاتجاهين امام حركة السير في اتجاه الحمراء.

مواجهات كورنيش المزرعة

وسجلت "النهار" عند التاسعة الا ربع صباحا تجمعا كبيرا لأنصار "تيار المستقبل" امام تقاطع مسجد جمال عبد الناصر في كورنيش المزرعة على مرأى من أنصار "حركة الشعب" و"المرابطون" وحزب "الاتحاد" و"تجمع اللجان والروابط الشعبية".

وافترش عدد من هؤلاء الارض وقطعوا طريق الكورنيش باتجاه الكولا ولف عدد منهم شالات حول أعناقهم عليها شارة "حركة الشعب" في حين اصطف عناصر للجيش في محاولة للفصل بين المعتصمين المحتشدين في الجهتين المتقابلتين.

وبدأ أنصار "المستقبل" يهتفون بحياة النائب سعد الحريري وتأييدا للرئيس فؤاد السنيورة، في حين فضل آخرون اطلاق الشتائم التي لم توفر الامين العام لـ"حزب الله" السيد حسن نصرالله، وقال أحدهم:

واقام عناصر الجيش حاجزا بشريا امام مدخل شارع عفيف الطيبي محاولين منع المتظاهرين من "تيار المستقبل" من معاودة الخروج من المنطقة في اتجاه الكورنيش، الذي جهدوا لمحاولة اعادة فتحه امام حركة السير.

وتجلى المشهد نفسه امام محطة الحلبي للمحروقات، وتحديدا عند ستنتر وقف الروم، حيث موقف قديم للسيارات عمل الجيش على اغلاق منافذه المفتوحة.

وفي التاسعة والنصف نفذت قوة كبيرة من الجيش انتشارا واسعا في المكان والشوارع المحيطة به، وسيرت دوريات راجلة بعدما أطفأت محركات آلياتها التي ركنت الى جانبي الكورنيش.

حرب هتافات وقودها الحجارة

في تلك الاثناء اعاد انصار "المستقبل" تجميع صفوفهم مجددا امام ساحة عبد الناصر،

كالمعتاد داخل الصفوف لا سيما في مدارس المقاصد المنتشرة في الشارع.

وفي احياء الطريق الجديدة الداخلية، وصلنا الى مدرسة عمر حمد الرسمية في محلة الدنا – صبرا، وكان التلاميذ يخرجون من الصفوف الى الملعب لتمضية استراحة فرصة منتصف النهار اليومية، وبدت المنطقة تعج بالمارة وباعة الكعك والخضر والفاكهة والاسواق التجارية المختلفة، خصوصا في شارع صبرا المعروف بكثافته الشعبية، ومستديرة الدنا ومحلة السبيل وحي البرجاوي وشارع حمد وساحة الملعب البلدي، ومسجد الامام علي، وساحة المفتي حسن خالد وساحة أبو شاكر والجامعة العربية والفاكهاني وشارع ابو سهل وغيرها من الاحياء والازقة الداخلية للطريق الجديدة المعروفة بشدة ولائها المطلق "لتيار المستقبل" بقيادة النائب سعد الحريري والمؤيدة

يجري هناك، احصت "النهار" 36 اصابة نقلت الى قسم الطوارئ من ارض المعركة في الكورنيش، وكانت جروح ثلاثة بالغة استدعت بقاءهم في المستشفى، في حين خرج الآخرون بعدما عولجوا في قسم الطوارئ. وعرف من الجرحى: محمد فواز (كسر في الانف والاسنان)، عبد القادر فارس (اصابات في الوجه والرأس بالحجارة والعصي واصابات وكسور في اليدين)، احمد ضاهر، احمد كيال، رامي عيتاني، حسن سيف الدين، محمد البوظ، محمد حيدر، محمد كنعان، محمد جمال الدين، عبد الهادي خالد، سامي جبر، فادي دية، محمد المصري، محمد حرب، حسين حجازي، عمر رمضان، علي عكيلي، مصطفى المصري، احمد سهيل، محمود الحارس، محمد شقير، عمر قرقوطي، عبد الناصر برجاوي، محمد كساسير، محمد دوغان، رامي زيدان، مروان الحلبي،

Fig.38
An-Nahar daily newspaper article, Wednesday, 24 January 2007.

VIOLENT CLASHES CENTRED IN CORNICHE MAZRA AL-MAT'HAF AREA BRING BACK THE MEMORIES OF CIVIL WAR DEMARCATION LINES...

Beirut residents woke up yesterday to a scene they have not witnessed since the civil war years...the sky was covered by a thick black cloud caused by the smoke of hundreds of burning car tyres in a number of main streets especially on corniche Mazraa road and the streets leading to it.

Translated excerpt from *An-Nahar* daily newspaper, Wednesday, 24 January 2007.

H.K.   12 January, 2010, 2–2:50 pm

Don't turn left. Step back. Stop photographing. It is there – the surveillance camera
is fixed somewhere on the opposite building. Just photograph from the right side
that looks onto the main street.

Be careful – they might see you and I don't want to get in trouble. The old yellow building
at the corner is an Amal movement building, can you see the green painted wall? It's
covering an Amal logo that was printed on the wall during the past period.

There is a new *arguilé* café at the end of the street across the pavement; it was opened
recently as a camouflage after the decision to halt street confrontations
and gatherings. It is where they gather and observe the neighbourhood nowadays.

I heard that they used to store weapons during the clashes inside one of those
arguilé café. Usually they grab plastic chairs and small tables from the shops and
sit at street corners. At night their motorcycles still pass by to challenge residents
and the state decision, they are the only group who have the courage to do so.

During the 'May 7 events', Amal used to take all the strategic buildings that over look Tarik
al-Jdide, to fire their RPG.

The opposite party – Mustaqbal movement – didn't have weapons; they just used Molotov
cocktails, which reached just outside the periphery of our area, nothing
went further inside the neighbourhood.

I don't sit on the balcony anymore; I close the living room curtains almost all the time.
Also I live alone and it's not appropriate to be seen outside on the balcony often.

She took me to the other balcony for a better view on the building she is referring to, the surveillance camera was not visible to the eye and she didn't allow me to photograph.

A military soldier with his weapon was standing at the corner of the building.

Later, I went to the place she described; I couldn't find the café but I found a pastry shop instead.

The government imposed a motorcycle curfew after 6 pm to stop neighbourhood raids by young guys.

S.H.   12 January, 2010, 3:15–4:00 pm

I have my morning coffee on the balcony... come and have a look at the surveillance camera; it is on that tree – can you see it?

Oh, do you want to photograph it? I'm not sure... the lens is facing the street, I think you could photograph it, right? Let me roll up the balcony awning. They added a metallic cover to protect it from rain, I guess. I asked the man who installed it whether it records both audio and video. He laughed and said that I should not worry, that it's just video.

Oh be careful don't photograph, naughty you. You are photographing an Amal building, the green one. Be careful they might notice.

We sleep with 'unlocked doors' as the Amal men protect the area, they never interfere with us, they are obliged to keep an eye on everyone and treat us well, for if anything bad happens to our houses we would accuse them.

They gather at street corners to observe and protect the area: a normal procedure. Even if you pass by Berri's former residence, that is two streets behind us; you will not notice their presence – no flag or gatherings.

A lot of shelling comes from the opposite neighbourhood, Tarik al-Jdide, down the road; we hear 'wzzz' all the time – snipers – but we have never seen anyone here. I hide in the kitchen; it is more sheltered.

I don't walk down there anymore to Tarik al-Jdide to visit my sister, neither do I allow my daughter to go; it's no longer a safe area there, it is a 'canton'; they might attack us.

It's a mixed neighbourhood here; very calm and safe, it's remained the same for years. Nothing has changed in the neighbourhood; everything is as it used to be...

I tried to photograph the camera spontaneously without her permission.

I noticed a green painted building that indicates the Amal movement who has power over the area since the civil war period.

I went afterwards to Berri, Amal movement leader, residence; there was a steel gate that regulated street access at night by Amal guys.

She didn't specify the period for the shelling; whether it happened during the short-lived clashes in 2007–8, or currently.

INTRODUCTION

At Her Balcony captures the dynamics of negotiation between surveillance mechanisms in urban space and residents in their interior spaces. The surveillance mechanisms include devices such as cameras and closed-circuit television (CCTV), sites such as militia buildings and observation coffee shops, and people such as security personnel and civilians on the streets and on motorcycles. Residents relate to surveillance in different ways that manifest as a contrast between safety and threat. This chapter explores the bordering practices produced by surveillance, the responses to it in Beirut neighbourhoods divided across political and sectarian lines, and how art practice – and, specifically, a critical bordering practice – can communicate an understanding of the spatial experience of surveillance.

Both S.H. and H.K. are female teachers in their late fifties. My research aimed to access the neighbourhood from the space of their balconies, which as sites of potential surveillance themselves occupy a border between the public space of the street and the private space of their apartments. From their balconies, I employed photography not only as a medium of documentation but also more critically as a device for measuring spaces of negotiation created by surveillance. Differences and distances – emotional, geographical, and political – are negotiated in these spaces; the differences and distances are both between the two women, and between their private interior spaces and the surveillance elements around them in public external space.

One of the main modern tools of surveillance is the camera. For this reason, I used the camera as my research tool in this project, as a device to survey surveillance and to explore the possibility of obtaining a neighbourhood panorama from the women's balconies. Photographic panorama was an exercise in gaining visual control over the neighbourhood scene, but it was also chosen as a political and metaphorical construction that situates the 'seeing' of the neighbourhood between residents' political differences and their lived experience.

The panopticon – a prison with a tower to observe the prison wings and their inmates – and the panorama – a tower or a space from which to observe urban and natural scenes – are both architectural spaces for observation that came into being in the late eighteenth century, and both mean 'all seeing'. Katrin Kaschadt comments on their similarities and on an important difference:

> the rooms constructed for each of them and their purpose of gaining visual control over the surroundings – nature in one case, the people under surveillance in the other – also resemble one another. But while the gaze is taught in the case of the Panorama, in the Panopticon it is used to teach.[1]

I refer to the panopticon as a metaphor and as a spatial setting of observation and control, in order to discuss surveillance practices in Beirut.

However, the distinction between the panorama and the panopticon as visual regimes, each with a distinct purpose for observation and control – the former over nature and the latter over people – became more complex with the intrusion of my camera to document and construct the photographic panorama at the women's balconies. Allan Sekula has commented that photography, as central to the development of technological surveillance apparatuses, has 'served to introduce the panopticon principle into daily life'.[2] Consequently, between the observer and the observed (the photographer and the photographed) there is an uneasy relationship. In the spatial conditions 'at the balcony', the visual observation operated by political surveillance in public urban space, and that of my photographic panorama at the balcony, were negotiated and became part of a surveillance gaze. This gaze comprised the personnel and devices in the public urban space, the women at their balconies, and myself – the researcher–artist with my camera. Each was operating a specific kind of observation of different politics and for different reasons. As this chapter will show, practices of observation and documentation are part of the practices of political surveillance, art and research.

Different modes of surveillance occur on 'a surveillance spectrum, from hard, centralized, panoptic control to soft, dispersed, persuasion and influence'.[3] Observation may be centralized and hard, such as the presence of the 'employer' and CCTV to observe employees in the workplace, or there may be a mix of hard and soft observation. State surveillance, for example, deploys, in addition to observation that can be seen, dispersed and invisible modes of observation such as computer-based, communication, electronic and biometric surveillance. Despite the current 'electronic technology-dependent surveillance' and the modern shift to a 'post-panoptic world', the panoptic concept of surveillance remains important as 'an ideal, a metaphor and a set of practices' that relate to knowledge, power and the role of visuality in modernity.[4]

The part of the surveillance spectrum that I am articulating in this chapter, and which has been particular to Beirut's practices of neighbourhood surveillance since the 2005 conflict, is that of hard 'panoptic control'; however, rather than being centralized, it has been diversified by the many opposing political forces operating it. Moreover, the surveillance presence varies between revealing and concealing itself to those it surveys: at times it is visible and revealed to everyone, while at other times it is camouflaged and concealed. The negotiation between the revealed and the concealed happens through spatial practices of surveillance that often borrow tactics from socio-spatial practices in the public realm, which include men sitting on street corners 'watching over' the neighbourhood.[5] Hence, I introduce to the surveillance spectrum 'domesticated surveillance' practices to explain the revealed and concealed nature of surveillance practices deployed by political parties in Beirut.

The presence of surveillance, set up in the name of security, influences the everyday spatial practices of the city's residents. It also influenced my research practices in this site with the residents. These practices, which included photography, video recording, note-taking and talking to people, occurred under observation by security devices, yet they also allowed a degree of resistance to take place while under surveillance. My project maps the surveillance practices, which, through being noticed, start to become visible.

The project was advanced through two exercises at the site. In the first, I met the two women in their living spaces, bringing my camera with me. Following the meetings, I planned the second exercise, which took place ten days later: a car journey, travelling from Tarik al-Jdide to Barbour and crossing the border at the Mazraa Main Road, which I documented with a video camera camouflaged in the car's dashboard. The project led from the urban site to the installation in a gallery space of *At Her Balcony*, a visual and textual panorama out of the revealed and concealed aspects of the neighbourhood gathered through my site-specific research. My research addressed the bordering practices of surveillance evident in the site; my responses to those practices involved my own bordering practice and critical spatial practice as an artist.

This chapter is in three parts that correspond to three conceptual panoramas connecting my different but related stages and modes of research, from site to theory to art installation. Panorama I sets the scene and highlights the border to be explored; it discusses *seeing* security and surveillance, and how these are deployed in Lebanon through *domesticated surveillance* practices. Panorama II focuses on *distance* and *difference* as variables in the implementation, assessment and reading of surveillance. Building on the first two panoramas, Panorama III concerns the presentation of the panorama of the gallery installation.

I propose in this chapter a bordering practice that happens through visual (immaterial) and physical (material) crossings of the neighbourhood's border. Crossing operates to describe first the various lines of vision created in the urban site itself through surveillance practices, and later the representational techniques used to construct the artwork and the audience's exploration of that artwork in the gallery space.

PANORAMA I

SEEING

I met S.H. and H.K. in January 2010. A new government had been assembled and a series of decisions and procedures among the opposing political groups was set to ease the tension in the country. A media truce had been announced and there was a reduction in the number of political slogans, banners, and militia personnel in city spaces. I wished to meet these women because their apartments were located in the Barbour neighbourhood: they both lived close to buildings belonging to the Amal movement, the dominant political party in the site. I was interested in the impact of the conflict and politics on the spatial practices and life in the neighbourhoods in the Mazraa district. The violent clashes of 2007 and 2008 had demarcated as a border the main road separating Barbour from the adjacent Tarik al-Jdide; I wanted to ask residents about the traces left by this and about how their lives had been transformed.

The question I asked each woman – Can I take a photograph from your balcony? – was a way of trying to find out whether the balcony offered a geographical vantage point and a platform to see. Their response to the presence of my camera at the balcony is what triggered the project to construct a panorama between the two women. At the time of its invention at the end of the eighteenth century, the panorama comprised a continuous and circular painted scene (initially of towns), hung and exhibited in a purpose-built rotunda, a place where it could be viewed by a town's inhabitants.[6] According to Bernard Comment, the panorama was a response to the expansion of towns to become metropolises during the industrial revolution that created a visual condition in which the whole landscape could no longer be viewed:

> The city exploded, becoming opaque, no longer visible. In conditions like these, the panorama had a decisive role to play. Not only did it express the perceptual and representational fantasies that befitted such troubled times; it was also a way of regaining control of sprawling collective space.[7]

The panorama offered people a position in the middle of the circular rotunda to gaze at the town which they were unable to see as a whole in real life; it provided the viewer with an illusion of superiority over a representation of reality over which they had no control outside the rotunda: 'They [the viewers] could be deluded into thinking that nothing has escaped them, that nothing would ever again be inaccessible to their gaze.'[8] The panorama offered, therefore, the possibility of control through visual means. For my project, the taking of a photograph from a balcony to see the neighbourhood could be understood as an attempt to gain control of the neighbourhood scene that had been restricted.

The balconies I visited belonged to female residents, and the project involved a gendered situation. This does not imply that exterior is male and interior is female, nor that male surveillance targets only females. But, as Fawaz, Harb and Gharbieh have commented on the issue of security and gender in Beirut, 'that security personnel are exclusively male dictates the necessity for a gendered analysis of urban public spaces.' They note that some females feel more secure walking at night in the presence of (male) security in their neighbourhoods, whereas other females find security personnel claustrophobic, and in conservative neighbourhoods some fathers prevent their daughters from walking in front of male security personnel. In this respect political security and 'social securitization' intersect.[9]

The balcony is not, however, a purely female place any more than the streets are a purely male space; both men and women exist in and use both spaces. The private/public interior/exterior border, with all its cultural, gendered and religious underpinning, is negotiated at the balcony by men and women. The balcony is a threshold across and between these spatial and cultural binaries; it is a space to negotiate and to connect to the other spaces beyond it. Through their presence at the balcony, women are protected both physically, by their higher position, and symbolically, by the patriarchal society; unattainable from the street and the surroundings, they are nevertheless exposed to the public gaze.

The anthropologist, Suad Joseph, complicates the notion of a public/private divide that is gendered into male-city/female-home by looking at it in relation to government, non- government, and domestic (family) life. She argues that the public/private divide, particularly in the case of Lebanon, is porous and has an imagined boundary that keeps shifting. Patriarchal connectivity flows across these categories, and under religious authority and kin relationships 'the domestic became a sacredly sanctioned domain of gender and age-based hierarchical relationships of women and men'. According to Joseph, 'men were relational and carried their familial model of relationships beyond the domestic domain', particularly at the time of nation-state establishment, into the economic and political realm. States build 'through culturally and historically specific ways, [and they] erect and gender their institutions and ideologies in their will to statehood'.[10] Patriarchy (male authority in the home) is, therefore, extended to other social domains, notably surveillance. It is within this extension of patriarchal familial influence into the political institutional context that the male surveillance on the streets of Mazraa and the women's habitation of their balconies operate. And it is on this threshold and in this particular in-between place – the women's balconies – that I sought to position myself to survey the neighbourhood and negotiate the politics of surveillance.

To understand the operation of the surveillance gaze across balconies and streets, Kaja Silverman's discussion of the politics of constructing and perceiving images is insightful. Following Jacques Lacan's concept of the gaze, Silverman defines the 'gaze' as an authoritative and broad process in the field of vision, which she differentiates from the 'look' that is part of the gaze but a more directed activity by subjects. Lacan deconstructed the system of perspective, proposing that the object (looked at) and the subject (who looks) are both the subject of representation for each other and that they are always mediated through images and screens in the field of the gaze which is separate from (or outside) the human eye.[11] The object and subject are both spectacles and spectators in and of the gaze, and they are both involved in constructing the image that others see. Silverman considers how the process of looking is part of a larger social and political network that includes the look, the gaze and the screen:

> the gaze manifests itself more through its effects than through its source. It impresses itself upon us through the sensation each of us [has] at times of being held within the field of the vision, of being given over to specularity.[12]

In this respect, the gaze of political parties' surveillance in the site of the Mazraa can be related to the wider (gaze of) political strategy of observation and control in the country, as well as to cultural practices. In addition, there are two senses of 'seeing': there is the physicality of 'seeing' material evidence (object) as part of the 'look' and the 'gaze'; and there is 'seeing' as an interpretive process that is politically and culturally negotiated and not merely optical.

The photographs I took from the two balconies revealed the borders of surveillance in two ways (Fig. 39). First, the taking of the photograph at the first balcony was a form of capturing (or stealing) a view from the neighbourhood, thereby highlighting the existence of a border by identifying the limit of the camera's reach in the neighbourhood – outside that limit are the surveillance apparatuses that I was unable to capture. Second, the visual inclusion of surveillance devices (CCTV) in the photographs at the second balcony highlighted their role and existence in urban space as physical and material borders. The panorama exercise made me realize that surveillance is a kind of bordering practice. This practice ranges from the materiality of the surveillance apparatus itself, and the activities associated with it (even if remotely located, such as sitting on the street), to the impact of that apparatus on residents and on their practices of seeing, to the impact of those actively researching the area and wishing to take images to circulate more widely. The content of the photograph is important, but so too is everything that is left outside its framing. Though the photographs in this exercise fail to produce a conventional visual panorama of the whole neighbourhood, the experience of the photographic process allows an exploration of a new type of panorama: a panorama containing both what can and cannot be seen – the revealed and the concealed, the visual (that which is included in the photograph) and the blind spot (that which is left outside the photograph).

Je veux voir ('I want to see'), a 2007 film by Joana Hadjithomas and Khalil Joreige, addresses the issue of seeing and producing images of war (Fig. 40). The directors' premise is that we no longer know 'what images to show and what cinema to do about war';[13] people are so bombarded with violent and traumatic images that they turn their heads away and no longer want to see. *Je veux voir* slips between real life and cinema, with the actors playing themselves. The film follows Catherine Deneuve, who wants to see the aftermath of the 2006 Israeli war on Lebanon. In a seductive game, the allure of cinema embodied by

Fig.39
Photographs taken from S.H. balcony (above), and from H.K. balcony (opposite).

Deneuve's presence shows her always as an image to be seen, a foreign visitor, superimposed on the war scene. This makes the viewer begin to see, and perhaps to comprehend, the results of war and to consider how film – in imaging violent destruction – offers these images an allure. Seeing 'seeing' is a reflexive act: in seeing someone else seeing, one starts to reflect on the act of seeing itself.

In my own research, seeing can be understood via various definitions that concern the political differences of residents and their relation to subjects or objects both seen and not seen. Not seeing becomes as important as seeing: we do not see something because it is physically not there and belongs to the realm of the invisible; we do not see something because it is so ordinary that we do not pay attention to it; we do not see something because it has actively been hidden; we do not see something it has been prohibited to see; we do not see something because we do not even realize we are seeing. The difference in subjectivity between various kinds of seeing involve positioning, politics and interpretation:

> the idea that visibility equals truth is a deep-rooted fantasy. Seeing the world, bodies, etc., is not a mechanical operation simply registering what is out there. What one sees is a product of positioning, and different accounts of the world involve political struggles of *how* to see and *how* to interpret.[14]

My exercise differentiated between elements and practices that are visible (revealed) and customary in Lebanese everyday life (such as checkpoints and road barriers), and those that are invisible (concealed). Elements and practices are invisible because they are new, or because they are unnoticed as activities of surveillance (such as the coffee shops, which are not known to everyone as places for surveillance), or because they are literally hidden from passers-by in the urban fabric (such as CCTV concealed in a tree).

In *Panorama: Philosophies of the Visible*, Wilhelm S. Wurzer introduces the notion of the 'expressive' to consider how the visible and the invisible relate to reality. Differentiating between the visual and the visible, Wurzer argues that they are not the same thing: the visual belongs to optics and what we see with the eye; the visible expands to include the expressive, the textual, and other forms of the arts. By being expressed, the invisible relates to the visible:

> Without the discursive link between the visible and the in-visible, we are apt to overextend the ahistoric significance of one or the other. It is possible to avoid ocularcentrism as well as blind transcendence if the visible is not merely identified with the visual and the in-visible is not merely

Fig.40
Joana Hadjithomas and Khalil Joreige, stills from *Je veux voir*, 2007.

reduced to an absolute sovereignty. In the realm of the expressive, therefore, Hermes excels not only in sending and receiving messages, but in reading them, revealing that the in-visible *is* expressive in *visible* regions ... the in-visible is not the essence of the visible but rather the expressive 'body' of the visible, as Derrida points out, '*right on* the visible.'[15]

The concept of the expressive is important for my own research. It allows me to understand how the visible incorporates the invisible, particularly through the women's narratives, which are linguistic expressive processes that not only take place in space but also shape space and the lived experience. Through their narratives, the women express the concealed practices and devices of surveillance mechanisms, revealing them so that the invisible becomes part of the visible.

For my part, I differentiate between kinds of surveillance: there is surveillance that operates as an extension of the power and control of dominant political forces; there is surveillance used by residents in general; and there is surveillance used by visual practitioners such as artists and film-makers, for whom seeing and being seen is the subject of their work. If we follow this pattern of gazes from and to the balcony across the street, we can understand how one side might be operating a political surveillance of control while the other is witnessing through seeing as an act of surveillance.

With the two women at their balconies, I did not at first see the surveillance directly; rather, I saw the women seeing surveillance, and I saw the impact of the surveillance through the women's eyes and responses. I, too, surveyed the women, their houses, and their responses to surveillance, and then I tried to survey the surveillance camera directly.

DOMESTICATED SURVEILLANCE

The two women's responses to surveillance revealed what I term the 'domestica-tion' of surveillance practices. 'Domestication' captures here how specific types of surveillance practice borrow from domestic practices, such as the use of young men sitting and playing cards for surveillance purposes, both outdoors on the street and in shops. These informal, domestic practices – practices common at home, and taking place in public space – have a politicized intent: they lay claim to that place for the purpose of control. Under the guise of neighbourhood protection – 'watching over' – these practices are used by political parties to ob-serve the neighbourhood, in the process staking their permanent occupation of the space. Variants of this practice are the transfer of surveillance practices from street corners back to the interiors of coffee shops, and use of motorcycles for surveillance. A mapping of surveillance locations would show that surveillance practices are tactics by political parties to remain continuously present in urban space but to do so invisibly, as if they are not operating surveillance. Domesti-cated surveillance is either added to more conventional and visible surveillance practices – such as checkpoints – or it temporarily replaces them when there is a political decision to retreat for a while. Consequently, surveillance by political parties is an elastic bordering practice: it moves through geographic sites and modes of practice that vary from the revealed to the concealed.

The bordering practices that domesticate surveillance are part of security strat-egies that have operated in Beirut since the civil turmoil in 2005. The security apparatus in the city currently consists of both state and private forces.[16] The private forces comprise political parties and private security companies, some of which are camouflaged or related to the political parties; accordingly, these different security forces sometimes overlap.[17]

The self-securing of neighbourhoods by residents and political parties began in order to counter the sporadic car bombing between 2005 and 2007.[18] Later, the intensification of the internal political turmoil provided an excuse for the political parties to expand their presence by arguing that specific areas needed protection from possible assaults. A parallel development was the employment of private security agencies by the private sector to protect business and com-mercial premises, such as malls, hotels, banks and companies; the aim was not only to protect the buildings but also to give the impression to consumers that these were secured safe zones.[19] The security situation led to a gradual militarization of urban space not seen since the civil war period.

The visibility of security, and the architecture that this imposes on the city, says much about the purposes behind it, since despite the increase in security, car bombs and street clashes continue. On a map entitled 'Visible security mech-anisms in municipal Beirut' part of *Mapping Security* project, the legend alone projects an aggressive image of the security measures used, including the number of physical elements in the city spaces and streets (Fig. 41). The following are listed: secured landmark; under bridge; secured street; checkpoint; parking pro-

A. VISIBLE SECURITY MECHANISMS IN MUNICIPAL BEIRUT
Survey conducted between February and July 2009, revised in September 2010

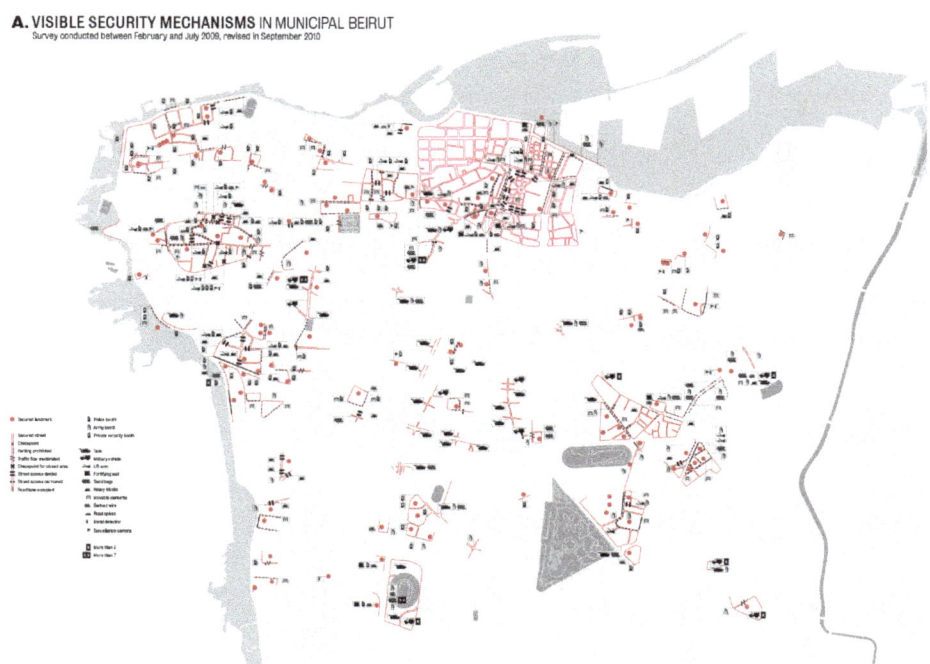

Fig.41
Mona Fawaz, Mona Harb, Ahmad Gharbieh, Map of 'Visible security mechanisms
in municipal Beirut', 2009-10.

hibited; traffic flow moderated; checkpoint for closed area; street access denied; street access narrowed; road lane occupied; police booth; army booth; private security booth; tank; military vehicle; lift arm; fortifying wall; sand bags; heavy blocks; movable elements; barbed wire; road spikes; metal detector; surveillance camera; more than three; more than seven. The accompanying text highlights 'elaborate systems' to secure well-defined sites or neighbourhoods, and 'less intense' security for smaller sites. The map's classification reveals a series of secured islands in the city and fragments and stretches of military points.

The visibility of surveillance helps to construct an image of power in the eyes of others – those under surveillance as well as those from opposing political groups. The low-tech personnel surveillant – that is, the body assisted by surveillance devices such as detectors and CCTV, and protected by fortified booths – marks the current mode of surveillance, whether by private agencies in public spaces or by political parties in local neighbourhoods. The embodied spatiality of surveillance, the physicality of the barrier and the face-to-face confrontation are key to maintaining the culture of conflict where 'security', or securing a person or an area, is no longer the aim in itself. Instead, the aim is to be present in the public space through surveillance as a bordering practice that aims for political control and division of areas. The purpose of political parties is to be physically present, armed and sometimes camouflaged in public, under the excuse of providing security, and this can easily lead to street war, as in May 2008, when Hezbollah fought with armed security members of other political parties.[20] Consequently, the bordering practice of domesticated surveillance facilitates the shift from the security of sects to a sectarian war.

Despite the physicality and visibility of security measures and surveillance practices in Beirut – the cameras that one can see on the street with the naked eye and the personnel in their booths – there remains in popular neighbourhoods a surveillance that cannot be seen by passers-by or strangers. This surveillance is concealed within the 'domestic' practices of political parties in the urban space, such as men sitting out on the street, cruising on motorcycles, and in shops smoking *arguilé*: these men are all undertaking political and visual surveillance, waiting to cross the border between the visual and the physical, a crossing which might involve violent assault and maybe even shooting. The practice of domesticated surveillance is used to conceal more organized political surveillance. Thus, the bordering practice of domesticated surveillance relates the tactical to the strategic: informal resident behaviour is used tactically as part of a political surveillance strategy.

The map of Beirut in the *Mapping Security* project sharply exposes security and surveillance measures at a topographical level, presenting them as visible and as information that is available to everyone. Such mapping reveals one set of information and hides another; it makes certain things spatially visible in order to further the specific interests of those who have organized the mapping exercise.[21]

In contrast to the map, if we return to consider the two women at their balconies – and the two photographs I presented at the start of this chapter (Fig. 37) – their act of looking outdoors returns surveillance to the mundanity of everyday life and to a neighbourhood scene. The act of looking is normalized, and the scene conceals acts of looking through security devices as though surveillance did not exist.

PANORAMA II

DISTANCE

H.K.'s living room curtains were closed when I was in her home. She described the neighbourhood in which she lives as a place detached from her own life, a neighbourhood which she observes from her apartment and which she fears on account of the activities of the Amal movement in the public space. She lives on the third floor in an apartment with balconies overlooking the street. The street is one block away from the Mazraa Main Road separating Barbour from Tarik al-Jdide. In light of the political unrest and the occasional street clashes in this neighbourhood, the Amal movement has been strengthened in the area and has gradually spread outside apartment buildings to occupy public spaces.

The presence of the Amal group in the Barbour neighbourhood goes back to the civil war period of the 1980s, and their buildings (offices) are still there.[22] H.K. lives opposite a yellow building belonging to Amal, as she indicated to me when I met her. This building is where the surveillance camera she mentioned, and feared, is installed. After the political tension had risen in 2005, the Amal logo was painted on the building's façade to mark their presence and to politically claim the area; more recently, at the time of my research, it was painted over in green to make it less visible, with the aim of easing the tension and the sensitivities of those residents in the area unaffiliated with Amal; this, at any rate, was H.K.'s analysis. However, even this gesture of painting over the logo seems provocative, as green is the colour of the Amal party. Since the start of the current conflict, the presence and practices of Amal members in public space, as well as those of other political parties in the country, have resurfaced in practices similar to those of the civil war time, albeit with slight differences (the men are not visibly armed, for example). These practices include having personnel on the streets, opening offices in buildings and shops, hanging flags and slogans, blocking roads and controlling access around their buildings or areas they identify as critical points. All this is in proximity to H.K.'s house and balcony and within her field of vision and hearing.

My meeting with H.K. became more tense when I suggested to her that we move out onto her balcony. In her attempt to show me the surveillance camera that I was unable to see, she asked me to move from the living room balcony to the bedroom balcony where there was a better view of the opposite building. We moved from one balcony to the other by returning inside her house and then coming outside again, as if chasing and being chased by the surveillance camera that the militia had installed on the opposite building so that it is visible. But strangely, I was able neither to see the camera nor to take a photograph of the street. H.K. feared that we were being watched and that if I took a photograph someone would notice. Her fear transferred to me and remained with me as I walked down the street after the meeting, with my camera hidden in my bag, on my way to S.H.'s place.

S.H. lives in an apartment building on a street at right angles to H.K.'s street, almost 300 metres away and further down from the Mazraa Main Road. The day I visited, S.H.'s living room balcony was covered with washing lines, which blocked her view of the outdoor scenery; in addition, curtains were rolled down on the windows to the balcony. To look outside, she had to gradually remove the washing to reveal the scene and, as she put it, for the photographs to 'come out better'. Her interior space – specifically the kitchen, which she described as the most sheltered space in her apartment – is her refuge when she retreats from the outside, especially when she navigates that interior while negotiating the whisper of the bullets fired, according to S.H., from the adjacent Tarik al-Jdide by members of the Mustaqbal movement.[23]

Fig.42
S.H. living room, *At Her Balcony*, 2010.

Fig.43
H.K. living room, *At Her Balcony*, 2010.

When the Amal man installed the camera on the tree adjacent to her balcony, S.H. joked with him that the surveillance camera captures images but not sound; she was worried that if the camera were to capture sound, it would affect her freedom of speech inside her house and on her balcony.[24] S.H.'s informal chat with the Amal member is an indication of the type of dynamic that can exist between residents and members of political parties, as these political parties include men from the neighbourhood. The ability to chat depends not only on the political affiliation or sympathy of residents with a specific party, but also on residents becoming habituated to the presence of political parties in their neighbourhood.

At the street corner to the north of S.H.'s apartment is an Amal building painted green and surrounded by green barrels to prevent parking. The presence of an Amal building in the street perhaps explains the bullets that S.H. claims were fired by Mustaqbal. Her house is also close to Amal's main building, where Nabih Berri had once lived. S.H. mentioned the camera on the tree, the building at the corner, another building behind the street where she lives, and the occasional bullets coming from the adjacent neighbourhood of Tarik al-Jdide – an area into which she no longer ventures to visit her relatives, because she fears trouble there or an attack by Mustaqbal supporters. Her fear resonates with what Samir Khalaf terms the 'geographies of fear' that configure residents' mobility, perception, and experience of city spaces across political and sectarian lines.[25]

The surveillance devices and practices located around H.K. and S.H. are of varying geographical distances from the two women. For example, the camera is about two metres from S.H.'s balcony on an adjacent tree, the militia building is about 30 metres from S.H.'s living room; bullets crossing from one neighbourhood to the other are only 6–10 metres away from S.H.'s sight when they cross by the balcony. The men on the street corner are 25–40 metres from H.K.'s living room, and the cruising motorcycles are 10–50 metres from S.H.'s living room and her hearing. These distances are important as they are part of the political parties' strategy for occupying public space; a spatial occupation could not be achieved without utilizing these varying geographic distances, whether in the same neighbourhood or across neighbourhoods within Beirut (Fig. 44). These distances, and their proximity to a resident's living space, start to dictate and shape the resident's practices in their own interior space and their relationships to the street, the neighbourhood, and the wider city beyond. For H.K., such practices include closing the living room curtains to isolate herself from the outside, and moving between her balconies and the inside of her apartment while chased by surveillance; for S.H., they include hiding in the kitchen from bullets, and avoiding the adjacent neighbourhood.

The distance of time is also significant and is manifested in two ways: the time when a surveillance practice/device begins; and the duration of that practice and whether it is still going on or has ended. It is especially relevant to the residents' experience of the past civil war and the recurrence of war practices today. Both women specified dates when describing certain practices, particularly practices that relate to memories of the civil war from 1975 to 1990, such as the presence of Amal movement buildings and personnel in the Barbour neighbourhood. The women also identified three new important dates or periods since the assassination of Hariri in February 2005 and the start of the current conflict: the clashes in January 2007 and in May 2008, and the two-month period prior to my meeting with them, as this was the period of time it took to form a new government at the end of 2009.

By utilizing the distances of geography and time, the practice of surveillance by political parties can transform the urban setting: it has the potential, frequently actualized, to turn public space into a place of imprisonment through the act of observation and by 'domesticated surveillance'. These surveillance practices in Beirut are reminiscent of Jeremy Bentham's concept of the panopticon prison.[26] This spatial setting that is based on attainable geographic distances serves as a 'pantheon of *punishment* to reform society'; it creates, as Michel Foucault later termed it, 'the disciplinary society' in which the power of observation is exercised by an unseen observer.[27]

Bentham's panopticon is an early historical (and theoretical) model; specific visual regimes, and the spatial arrangements associated with them, have changed over time and according to different cultures. The new surveillance models in modern society have been defined as a 'surveillant assemblage', formed out of 'the convergence of once discrete surveillance systems', and operating 'by abstracting human bodies from their territorial settings, and separating them into a series of discrete flows'.[28] This concept, which stems from the philosophy of Gilles Deleuze and Félix Guattari, relates to the technology and information flow characteristic of modern societies, through which people are managed from far distances and out of sight. It is connected to the post-1945 breakdown of eighteenth- and nineteenth-century bounded institutions (confinements); as Deleuze explains, this breakdown led to a shift from Foucault's 'disciplinary societies' to 'control societies'.[29]

However, Beirut's surveillance is not monitored from a central location or by one pantheon of power or authority as in Bentham's concept of the panopticon; rather, it is scattered in different locations/distances following the complex plan of the urban city and the multiple forces behind it. In this respect, a specific aspect of Lebanese history has led to a specific practice of surveillant assemblage; but the corporeal observation of political parties' personnel is essential and is the means through which this practice is linked to the panopticon model. This is what differentiates Lebanese surveillance from the surveillant assemblage in Western societies.

The impact of surveillance has long interested analysts, particularly in the West, since it concerns the freedom of individuals and the conditions of privacy and anonymity in the modern urban experience, and characterized by Walter Benjamin's notion of the *flâneur* or the city stroller.[30] Digital surveillance captures the

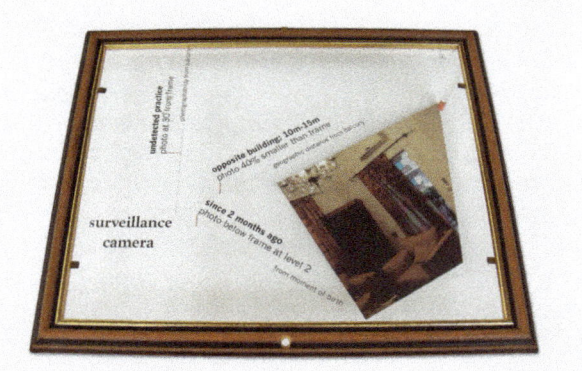

Surveillance Camera
10-15 metres
Since 2 months
Unphotographed

Green Painted Wall
25-40 metres
Since Civil War, 1980-90
Unphotographed

Motorcycles Convoys
10-50 metres
Since 2 months
Unphotographed

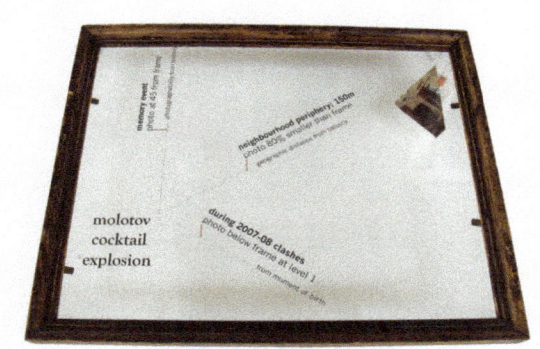

Molotov Cocktail
150 metres
During 2007-2008 clashes
Unphotographed

Firing RPG
25 metres - variable
During 2007-8 clashes
Unphotographed

Surveillance Camera
2-6 metres
Since 2 months
Photographed

Fig.44 (Previous and Here)
Measuring distances, *At Her Balcony*, 2010.

Snipers Shelling
10 metres
During 2007-8 clashes
Unphotographed

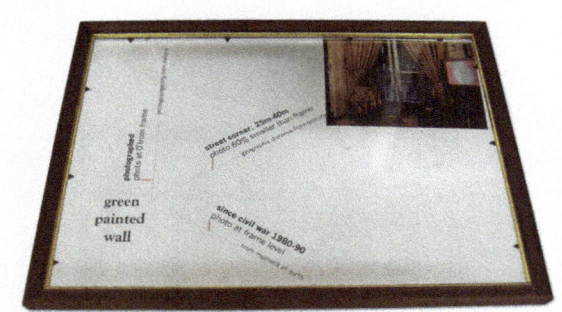

Green Painted Wall
25-40 metres
Since civil war, 1980-90
Photographed

body at varying geographical distances and transforms it into data, leading to the disappearance of anonymity and of the possibility of disappearance itself in public spaces.[31] But the implication of a surveillance system such as that operative in Beirut – one still based on corporeal observation, and combining the use of the human eye with low-technology surveillance such as cameras – is not merely limited to the public space where it is usually deployed and where it directly reaches/sees the body; rather, it can spread to affect residents in the interior and private spaces of their homes, as in the cases of H.K. and S.K., without the digital capturing of the body.

One response to surveillance in public spaces is the internalization of the gaze, which is similar to the type of boundary that architectural projects of late capitalism have imposed on users as boundaries of negotiation. Architectural historian Iain Borden has highlighted, using the example of the Broadgate office development in the City of London, how capitalist space takes over state space in 'managing not just built structures but also social structures and relations, behavioural patterns and conflicts, interiors and boundaries'.[32] Through hard architecture, soft gates and other boundaries that relate to the control and managing of the time of users/workers in this place, as well as to class seg-regation and differentiation, users internalize surveillance/control and deprive themselves of the right to be in a particular place; they ask, as Borden puts it: 'Should I be here, and now? Do I have the right of passage?'[33]

Surveillance in Beirut has been utilized as a mechanism to control residents in their neighbourhoods rather than as a means to protect them, as is usually claimed, from an outside danger; this is evident S.H. and H.K. fearing the outside. Surveillance has been subverted from protection to threat. Hence the question 'Who is being watched?' becomes important, as does the distinction between the practices of 'watching over' and 'watching'.

Surveillance is, therefore, a kind of bordering practice by which the common notion of a local neighbourhood as a communal social space of interaction between local partners (neighbours) – as is (or is thought to be) the case in pop-ular neighbourhoods such as the Mazraa district in Beirut – is destabilized and turned into an interior occupied by others or strangers rather than by residents or neighbours. This establishes a culture of surveillance and observation that gives residents – and, in this case, specifically male residents who are also members of political parties – the right to observe and interfere in the lives of other residents for reasons that go beyond 'protection' and 'watching over' to just 'watching'.

This situation has been well described in a collaborative work by artists Mazen Kerbaj and Jana Traboulsi that concerns the extent of current surveillance on the freedom of residents in Beirut (Fig. 45, 46). Kerbaj presents an illustration of a Beirut road map with the figure of a man reading a text which says: 'YOU ARE NOT ALLOWED TO BE HERE'. Traboulsi responds with another illustration of a similar map with figures and texts inside the map grid, completing the pro-hibition with the following phrases: 'as a woman', 'as a tourist', 'as a Muslim',

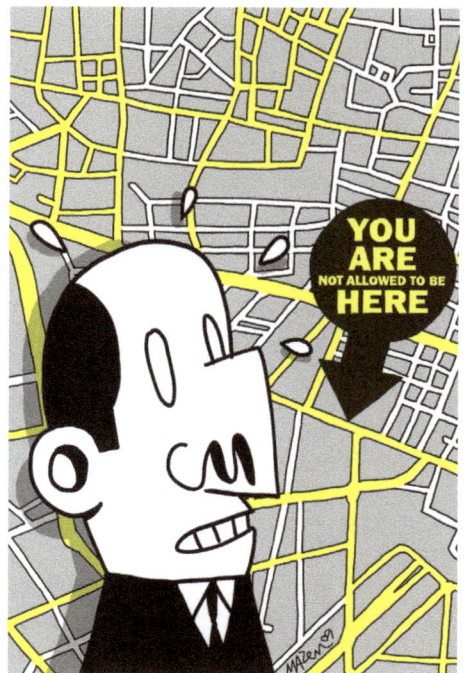

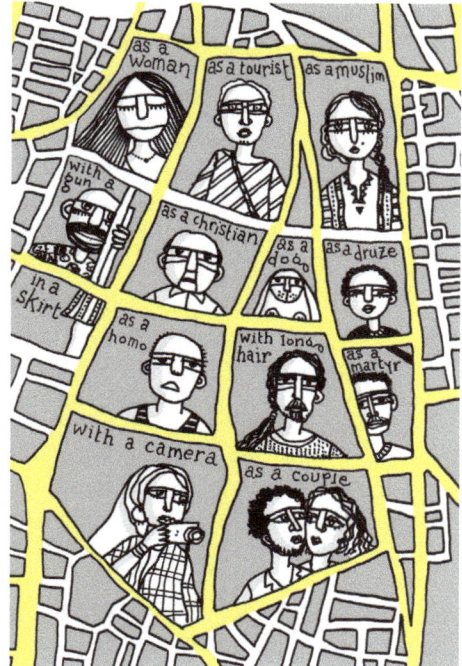

Fig.45
Mazen Kerbaj, *You here*, 2009

Fig.46
Jana Traboulsi, *You here*, 2009.

'with a gun', 'as a Christian', 'as a Druze', 'in a skirt', 'as a homo', 'with long hair', 'as a martyr', 'with a camera', 'as a couple'.[34] The artwork thus lists the people residents are not allowed to be and the activities that residents are not allowed to do. These prohibitions relate not only to the apparent threat attached to the political situation in the country, but also to the desire of the men who do the watching and to the wider cultural and social prohibitions that are mixed up with political surveillance.

Currently, surveillance practices push occupants from their balconies further into their interiors. This border, which exists between private and public, and between inside and outside, is stretched so that the public enters the private. The definition of privacy in relation to the interior/exterior and private/public binaries invites rethinking. Judith Squires has argued for the 'possibilities of realisation and preservation' of *privacy* in liberal democracies, maintaining that privacy has been lost in 'practice' and in 'theory' and needs defining and defending. This loss, in her view, relates to technology, communication and information flow, as well as to modes of surveillance, whether for the benefit of citizens' safety or as working against them:

> the condition of postmodernity is characterised by forces that would erode many of the spaces and places in which privacy was previously grounded. Where there was distance we witness time-space compression; where there were boundaries we perceive transparency; where there was confidentiality we find information flow.[35]

Squires notes the multiplicity of definitions that the public/private distinction has taken in different disciplines: in law, in economy and in geography, whether to set legal rules or property ownership and so on. She compares and distinguishes the public/private binary from the public/domestic one, showing how the domestic – the house as a private sphere for family – does not necessarily provide privacy; the house is, for example, in some cases a place of tension and violence between husband and wife or between parents and children. Hence, the 'private sphere' is not synonymous with 'privacy'.[36] Squires argues for 'privacy as political possibility' and as 'a value crucial to the development of a fully articulated radical pluralism', in an age when the distinctions and definitions of private/public are constantly changing, and where privacy within domestic borders is not granted:

> For the body can be viewed as one of the core territories of the self: control over one's own body can be viewed as one with a sense of self and hence the ability to interact openly with others. To have control over one's own bodily integrity (to regulate access to it) and to have this integrity recognised, is a minimal precondition for free and equal social interaction. To ensure the possibility of such an embodied autonomy for all persons in contemporary society – with all its multifarious mechanisms of observation and control – *we need a political defence of privacy rights.*[37]

The geographical distance between surveillance elements and the interior space of the person exposed to them is as important as the length of time a person is exposed to those elements. Through both spatial and temporal distances, surveillance extends its impact to the interior, either directly through the ability of the camera or the person who is watching to observe the interior, or by self-surveillance as an internalization of the surveillance gaze applied by residents in their interior spaces. This self-surveillance is characterized by fear of the outside, changes in their practices and mobility, and withdrawal to the confinement of interior space.

DIFFERENCE

The political difference between the two neighbouring women is revealed through their contradictory readings of the same domesticating surveillance practices used by the same political group: one sees them as a threat, the other as security. Their difference in the neighbourhood space is similar to, or a result of, the political division in the country between two main blocs – the two political parties set in opposition. This contrast is integral to the field of surveillance: threat versus security, or control versus safety, and the one who looks versus the one who is looked at – the latter being the key distinction in visual theory between subject and object of the gaze.

Another manifestation of the difference is in the women's practices on their balconies once confronted with the outside politics in the presence of my camera. While one woman responded with curiosity, the other was more apprehensive. That difference signalled something important to me, and it required me as researcher to read more of their political affiliation and perhaps their sectarian background into their responses. However, I did not ask them directly about their religious or sectarian background, as I wanted to avoid my enquiry and subsequent interpretation being based on the sectarian rhetoric of considering religious background. Both women commented that the presence of members of political parties (militias) in the city was a sign of war; nevertheless, while one woman was sympathetic to the neighbourhood militia, the other was allied with the militia located in the adjacent neighbourhood and opposed to the one based in her own neighbourhood. If I wanted to simplify and explain this situation, I could say that each group of residents justifies the practices of the political party to which it is affiliated by blaming the other political party's practices for any problems – 'it is because the *other* has done this or that'. So, in areas where residents of mixed sectarian and religious backgrounds live on the same street, different residents deal differently with what might seem to be a shared understanding of an event, especially a traumatic event such as an armed clash. Contradictory versions and interpretations of the same event present alternative readings of the militia's presence – the same presence might be understood variously as protecting or as watching a neighbour's activities. Following this mode of thinking, a focal point which we might call a blind spot in the neighbourhood is not really blind; rather, it must be understood according to whether a resident is affiliated or not with the political group operating the camera. The blind spot of H.K. includes all the devices and practices she mentioned but that I could not capture in my photographs, whereas most of what S.H. described is within a visual field that I managed to document.

The women's political difference influenced the way I learned the surveillance practices in the site, as well as the possibility of obtaining a visual panorama. In *Knowing the Difference*, feminist scholars Kathleen Lennon and Margaret Whitford question the objectivity of knowledge as that which has been dominated/produced by males, and they turn to consider the contribution of feminist theorists to epistemology – to theories of knowing – to examine how 'power relations [are] at the heart of knowledge-production':[38]

> Differences are a challenge to our own position and require re-evaluation based on recognition of our interrelation with others ... we are required to evaluate and accommodate different experiences to reach a characterization of situations as a whole.[39]

The two women's different relationship to the same surveillance devices might depend, therefore, on their relationship to the political divisions of Lebanon. This difference exposed to me the complexity of residents' responses to the contested boundaries between political parties. It also revealed how political parties build on sectarian differences and sensitivities in order to be present in the public urban space, and how they establish emotional distances between residents through the different modes (and distances) of their occupation of space. Difference is, therefore, important both for the parties' practices and their presence in urban space.

Measuring geographical distance, and the cultural and political differences created by physical distances, has been behind the creation of the idea of the 'other' as something or someone that can exist only in the imagination. The process of producing the other has been described by Edward Said in his critique of Orientalism as 'imaginative geographies'.[40] Derek Gregory has applied Said's imaginative geographies to the discussion on the violence 'used by regimes in Washington, London, and Tel Aviv, to advance a grisly colonial present (and future)',[41] as part of their justification of the 'war on terror' and, for example, their invasion of Iraq. Gregory argues that imaginative geographies are 'constructions that fold distance into difference through a series of spatializations ... [to] serve to demarcate "the same" from "the other"'.[42]

Such difference can be experienced at a closer range. Distance does not have to be as far as that between the West and the East; it is within that other, the East, particularly in Lebanon, that difference is experienced across religious, sectarian and political lines. These differences turn into distances that cannot be traversed, and they are associated with corollary violence. The distance–difference relation is one which can be reversed; if, as Gregory says, distance can be folded into difference, then that difference can also become distance – distance as physical and geographical, and, more metaphorically and emotionally, distance that entails the distancing of one from the other, which could include neighbours within the same building or neighbourhood. This is particularly the case if we consider how political differences in Beirut affect the social geography of the city; for example, the decisions of residents concerning where to live are related to their political-sectarian affiliations, thus creating separated geographies from political and sectarian differences.[43] Whether distances are large or small, and their varying power to create difference, is important. Furthermore, how different kinds of difference can create different kinds of distance should also be considered. Gregory explains the negotiation of distance and difference: 'distance – like difference – is not an absolute, fixed and given, but is set in motion and made meaningful through cultural practices'.[44]

In the Lebanese context, the 'other' to which I am referring here – someone who comes from a different sectarian and/or political affiliation but is located nearby in the same neighbourhood – is not a fixed construction or category throughout time: the 'other' is constructed at one time and place, and is overlooked at another; the 'other' is the familiar neighbour who is turned, or turns into, an 'other', but may re-turn or be re-turned at another point in time and place. The moment and place at which someone becomes an 'other' depends on wider political and media influences and to sensitivities belonging to history and religion. To give a practical example: some of the major political parties that have religious underpinnings and who fought against one another during the civil war are allied with one another in the current conflict against political parties with whom they were once allies.[45] Residents who support these groups shift easily in their affiliation and sympathy: yesterday's enemy is today's ally and vice versa. In as fluid a situation as that in Lebanon, the 'other' can change in relation to the shift in political alliances that parties establish through time,[46] and this can affect residents' consideration of who is their political 'other' at every particular period in the history of the country.

Judith Butler has argued that we cannot exist without the 'other'; it is for the 'other' whom we address as 'you' that the 'I' exists:

> I speak as an 'I', but do not make the mistake of thinking that I know precisely all that I am doing when I speak in that way. I find that my very formation implicates the Other in me, that my own foreignness to myself is, paradoxically, the source of my ethical connection with others. Do I need to know myself in order to act responsibly in social relations? Surely, to a certain extent, yes. But is there an ethical valence to my unknowingness?[47]

For Butler, opacity plays an important role in the construction of the self/other. Opacity – which brings visuality and seeing into the discussion of the negotiation of difference and distance – does not rebut ethical responsibility between a subject and others. There is opacity between the subject and others outside the self, and there is opacity within the self (the subject): 'it is precisely by virtue of the subject's opacity to itself that it sustains some of its most important ethical bonds'. The unknowingness/opacity of ourselves, and of others outside ourselves, is not an excuse for harm or violence. Rather, they demand 'an account of responsibility' in dealing with differences and the opacity of 'others'.[48]

PANORAMA III

<u>**MEASURING**</u>

At Her Balcony, the art installation, constructs a panorama out of that which was revealed and concealed, made visible and accessible, through two women's negotiations of surveillance at their balconies. From conceptual and material considerations of the work, through to the way different viewers at various distances spatially and emotionally engage with the work, *At Her Balcony* was developed out of the differences and distances between the women and my attempts to measure these differences.

The series of art components – or fragments – that make up the installation *At Her Balcony* are positioned on a 1200 mm × 2200 mm table covered with white paper. The components comprise:

- First, two photographs of the women's living room interior space and a map of the area, which can be viewed using a magnifying glass, and a newspaper report.[49] These documents provide a context for the installation, since they refer to the geographical location of the balconies and the physical border that emerged during the violent clashes on the Mazraa Main Road in 2007.
- Second, a panel consisting of three layers of paper with cut-outs and a printed text in English of written narratives. The two external papers contain a narrative based on the conversation that took place between each woman and myself. On the middle paper, and visible through the cut-outs, is a text based on my experience with the women in the site, which provides comments and extra information.
- Third, a series of wooden frames with photographic diagrams and texts which aim to measure the differences and distances – emotional, geographical and political – between the two residents, their interior living spaces, and the surveillance practices and elements revealed by my act of trying to photograph them.
- Fourth, a monitor showing a video work of a visual panorama constructed out of the still photographs I took from the balconies and the video footage that I took in the car crossing the neighbourhood.
- Fifth, the two photographs obtained from the women's balconies.

All these components are laid out across the table with a clear line of division down the middle, highlighted vertically with a paper panel. The different components measure (and are measures of) distances and differences. This measuring exercise is borrowed from *Measures of Distances* (1988), a work by Mona Hatoum that explores different notions of distance created by displacement (Fig. 47).[50] The magnifier with the map, and two small photographs of the interior space, show the geographical distances relating to the women and the neighbourhood. The distance between the three-layered panel and the textual narrative on each paper reveals the emotional and political differences between the two women,

Fig.47
Mona Hatoum, *Measures of Distance*, 1988.

and between the two of them and myself as a researcher. The wooden frames are used to *measure the distance* of the surveillance mechanisms from the interior spaces inhabited by the women, and the differences between the women in their relations to surveillance. The video work and two photographs are used to *cross the distance* of the neighbourhood and surveillance, physically and visually (as I will explain below).

The installation allows viewers to look at a range of highly political yet personal material. In this work, the embodied position of the viewer is defined and limited by the edges of the table and the frames of the artwork displayed on it. These physical limits can be negotiated through acts of seeing. A viewer can move around the table and his or her engagement may become intensified by the presence of other viewers located opposite him or her across the table. Viewers can explore the practice of seeing as an interpretive and optical action that is often mediated through a physical device: in the neighbourhood, the lens of seen and unseen cameras; in the gallery, the lens of cameras which belong to the researcher–artist, as well as various lenses and physical frames – magnifying glasses, wooden frames, paper cut-outs, and video screens – which comprise the work. Thus, the installation invites viewers to practise the intrusion of seeing as an inherent part of visual and spatial art.

Fig.48 (Here and Overleaf)
At Her Balcony gallery installation at Cities Methodologies exhibition, UCL, London, 2010.

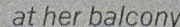

at her balcony

January 12 , 2010, from 2:00 pm to 2:50 pm

Name: H.K.
Gender: Female
Profession: Schoolteacher
Age: 52
Balcony location: Barbour
Work location: Burj Abu Haidar

H.K. asked to photograph her painted photo instead of her portrait one.

H.K.:

Don't turn left. Step back. Stop photographing. It is there- the surveillance camera is fixed some-where on that building. Just photograph from the right side, which looks onto the main street.

She took me to the other balcony for a better view on the building she is referring to, the surveillance camera was not

visible to the eye and she didn't allow me to photograph.

Be careful - they might see you and I don't want to get in trouble. The old yellow building at the corner is an Amal building, can you see the green painted wall? It's covering an Amal logo that was printed on the wall during the past period.

A military soldier with his weapon, was standing at the corner of the building.

There is a new coffee shop at the end of the street across the pavement; it was opened recently as a camouflage after the decision to halt street confrontations and gatherings. It is where they gather and observe the neighborhood nowadays.

Later, I went to the place she described, I couldn't find the cafeteria but I found a pastry shop instead.

I heard that they used to store weapons during the clashes inside one of those Arghileh cafeterias. Usually they grab plastic chairs and small tables from the shops and sit at street corners. At night their motorcycles still pass by to challenge residents and the state decision, they are the only group who have the courage to do so.

The government imposed a motorcycle curfew after 6 pm to stop neighborhood raids by young boys.

During the '7th May' clashes, Amal used to take all the strategic buildings that over look Tarik Ejdide, to fire their RPG.

The opposite party-Almustaqbal - didn't have weapons, they just used Molotow cocktail, which reached just outside the periphery of our area, nothing went further inside the neighborhood.

I don't sit on the balcony anymore; I close the living room curtains almost all the time, I live alone and it's not appropriate to be seen outside on the balcony often.

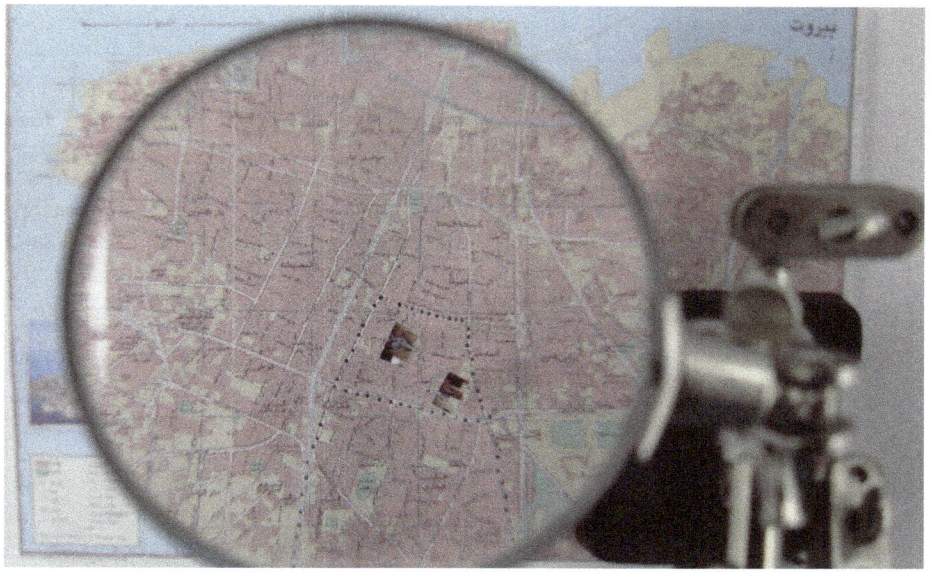

The installation also poses ethical questions about the intrusion on the subject. Since photography's invention in the early nineteenth century, the desire to see without being seen has marked photographic experiments:

> Seeing without being seen has been a central tenet of the practice of photography throughout its history, a guilty pleasure thought to provide insights into life beyond the reach of the posed picture.[51]

The ethical concerns of photography apply to experiments featuring subjects unaware of the camera, or to ethnographic work that has a political and ethical role in portraying the marginalized and overlooked. In these photographic works, subjects are looking directly into the camera with awareness and agreement to its presence (however unaware they are of the context in which the photographs are used), such as the work of Jacob August Riis and Lewis Hine who documented working-class life in New York City in the second half of the nineteenth century.[52]

Similar issues have been raised since the development of the medium of video in the 1960s, and artists have dealt with the intrusion of CCTV surveillance cameras in people's lives in a critical manner. The CCTV camera and the instant production of images on monitors have offered new artistic imagery, physical relationships and emotional experiences in the gallery space. Artists expose the politics of image production and question the credibility of photography and the photograph in portraying an image of truth. An example is Bruce Nauman's *Live/Taped Video Corridor* (1969–70),[53] a multimedia installation in which the audience is simultaneously the subject matter for the artwork and the audience of his/her own surveillance through the use of a live video camera and a monitor in the gallery space (Fig. 49).

Surveillance and images of political conflict and war are becoming more apparent in our everyday life and spaces. According to Harun Farocki, the live coverage by the media of the war on Iraq marked a new era in the history of both war and media: it was the first time that a war was watched live on TV as it was happening, as well as from an aerial point of view resembling that of power.[54] Farocki shows how new technologies of image production have interfered in the lived reality that exists between viewers, real-life events, and images of events, removing all from their spatial coordinates and 'abolishing the eyes as the organ that bears witness to history'.[55]

More recently, in the so-called 'Arab spring', the role of social media and the Internet was instrumental in connecting the events with the world and in providing images from the ground and from inside the events, particularly by those being attacked by authorities; the use of social media stands in contrast to the censored and studied views provided by the state and its media. These images expose the pain and death of those who were victims of violence; the ethics of exposition in such photographs assumes a significance according to the political

Fig. 49
Bruce Nauman, *Live/Taped Video
Corridor*, 1969-1970.

Fig. 50
Mosireen, still from *Don't forget and
keep remembering: the cabinet battle*,
posted on 14 December 2013

role they play as an act of resistance. Such a role is played, for example, by *Mosireen*, an Egyptian NGO and website founded in the early stages of the Egyptian revolution in 2011 to circulate, screen, archive and produce videos and films supporting the revolution (Fig. 50).

The domestic environment – the confinement and interior space of the home – is a site to which the various images of surveillance from different distances and of political differences are brought closer by the devices and screens of communication technology: TVs, smartphones, the Internet, etc. More specifically, in Beirut and in the site of my research the corporeal observation of political parties is located outdoors around the two women and is negotiated through their windows and balconies. These apparatuses and mechanisms of surveillance interfere in constructing the lived reality of those exposed to them and convolute the difference between the seen and the unseen, the visible and the invisible, and the real and the fabricated. Although *At Her Balcony* hides the women's identities, it exposes their interior spaces and stories. The ethical role of such an act of concealing and revealing is to make an urban phenomenon such as surveillance visible, to shift it from the lacuna and blind spot of public life, and to make it part of the public consciousness and its gaze.

The measuring of political parties' surveillance in the spaces outside the domestic interiors is conducted in relation to three variables that are highlighted from the research findings: (1) the geographical distance of the surveillance device and practice from the house; (2) the distance in time from the moment surveillance first appeared in the neighbourhood; and (3) the (im)possibility of photographing the surveillance devices, either because I was not allowed to photograph them, or because they did not physically exist at the time of the research but came from the women's memories or even their imaginations. As a result of this spatial and temporal measuring, the emotional, political and sectarian differences between the two women are also being measured, particularly if we consider that the possibility of my taking a photograph is directly related to each woman's response to the photography exercise at her balcony in the presence of surveillance around her.

The wooden frames on the table, which are dedicated to the measuring, employ text (titles) to name surveillance elements. Rather than showing fixed photographic evidence of surveillance, the frames include the two photographs of the interior spaces of the women's living rooms as reference points for measuring surveillance in the outdoors. The three variables of distance – geographical location, time of emergence, and photographability of surveillance – consecutively change the position, size and rotation of the photograph of the interior space in relation to the wooden frame.

The act of trying to 'measure' the distances between the interior spaces and surveillance mechanisms takes into account the two women's subjectivities and their political differences. This act of measuring concerns the border between public and private/domestic, as well as the acts of separation and negotiation that cross that border.

My research for this chapter and the associated installation is not a charting of surveillance but a charting/measuring of the distances created by surveillance and those distances integral to its operation as they extend to the interior space of residents. This research concerns the possibility of producing an account of knowledge of surveillance in a divided urban context. Thus, the bordering practice in this instance involves measuring the distances created by surveillance across spaces.

CROSSING

Exercise 1, 12 January 2010
Meeting H.K. and S.H. with a camera at their respective balconies, without any previous encounter.

Exercise 2, 24 January 2010
In a car crossing the Mazraa road, with a video camera camouflaged in the car's dashboard (Fig 51).

The photographs and the video footage result from the two exercises I undertook at the site provide the visual material for the video work presented in the installation. The video is played on a monitor positioned on the edge of the table in front of printed photographs taken from the balconies. The video work starts with a scene that appears in the middle of the screen; it shows footage, taken from the car's dashboard, of the street travelling from Tarik al-Jdide towards the Mazraa Main Road, crossing the latter and entering the Barbour neighbourhood. At two intervals, the scene slows down for a few seconds. In the first, a second scene starts on the right-hand side of the screen. It shows video footage of the neighbourhood from the first woman's balcony. In the second interval, a third

MAZRAA

S.H.   H.K.

TARIK AL-JDIDE

——— Route of filming journey

◁ Photography and filming

Fig.51
Map of the route taken when filming and the location of my cameras in exercise
1 & 2.

scene starts on the left-hand side of the screen, this time showing similar footage from the second woman's balcony. These two views were obtained by using
a video camera that scanned the photographic prints taken from the balconies
and presented in the gallery next to the video.

The car journey gives a geographical sense (scale) to the physical distances
separating these two women who live in the same neighbourhood. The scene
provides a context for the photographs by passing through the very street from
which they were taken. The video offers three points of view of the site: one
from inside the car crossing the street where the two houses are located, and
the other two from the women's balconies overlooking the street where the car
later passes.

Taken together these three sources construct a visual panorama on the screen in
the gallery by contrasting and connecting distances and differences that relate
to the sources and the type of visuals used, and by providing a visual survey of
the neighbourhood and what it includes in terms of the presence of political
parties and their practices and devices of surveillance.

The three visuals used in the video are censored by the political pressure and
fear experienced in the site. The video camera was camouflaged in the car's
dashboard as it passed by the army military tank and entered the neighbourhood
under the control of the political party/militia, passing by the militia's building

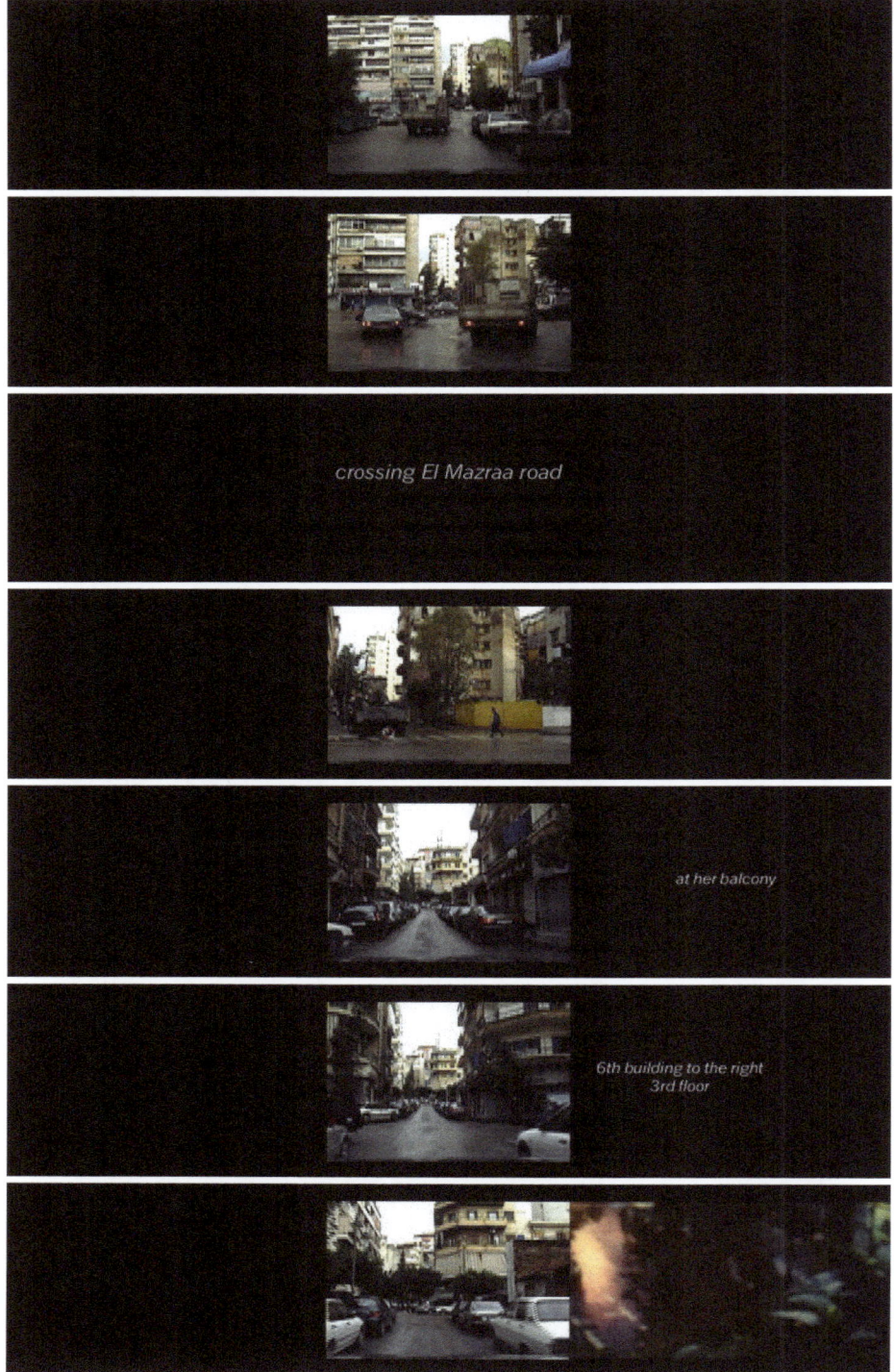

Fig.52 (Previous and Above)
Stills from *Crossing, At Her Balcony*, 2010.

and all the elements mentioned by the two women. The photograph taken from H.K.'s balcony indicates the limit that the lens is allowed to reach; what is left outside the frame are all the signs of conflict that the woman mentioned and that surveillance does not allow to be captured or to be made visually evident. The photographs from the second woman's balcony were taken with caution and in a short time, as though I was stealing something to which I had no right. The scene obtained is a slow journey through the details of the neighbourhood's photographs that would not otherwise have been allowed. In so doing, it expands the space of the neighbourhood into the field of photography, which is constricted by the presence of surveillance. The physical and visual borders of the photograph and those of the neighbourhood are both crossed.

Measuring Distances and *Crossing Distances* are two neighbouring pieces placed on the table in the gallery space; while the first maps surveillance information and names it with the use of text, the other shows surveillance visually without indicating or commenting on its location in the visuals. The work tests the 'seeing' of surveillance through the difference between the experiences offered by the two representational strategies and languages in both works. Measuring distances and crossing distances are two activities which, I argue, are part of the bordering practices that exist across lines of surveillance, political forces, geographies, and residents' differences.

I started to consider crossing as a spatial, political and emotional bordering practice when I spoke to the two women on their respective balconies, and when I began to use my camera as a device for revealing and measuring differences and distances in terms of borders. I constructed a spatial narrative out of the revealed and concealed aspects of the neighbourhood scene that both women, although differently, see, negotiate and narrate. The process of negotiation with the two women at their balconies revealed some borders, and it also created others through the fear accompanying the acquisition of my photographic experience. Surveillance crosses people's lives, it crosses individuals' zones of privacy, it crosses distances, and it convolutes the distinction between private and public lives, both practically and theoretically. So too does photography: as a visual practice, the line of the camera's gaze crosses spaces and diminishes distances into a photograph – in this case, a photograph of surveillance. As a bordering practice, the taking of a photograph and a video recording in the site is a critical spatial practice that considers its own methods in crossing spaces and negotiating the boundaries between private/public, interior/exterior, and residents'/political parties' surveillance. The artwork in the gallery space extends these acts of crossing and looking into a critical spatial practice that moves outside the site of research; in so doing, it creates a critical bordering practice that itself crosses some lines of surveillance and reveals others.

Fig. 53
At Her Balcony gallery installation at Cities Methodologies exhibition,
UCL, London, 2010.

Bordering
Practice 03

TRANSLATING

SOUND

This is How Stories of Conflict Circulate and Resonate

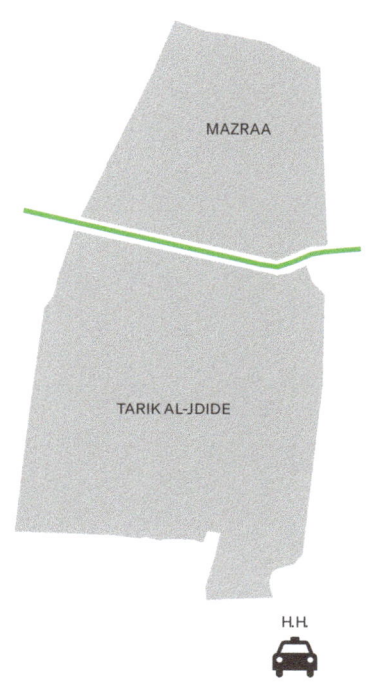

Fig.54
Map of H.H. vehicle location.

What are you listening to?

H.H., a taxi driver, travels from Dahyeh, a suburb in the south of Beirut where he lives, to the Mazraa district, mainly for work but also to join the political group he supported in the street fights that took place in 2007 and 2008 in both sides of the Mazraa district – the Mazraa and Tarik al-Jdide areas – and on the Mazraa Main Road which separates them. He plays loud 'patriotic music' in his car while driving across different neighbourhoods and displays images of political figures, in addition to religious proverbs, on the car's dashboard. At a later stage in the conflict – at least by the time I met him in January 2010 – he was having to hide these materials, due to their political and sectarian identification, in order to regain access to all neighbourhoods in the city. In so doing, he was prioritizing his livelihood over his political affiliation.

In January 2011, a year after meeting H.H., I planned a series of journeys with other taxi drivers, crossing the two areas, and I documented these journeys using a small video camera. A couple of days after the taxi journeys, after being stopped by the state's internal security forces to investigate the purpose of my filming, and a day after violent street clashes in the area, I planned a walking journey across the two adjacent areas using a hidden sound recorder. In what follows, the music and songs, the conversations and other aural material I heard and recorded are translated into written and visual material to be read and seen.

Fig.55
Detail from *Presence and Absence 01, 2011.*

shes of "7 May 2008"; I was curious to know what was happening in the city

om Dahyeh, the southern suburb, till I reached the Bachara El-Khoury

the internal roads with great care manoeuvering only within areas under our

nt of Gefinor hotel and picked up the first customer and drove her to east

the price but as a round of bullets began she rushed into the car and agreed

ain within Dahyeh's limits, I wouldn't work far from there for a week. a while.

treet clashes in Barbour and Tarik Al-Jdideh, I would immediately get excited and

h eagerness, as if something called me to support my people.

after the Arab University clashes of 2007 I didn't enter Tarik Al-Jdideh, I was

I don't work everyday I don't eat; and in these conditions I need to work in all

d all the sectarian signs from my car to re-enter Tarik Al-Jdideh. I used

Wilaya band while driving; I removed that tape from the car too, I also removed

mam Aili.

have my two years old daughter's Arabic calligraphy name instead,

na omri'. Al-Sayyed's photo is in my wallet.

Fig.56
Detail from *Presence and Absence 02*, 2011.

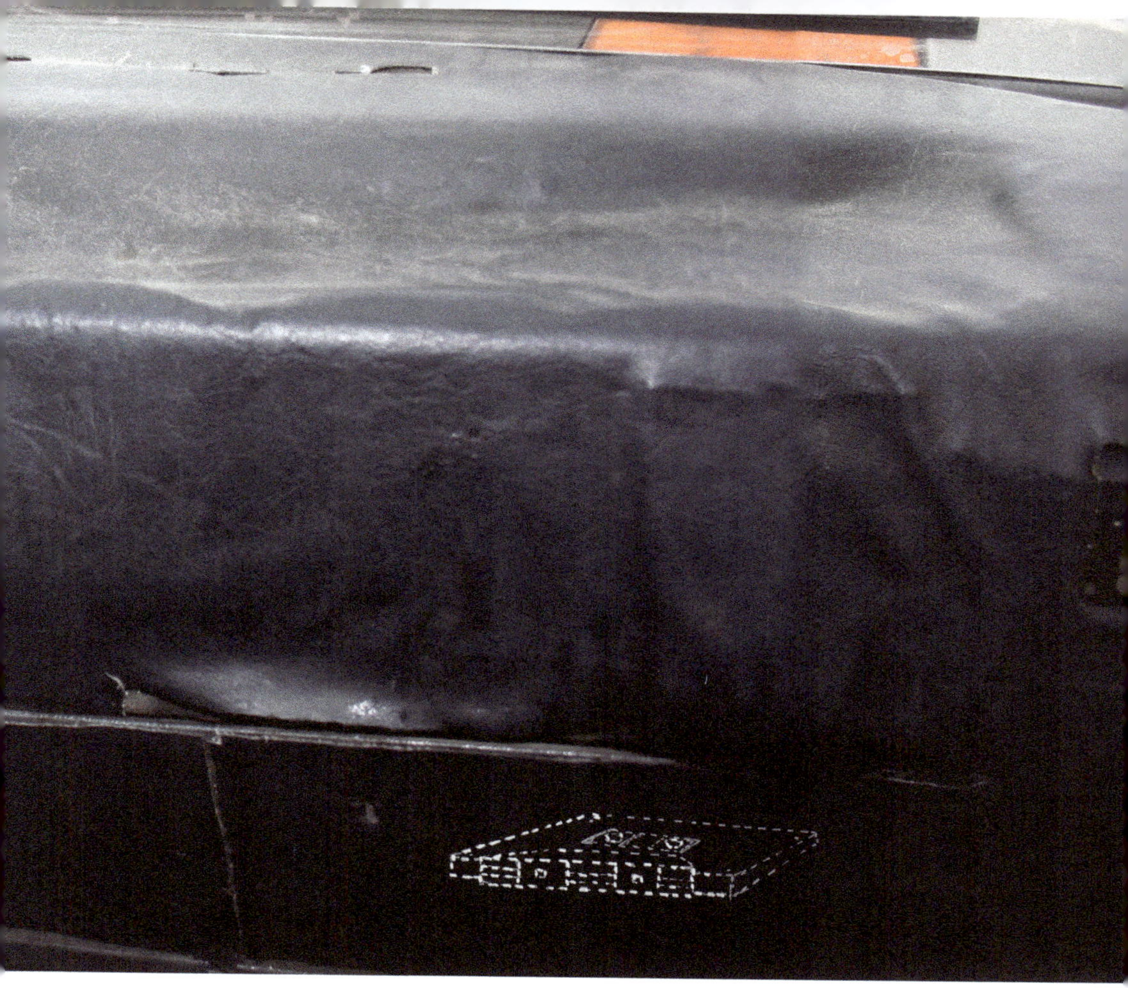

LG
فرقة الولاية
لبنان الواحد الموحد

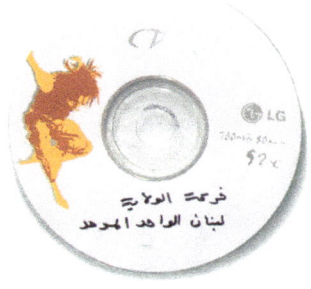

Fig.57
Detail from *Presence and Absence 03*, 2011.

INTRODUCTION

The unsettling, ephemeral nature of sound material inhabits and resonates in the spatial experience and memory of people, especially in times of political and sectarian conflict. Since 2005, with the beginning of a new round of civil unrest in Beirut, new forms of sonic spatial practices, coupled with mobile ones, have been utilized to confront or to communicate with the 'other' – that is, those who have different political-sectarian affiliations. These practices include the use of fireworks and gunshots following a political victory or a politician's speech, cruising in cars playing loud political-sectarian or religious songs and speeches of political and religious figures, closing streets for ceremonies that are either religious or political, and the invasion of neighbourhoods with the sounds of motorcycle convoys with flags and horns.

These sonic practices of a political-sectarian content or nature are used strategically by political parties to claim space for non-violent confrontation. This space is the subject of this chapter. Employing video and sound recordings to explore the boundary between sound (the auditory) and images (the visual), this chapter shows how social and political borders in a divided city like Beirut relate to one another and are played out through practices of hearing and seeing. It shows how political control interferes between the auditory and visual senses and practices, just as it does between the interior and exterior divisions of spaces. I explore the soundscape of sectarian neighbourhoods, and the personal space of residents, in ways that, going beyond the confines of their physical spaces, enter the political, social and economic domains. I consider how sounds can create immaterial borders and how soundscapes operate as spaces of contestation, paying particular attention, through site-specific and practice-led research, to the sounds of the adjacent areas of Mazraa and Tarik al-Jdide.

The chapter is based on visual and audio material I collected from research exercises conducted with taxi drivers crossing the two areas; on a walking journey I undertook; and on an associated gallery installation comprising two works: an audio photographic piece, *Presence and Absence*, and a film, *Look, Someone is Filming*. Through these exercises, I show how the political-sectarian divisions between and within communities are present in their sonic practices: the songs they play and listen to, the media stations they tune in to, the content of their conversations and the stories they tell. More specifically, I differentiate between those sonic practices intended only for personal listening and those sounds intended for the ears of others.

I focus on the differences between 'listening', 'hearing', and 'overhearing' political (and politicized) sound material. These practices are means of receiving sonic information that build personal political knowledge and correlate personal and emotional borders, and which are invisible in nature but clearly informed by the political and geographical affiliations of the listeners. The process of overhearing sonic material from someone else's space is an informal one that cannot be escaped, as opposed to the intentional listening mode adopted in relation to formal media news such as that provided by radio and television stations.

My research privileged neither sight nor sound over the other; rather, it was based on the idea of 'a democracy of the senses',[1] adopting the principle that 'no sense is privileged in relation to its counterparts'.[2] This enabled exploration of the distinctiveness of each realm, and of what each offers to the study and practice of bordering. In addition, through the artwork created from the findings of this sonic research, this chapter deliberately maintains a tension between heard and seen – between sound and image – specifically through particular recording techniques of sound, translated into written text and animated in film. The result is an inquiry into the way sounds and im/material negotiations are politically produced and practised.

The pursuing, recording, and re-producing or re-arrangement of the sonic for other listeners in the form of a gallery art installation (and for readers in the form of an essay) is not merely a recording of an existing space but is also the pro-duction of a new space. This new space is constructed through the translation of the sonic into a written text, a process that entails an extraction of content from the original context, which further changes the spatial and temporal references in the gallery space. The bordering practice explored in this chapter takes place between one site and another and between sound and image, employing at its core *translation* as a bordering practice that is both linguistic (Arabic and English) and material (sound and image). This bordering practice is a critical spatial practice that includes the listening, writing, reading and experiencing of the translated sonic material, to draw boundaries in the gallery space which, following de Certeau, have 'transportable limits'.[3] My aim, therefore, is to extend the notion of the border as material object to include the immateriality of sound as a bordering practice. In so doing, the following questions are raised by my critical bordering practice: How do borders – material and immaterial – produce particular kinds of sonic practices? What kind of borders and bordering practices do sonic practices produce? How do sonic bordering practices relate to visual ones? But to begin with: Why sound?

Sound as a border – utilized by one and experienced by another – operates through its invisible fluctuating matter that spans spatially from the point (body, device, space) where it is released (sourced) to the point where it is sensed (re-ceived). For sound has the ability to transcend the geographic borders of spaces and neighbourhoods, and even to transcend the limits of residents' sight – for example, residents may be unable to see the source of the sound.

A special kind of temporality is generated from the movement of sound as Brandon LaBelle has commented: 'In the movement of sound, the making of an exchange is enacted, a place is generated by the temporality of the auditory.'[4] This temporality is what gives sound its appeal in times of territorial conflict, for it has no 'real' or actual space in which to be located: 'Sound is no respecter of space'.[5] Thus different political groups embed their own sounds in others' spaces, such as in houses, shops, or cars. At times of lesser political tension, sonic practices can substitute for physical and visible confrontations. However, despite the seemingly 'peaceful' use of sound as part of political conflict, such as the playing of political songs, it is important to acknowledge the role of sonic warfare and the use of sound as fatal weaponry, as well as its use to instil fear in civilians, such as the use of sound bombs by the Israeli army in the Gaza Strip:

> Fear induced purely by sound effects, or at least in the undecidability between an actual or sonic attack, is a virtualized fear. The threat becomes autonomous from the need to back it up. And yet the sonically induced fear is no less real.[6]

The fear of certain sounds as indications of imminent attacks or other acts of violence has been part of Lebanese life since the 1970s: sounds have been induced in the sky over Lebanon by Israeli military aircraft in their continuous illegal crossing of the airspace, and the powerful sound that results when their military fighter jets break the sound barrier is often mixed up with those sounds produced through actual aerial bombardment. Consequently, and particularly at times of political unrest, the sound of commercial airplanes in Lebanon's sky becomes heard as a signal of a possible attack and is therefore accompanied by fear and anxiety. Sensitivities towards certain sounds become intensified in times of conflict, as they anticipate dangers associated with those sounds.

Other sectarian and divided societies illustrate the bordering nature of sound. Marching parades and drumming of opposing Protestants and Catholics in Northern Ireland, for example, come to perform a cultural identity of binary opposites, as has been noted by anthropologist, Paul Moore: 'particular sounds are designated as sound marks to construct complex social and physical boundaries'.[7] Moore argues that the drumming sounds and their differing intensities – such as the type of drum and volume of music – express something of the political, cultural and historic differences between the two communities: the one Protestant and associated with the sound of industrial machinery; and the other Catholic and connected with a more pastoral sound.

In other contexts, sound is not merely a signifier of difference or a tool and material of invisible confrontation but also becomes the subject matter of violent struggle over power and authority, through sonic practices of sacralizing urban space. For example, the conflict between the charismatic Pentecostal churches and Ga traditionalists in Accra in Ghana is enacted through sound and silence, which draw, in part, on their respective religious practices. The conflict over sound and silence contains, as Marleen de Witte has shown, a deeper conflict between '"native" Ga people and "strangers"', and between 'different understandings of citizenship and territory'.[8]

Sound can have a bordering nature in divided communities because our experience of it – and of hearing – is culturally specific. It is neither fixed nor 'a natural phenomena [sic] exterior to people';[9] rather, sound needs to be considered in relation to the nature and culture that together make up sonic experience. Jonathan Sterne explains how sound is 'part of a larger physical phenomenon of vibration … [as] a product of the human senses and not a thing in the world apart from humans, sound is a little piece of the vibrating world'; in other words, 'the hearing of sound is what makes it'.[10] It is this subjectivity of hearing and perceiving certain sounds, particularly when they contain political-sectarian content, as well as the ephemerality of sound's movement and the three-dimensionality of its occupation of the airspace, that make sounds as borders and sonic bordering practices resonate in Beirut's conflict today.

There is a dialectic between sonic borders and sonic bordering practices that relates the social and the spatial – what Edward Soja describes as the 'socio-spatial dialectic'. As an ephemeral border, sound contributes to bordering practices that share in the establishment of the social and political borders between residents as part of the everyday life and practices of division in the city. Soja argues that 'the two sets of structured relations (the social and the spatial) are not only homologous, in that they arise from the same origins in the mode of production, but are also dialectically inseparable';[11] similarly, I argue that sonic borders and sonic bordering practices are inseparable in producing the spaces of division as material entities and as practices of both division and connection.

The chapter is structured in three sections: 'Hearing and Listening'; 'Overhearing'; and 'Translating'. In 'Hearing and Listening', I discuss hearing sonic material of a political-sectarian nature in general across city spaces, and in particular the direct listening to stories of conflict in the car space of a taxi driver. The section explores the negotiation between sonic and visual borders through the production of the gallery piece *Presence and Absence*. In 'Overhearing', I discuss the process of overhearing from someone's else space, highlighted in the film *Look, Someone is Filming*. Finally, in 'Translating', I discuss how both artworks involve the specific bordering practice of translation. Translation occurs between Arabic and English and includes transcription; and it also occurs between the immateriality of sounds and materiality of images. The intention is that this bordering practice is spatially experienced in the gallery.

HEARING AND LISTENING

I met H.H., a 30-year-old taxi driver, twice. The first time was accidentally as a passenger in his taxi on 8 January 2010 when he told me his story, which I will go on to present. This encounter occurred at a time when I was initiating conversations with residents about the influence of the conflict on their spatial practices and movement in the city. I met H.H. a second time a week later, when I asked to see him on a Saturday afternoon by the sea to continue our conversation, having explained my research interests to him.

During our second meeting, H.H. asked why I was not taking notes as researchers normally do. The decision not to take notes at the start of the meeting was to avoid any tension that might come from the information discussed and which might affect the flow of the discussion, especially as H.H. came to the meeting accompanied by a man whom he introduced to me as a friend, who in turn asked me questions about the type of information I was after and the nature of my research before he left us. My suspicion was that this 'friend' was a member of Hezbollah and that he had been invited along to investigate me. In response, I took out my notebook and started taking quick notes in Arabic. After our meeting I continued to write down his words, from memory, in English – the language of my research studies. The shift from Arabic to English, accompanied by the shift from listening to writing notes, and then to the writing of a structured narrative, marks the beginning of my act of translating H.H.'s words into written text. As such, this translation process is both linguistic and material: it involved translation from Arabic into English and transcription from sound (speech) to image (written). This process marks the beginning of the two consecutive narratives and artworks that I present in this chapter.

> H.H.: I earned more than $400 in one day during the clashes of '7 May 2008'; I was curious to know what was happening in the city and so continued working. It was an easy ride from Dahyeh – the southern suburb – till I reached the Bchara El-Khoury intersection in Beirut. From there I had to navigate the internal roads with great care, manoeuvring only within areas under the control of the 8 March bloc. I decided to go to Hamra. There I parked in front of the Gefinor hotel and picked up the first customer and drove her to east Beirut. At first, she was bargaining with regard to the price but as a round of bullets began she rushed into the car and agreed to pay $100.
>
> After any explosion or assassination in the country I would remain within Dahyeh's limits. I wouldn't work far from there for a while.
>
> Whenever I heard about street clashes in Barbour and Tarik al-Jdide, I would immediately get excited and head there to participate with eagerness, as if something called me to support my people.
>
> For the first seven months after the Arab university clashes of 2007 I didn't enter Tarik al-Jdide, I was scared of being attacked there. But I needed to work, for if I don't work every day I don't eat; and in

these conditions I need to work in all areas, so my customers are from everywhere and from all sects. I removed all the sectarian signs from my car to re-enter Tarik al-Jdide. I used to listen to patriotic songs like 'oum t'harrar ya shaabi' by the Al-Wilaya band while driving. I removed that tape from the car, too. I also removed Al-Sayyed's photo and other religious sayings by Imam Ali.

Now I have my two-year-old daughter's Arabic calligraphy name instead, 'Jana omri'. Al-Sayyed's photo is in my wallet.

H.H.'s narrative follows the mobile space of a taxi driver whose sectarian affiliation and situation of economic urgency are in constant negotiation with the elastic geographic limit of his circulation in Beirut. He lives in the southern suburb of Beirut (a majority Shiite area under the political power of Hezbollah), and his relationship to Tarik al-Jdide and Mazraa is both professional and ideological, the latter having led him to join street fights in the areas in support of his sectarian group.[11] These fights were part of a series that Beirut witnessed in 2007 and that led to armed clashes in 2008.[12] The textual story I am presenting above describes H.H.'s use of sound material as well as the limits to his mobility in the city in different political and security situations.

The economic, sectarian and geographic negotiation takes place through the changing of political-sectarian songs and of visual expression of identity in his vehicle, manifest through presence and absence: the appearance of sectarian and political visuals (photographs) and music in his car, and their disappearance in line with his aim to expand the periphery of his work by securing access to areas outside his sectarian affiliation. The appearance of both the visuals and music in his car could be explained as a typical expression of this taxi driver's sectarian and political identity in his own space, but it could also be understood as 'a means to reclaiming significance in the present',[13] as Michael Bull argues in *Soundscapes of the Car*, where he discusses the listening to radio and tape cassettes while driving as a positive experience, as opposed to the more frequently expressed and negative idea often associated with driving that 'real life is elsewhere'.[14] Bull shows that, while the car has been linked to metaphors of individualism and domestic habitation that interpret the car's mass use and the act of driving as forms of 'democratization of autonomy and control', the car has a contradictory nature not only because it is a private space in the public realm but also because the driver is simultaneously understood as 'all-powerful and controlled' – by technology, other drivers and the road system.[15] Bull notes, from his empirical research with drivers, that the auditory plays a mediating role in the driving experience: music played in the car allows an engagement with that space rather than a disconnection from it. Bull's observation questions Theodor Adorno's idea of 'the auditory "colonization" of the "site" of experience', which implies the power of the auditory to mask and control users' experience in a specific place.[16]

In this respect, Bull argues, sounds played in the car mediate and engage the driver in the present time and space and are not merely forms of detachment from those times/spaces. The car can be understood, therefore, as a space where power and control are negotiated between the 'inside' of the car and the 'outside' world.

The content of the sound played in the car is another important element to consider, for it is not just 'a' sound – or 'any' sound. Charles Hirschkind has shown how Islamic sermon cassettes helped to spread the Islamic revival movement in Cairo in the 1970s and 1980s, 'reconfiguring the urban space acoustically through the use of Islamic media forms'.[17] Hirschkind notes that the playing of cassette sermons in shared taxis allowed for a public deliberation to take place between various passengers and the driver about issues around Islamic sharia law and its application in daily life that would not have been possible in the formal setting of a preacher and his audience. For in the car, discussion is 'situated outside the boundaries of prescribed ritual practice or scholarly instruction, this form of discussion cuts across generational and gender lines in ways not possible within the traditional institutions of Islamic authority'.[18]

Hirschkind's discussion of the Islamic sermon tapes in the Middle East, and specifically in Egypt, sheds light on the ordinary Muslim's practice of listening to religious material in cars. This practice has an autonomous public agency that goes beyond formal political purposes.[19] In Lebanon, Muslims and Christians listen to religious material; for example, both Sunnis and Shiites listen to the Quran and the *khutbah* (preaching) that precedes Friday prayers broadcast by radio stations. However, to consider the car as a shared space for dialogue facilitated by the content of Islamic tapes is to risk dismissing the imposing and powerful role played by the driver, who is in control of this material, particularly when the driver 'assumes' a common cultural and religious identity among passengers, simultaneously dismissing any differences and sensitivities among his passengers.

In H.H.'s case, the use of music and visual display is deliberate (as he explained to me). During the early stages of the conflict in Beirut, he used them as a confrontational element on his dashboard, intended in the first place to confront his passengers who were not affiliated to, or supporters of, H.H.'s political party. At the same time, his patriotic music, which is played while moving from one area to another, stands out from the sonic fabric of some of the areas into which he ventures, such as Tarik al-Jdide, overflowing and infiltrating the space yet leaving no physical or visual trace.

H.H. listens to firqat al-Wilayah (the al-Wilayah band), a group associated with Hezbollah and described in their media as a resistance group. Their song lyrics often contain speeches by key political figures associated with Hezbollah, as does the song 'oum t'harrar ya shaabi' that H.H. favours listening to. The song starts with the political speech of Al-Sayyed Nasrallah, the Hezbollah leader, criticizing the government at that time as followers of the West – particularly the United States. The lyrics that follow invite people to mobilize against the government and liberate the country. Part of the song translates as: 'Oh my people, revolt to change this dire situation … liberate yourselves … we want a wise government which brings glory to our nation, not one which follows instructions [from the outside].' This sound material is of a highly sectarian nature and extremely sensitive when played in an area such as Tarik al-Jdide, where the majority are Sunni and followers of the Mustaqbal movement, who oppose Hezbollah. In this respect, sound and mobility – especially when they are combined through the playing of loud music in a car – cross contested geographic, cultural and sectarian boundaries in transient ways that would otherwise be impossible. The role that sounds can play in acts of crossing is a bordering practice dependent on sound's immateriality and the impact its matter (content) can have on listeners or receivers in their own space.

In this process of what I am calling 'sonic crossing', a sound that is familiar to one person can be considered noise and even a confrontational element by someone else. Jacques Attali refers to sound as noise, specifically urban sound that is man-made as opposed to the sounds of nature: 'life is full of noise and that death alone is silent: work noise, noise of man, and noise of beast. Noise bought, sold, or prohibited. Nothing essential happens in the absence of noise.'[20] Charles Gurney has commented that 'noise is a sound which is out of place'.[21] In relation to the city, Rowland Atkinson writes that 'it is not simply that [the] city is louder than other places; rather, our sense of volume is always the result of subjective assessments'.[22] This subjectivity in assessing noise is not only related to volume but also concerns issues of quality: what sound in which place. 'Sensitivity to noise is often class and culturally based,' Atkinson argues, while Bull notes that the 'production of noise is often perceived as "uncivilized" within a bourgeois ethic'.[23] When a sound – whether or not of high volume – is unwelcome in a particular place, then it becomes a noise; more specifically in the case of sectarian sounds in Beirut, it becomes a confrontational noise.

H.H.'s decision later in 2007 to remove from his dashboard the sectarian visuals and music – which for some would have been seen and heard as confrontational noise – for ostensibly economic reasons might be understood as an act of self-surveillance. It was certainly a conscious practice in line with the other forms of surveillance that, as I discussed in 'Bordering Practice 02', control people's mobility and spatial practices and are enforced by formal political and security mechanisms in the city. This internalization of an external urban apparatus appears (or is translated) both physically, through the materiality of his car, and mentally, in his actions of self-surveillance, and raises the question: At what point does an action of self-surveillance lead to censorship? Yet the story that H.H. told me when I was in his car as a client becomes significant, not because it is true or false, but because it has been told; and his personal narrative, in

Fig.58
Presence and Absence part of *This is How Stories of Conflict Circulate and Resonate* gallery installation at Cities Methodologies exhibition, UCL, London, 2011.

being shared, thereby becomes part of a collective lived experience, along with other stories of conflict that circulate in the city and shape the current space of its residents. H.H.'s narrative is a bordering practice that involves the use of the sound of the voice for sharing stories rather than the use of noise in an act of division. The interrelated processes that operate between told stories and 'material' reality, and which produce the spatiality of narratives, are a dialectical process through which we can understand how places make narratives, as well as how, through the act of narration, places are made. As such, we can understand the dialectic, too, between sonic borders and sonic bordering practices.

The disappearance of political signs (sonic and visual) in H.H.'s taxi can be read as an act of retreat following his attempts to dominate his clients with his political views; it can also be read in terms of the distinction or contradiction that exists between, on the one hand, H.H.'s economic objectives and his desire to be safe, and, on the other hand, his wish to display his allegiance to his chosen political party. H.H.'s retreat relates to the particular historical moment and the political decision taken by his party to ease the tension in the country by temporarily retreating. De Certeau's explanation of the shift between strategy and tactical practices at a time of shifts in power – 'the weaker the forces at the disposition of the strategist ... the more the strategy is transformed into tactics'[24] – helps explain how the use of the voice, and the stories told through conversation, start to make up for the absence of fixed material signs, and how the voice and stories operate in place of material signs by performing a bordering practice involving resistance and power. The appearance and disappearance of signs on the dashboard resembles the nature of conflict in Lebanon: both are in constant flux, in which shifts in spatial manifestation and geographic domain can move from physical and visible confrontations to subtle ephemeral processes embedded in the practices of everyday life and back again to physical confrontations.

Sonic signs are also heard and listened to. As Sterne has commented: 'Listening is a directed, learned activity: it is a definite cultural practice. Listening requires hearing but is not simply reduced to hearing.'[25] My act of listening to H.H.'s story and my transcription of his words need to be understood as a qualitative research method. In some ethnographic and geographic studies, the transcription of the sonic is a form of silencing respondents: 'Transcription reduces sound recordings to communicated meaning, silencing everything that cannot be easily interpreted.'[26] This act of silencing as practised by the researcher – the one who transcribes – excludes elements that cannot be marked in written language, such as 'regional accents; the sexed, aged and gendered aspects of voice; and the acoustics, ambiences and resonances of the spaces in which research encounters take place'.[27] These elements of H.H.'s narrative, which I have not included in my transcription, raise the question: As a researcher, have I silenced H.H.? And by acknowledging the elements lost in transcription, it is possible to consider how stories are changed and transformed as they are exchanged through translation and transcription.

My encounter with H.H. involved hearing political songs experienced in the city of Beirut as well as listening to stories of conflict; it also highlighted the process of transcribing his spoken words into visual written material. The *Presence and Absence* artwork I made later and presented in a gallery space comprises three adjacent framed photographs of H.H.'s dashboard: the central one marks the absence of his voice through the presence of his words in the form of writing that fills the space of the dashboard; a second photograph marks the absence of his visuals with a dotted outline indicating their location on the dashboard; and the third marks the absence of his music cassette, also shown by a dotted outline on the dashboard. The song that H.H. listens to in his car space, 'oum t'harrar ya shaabi', is played on a loop through headphones for members of the audience to experience individually while located in front of the absent dashboard photographs in the gallery space. The work also features documentation of the visuals and music H.H. mentioned to me, and which I later obtained following an online search and a visit to a music shop. The visuals are laid out below the corresponding dashboard photograph. *Presence and Absence* marks the dashboard as both a material and immaterial border (Fig. 58).

OVERHEARING

In January 2011, one year after my encounter with H.H., the political tension between the two main opposing political blocs in Lebanon intensified and led to a shift of political power in the government from the 14 March bloc to the 8 March bloc. This political change was directly reflected in the Mazraa district, with tension and clashes because of the feeling of loss of power in Tarik al-Jdide – where the Mustaqbal movement, the main Sunni party in the 14 March bloc, is dominant – and the gain of power felt in Mazraa – where Amal, the main Shiite party along with Hezbollah in the 8 March bloc, is dominant. This political shift was visible in the reappearance of the personnel of political parties, who were controlling security and affecting people's mobility. Their presence was coupled with the existence of the Lebanese army on the streets where possible conflicts might arise among opposing groups. It is worth noting that the presence of the army and of political parties has been constant since 2005, but that at times of tension this presence is more extensive and visible. This limits one's movement in the city and makes the simple act of taking pictures with a camera a suspicious one. Once again formal politics solidify the geography of division and redraw material borders in the streets of Beirut. Before and during the week when the government changed, and after a day of street clashes on the Mazraa Main Road – due to anger that the leader of the Mustaqbal movement had been left out of the government[28] – I took a series of site journeys across the borders of the two adjacent areas, Tarik al-Jdide and Mazraa (Fig. 59).

The first journey, during the week of tension before the governmental change, involved a series of rides with several different taxi drivers, in which I observed

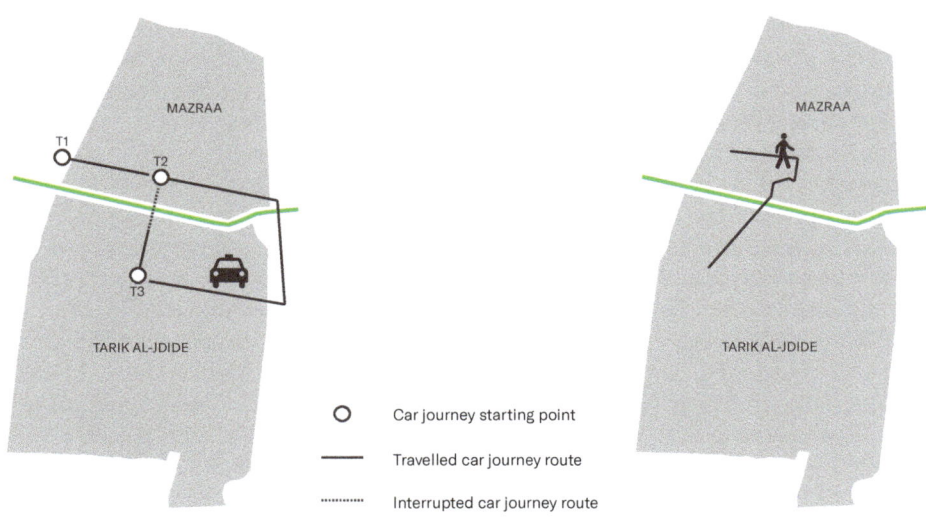

Fig.59
Map of taxis and walking journey.

and recorded their music, radio stations and personalized decorations, and engaged in conversation with the drivers. The journeys followed the taxi route between the two areas, particularly between the Makassid neighbourhood in Tarik al-Jdide and the Barbour neighbourhood in Mazraa. The second journey took place a day after the governmental change and the clashes, and it involved the collection of street sounds during a walk in the two areas. These included voices and sounds heard from inside shops, as well as those collected on the outside and on pavements and streets, using a sound recorder.

These journeys, or what I call research exercises, began with the intention of studying the political-sectarian differences in sonic material between the two contested areas. I was also interested in whether the drivers, depending on their political affiliations and background, changed the content of the sonic material played inside their taxis while crossing from one area to the other – and whether they did so in relation to their view on my affiliation. Furthermore, I wished to examine the presence of music and visual evidence of the drivers' political-sectarian affiliation displayed in the vehicles at the time, and to understand whether, in the absence of such evidence, the drivers substituted other forms, such as speech, for it.

The research adopted two different methods for approaching the sites, each one utilizing a particular and appropriate medium of recording. In the first method, I formed partnerships with taxi drivers by obtaining their permission to video record their memorabilia while having a conversation with them (Fig. 60). My aim was to access their cars and, through them, the streets we traversed, using a video camera to document the journey. The video recordings capture the street background as I film the conversation in the foreground. In the second method, I walked through the streets alone with a hidden sound recorder, capturing the sounds heard, directly yet unintentionally, as well as those overheard coming from spaces not visible but physically adjacent. Both methods use digital recording, but they challenge, or silently resist, the politics of surveillance in the site, by playing with the question of when and where to record audio or to record video. The methodological differentiation between employing video and sound recording was a response to the site's constraints, determined by the prohibition on photography, and the difficulty of site accessibility due to security and surveillance carried out by the army and political parties in both areas.[29]

My use of video and sound recording connects to what Sterne describes as the 'clichéd attributes' usually associated with the hearing/seeing binary.[30] Sterne refers to an 'audiovisual litany', a term chosen for its theological overtones; the concept of 'litany', he argues, is embedded in Western intellectual history:[31]

- hearing is spherical, vision is directional;

- hearing immerses its subject, vision offers a perspective;

- sounds come to us, but vision travels to its object;

- hearing is concerned with interiors, vision is concerned with surfaces;

- hearing involves physical contact with the outside world, vision requires distance from it;

- hearing places us inside an event, seeing gives us a perspective on the event;

- hearing tends toward subjectivity, vision tends toward objectivity;

- hearing brings us into the living world, sight moves us toward atrophy and death;

- hearing is about affect, vision is about intellect;

- hearing is a primarily temporal sense, vision is a primarily spatial sense;

- hearing is a sense that immerses us in the world, vision is a sense that removes us from it.[32]

TAXI JOURNEY T1

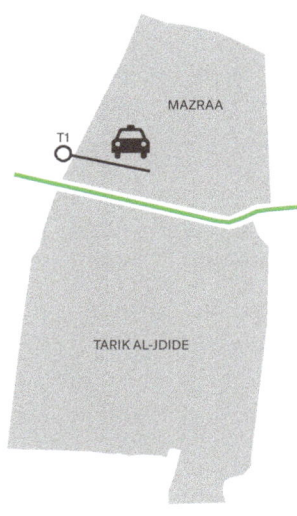

○   Car journey starting point

—   Travelled car journey route

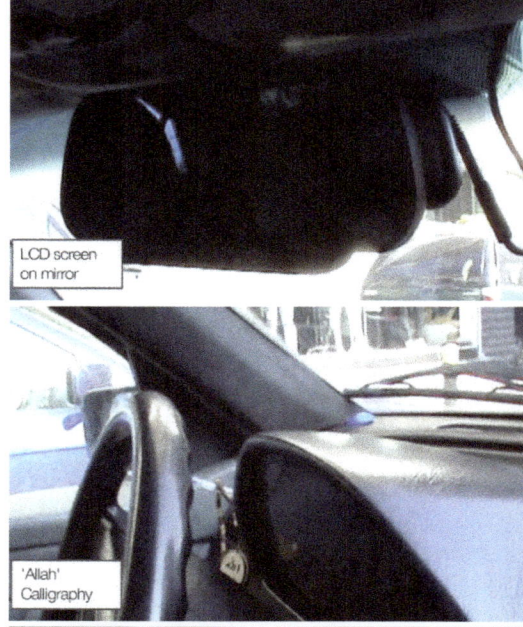

LCD screen on mirror

'Allah' Calligraphy

Stereo

مادة سمعية ت١
محادثة مع سائق سيارة أجرة

(٠٠:٥٥)   م   بتحط موسيقى بالسيارة؟

(٠٠:٥٨)   ت١   ميلا، مرّات. أنا أكتر شي بسمع
أناشيد دينية.

(٠١:٠٩)   ت١   مرّات بسمع أغاني، ليش لأ.

(٠١:٢٣)   م   هول أي فرقة أناشيد؟

(٠١:٢٦)   ت١   هول جمعية المشاريع.

(٠١:٢٩)   ت١   أنا مش معهن، بس أناشيدن حلوة.

Sonic material T1
Conversation with taxi driver

(00:55) **M** Don't you play music while
            driving?

(00:58) **T1** Yes, I do sometimes; usually
            I listen to religious chants.

(01:09) **T1** Other times I listen to
            pop music.

(01:23) **M** Which band is singing?

(01:26) **T1** It is the Association of
            Islamic Charitable Projects
            (Al Masharee).

(01:29) **T1** I'm not a member of their
            organization but their
            chants are nice.

TAXI JOURNEY T2

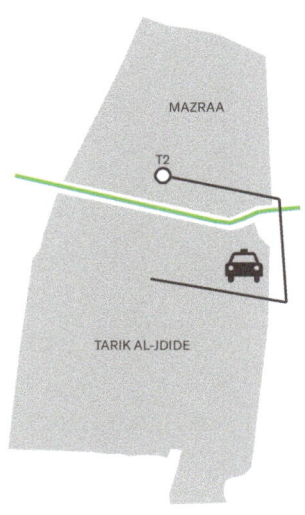

MAZRAA

T2

TARIK AL-JDIDE

O   Car journey starting point

—   Travelled car journey route

Cup holder

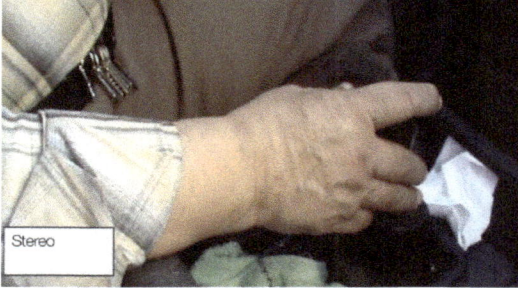

Stereo

Evil eye

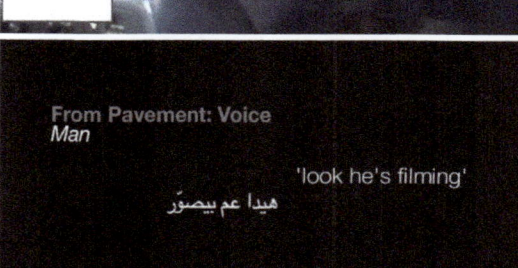

From Pavement: Voice
Man

'look he's filming'

هيدا عم بيصوّر

مادة سمعية ت٢
محادثة مع سائق سيارة أجرة

(٣:٠٦.)   **ت٢**   يعني بدنا نساويها وبتعرف أنت الأوضاع.

(٣:١٦.)   **ت٢**   مش عم بيقدر الواحد يوّقف شغل ليساوي هالمسجلة. حتى المصلّح ما يقول بدة ٤٠ أو ٥٠ دولار، وهي حقّها جديدة هالقيمة.

(٣:٣٥.)   **م**   ما بتحط صور لولادك ولعيلتك؟

(٣:٣٨.)   **ت٢**   كنت حاطط صورهن.

(٣:٤٢.)   **م**   شلتهن؟ ليه شلتهن؟

(٣:٤٧.)   **ت٢**   بتفوت عالطرنبة لتغسل السيارة، بيمسحولك ياها وكل شي بيخزقو.

Sonic material T2
Conversation with taxi driver

(03:06) **T2** I want to fix it but you
         know we are in difficult times.

(03:16) **T2** I cant take time off to get
         the stereo fix, because
         the technician will ask
         forty or fifty dollars
         almost the price of a brand
         new stereo.

(03:35) **M** Don't you put family
        photographs in your car?

(03:38) **T2** I used to have their
         photographs.

(03:42) **M** Why did you remove them?

(03:47) **T2** When I go to get the car
         washed at the gas station
         they wipe the photos and rip.

TAXI JOURNEY T3

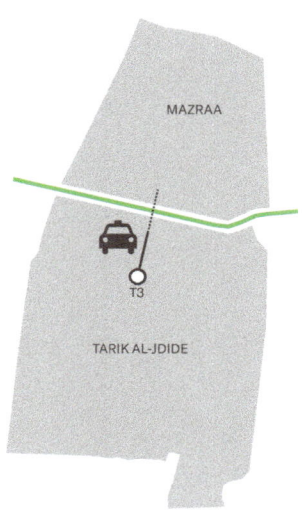

○   Car journey starting point

──   Travelled car journey route

········   Interrupted car journey route

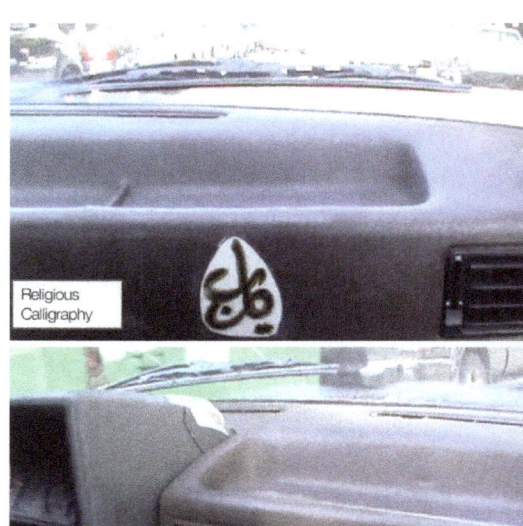

Religious Calligraphy

Religious Calligraphy

Stereo Cavity

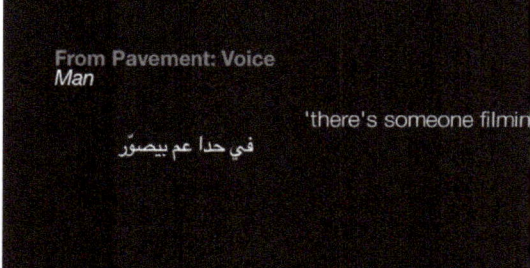

From Pavement: Voice
Man

'there's someone filmin

في حدا عم بيصوّر

مادة سمعية ت٣
محادثة مع سائق سيارة أجرة

(٠٥:١٩) **ت٣** هو بعد لسّا عم بساويهن. بعد بدّي صفّقهن وأعملّن لوحة وساويها.

(٠٥:٢٥) **م** كلمات شو؟

(٠٥:٢٧) **ت٣** كلمات حلوة. في عندك مثلاً "بسم الله الرحمن الرحيم". في كمان مثلاً "وان تعدوا نعمة الله فلن تحصوها".

(٠٥:٤٠) **ت٣** حسب، في أشيا حلوة. في كمان "الجنة تحت أقدام الأمّهات". يعني هاي بشكل...في أشيا حلوة .

(٠٥:٥٢) **م** ما في شي سياسي؟

(٠٥:٥٥) **ت٣** لا لا ما بتعاطا بالسياسة. شو بدنا يا خيّي. مش انو شو بدنا، بس عايشين بالوضع يلّي هو، بس يعني .

Sonic material T3
Conversation with taxi driver

(05:19) **T3** I'm working on new
         calligraphy; I want to
         arrange them on a sheet and
         display them.

(05:25) **M** What kind of calligraphy do
         you write?

(05:27) **T3** Nice words, like 'In the
         name of merciful God'.
         There is also 'You can not
         count the blessings of God'.

(05:40) **T3** Other nice sayings like:
         'Heaven lies underneath the
         feet of mothers'.

(05:52) **M** Do you put any political
         slogans?

(05:55) **T3** No, no, I don't like
         politics;anyway we are
         living it everyday.

TAXI JOURNEY T3

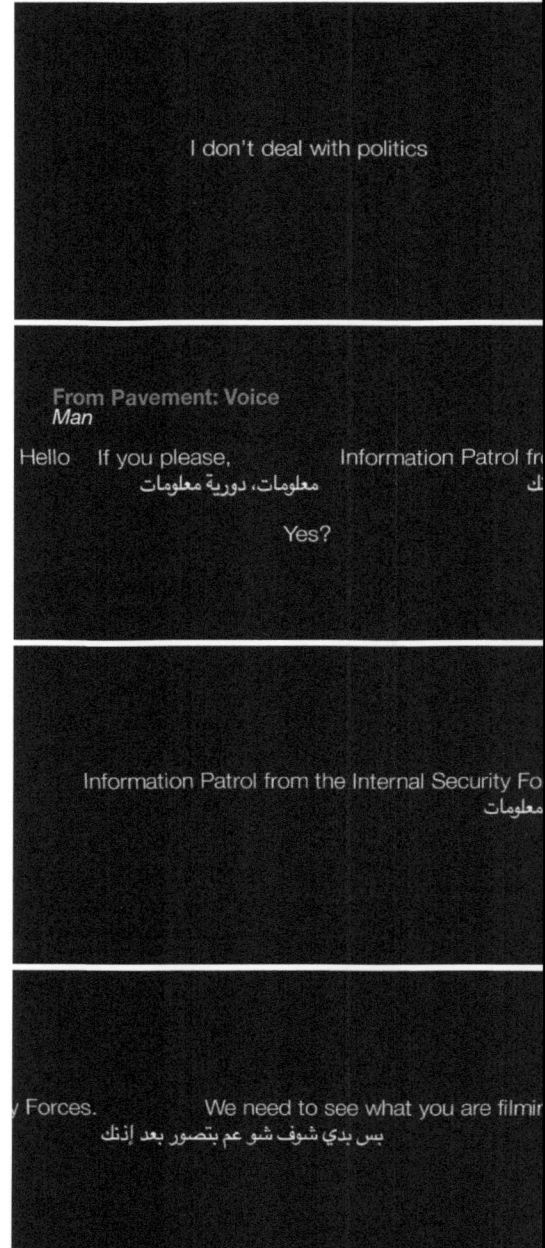

Fig. 60
Stills from *Look, Someone is Filming*, 2011.

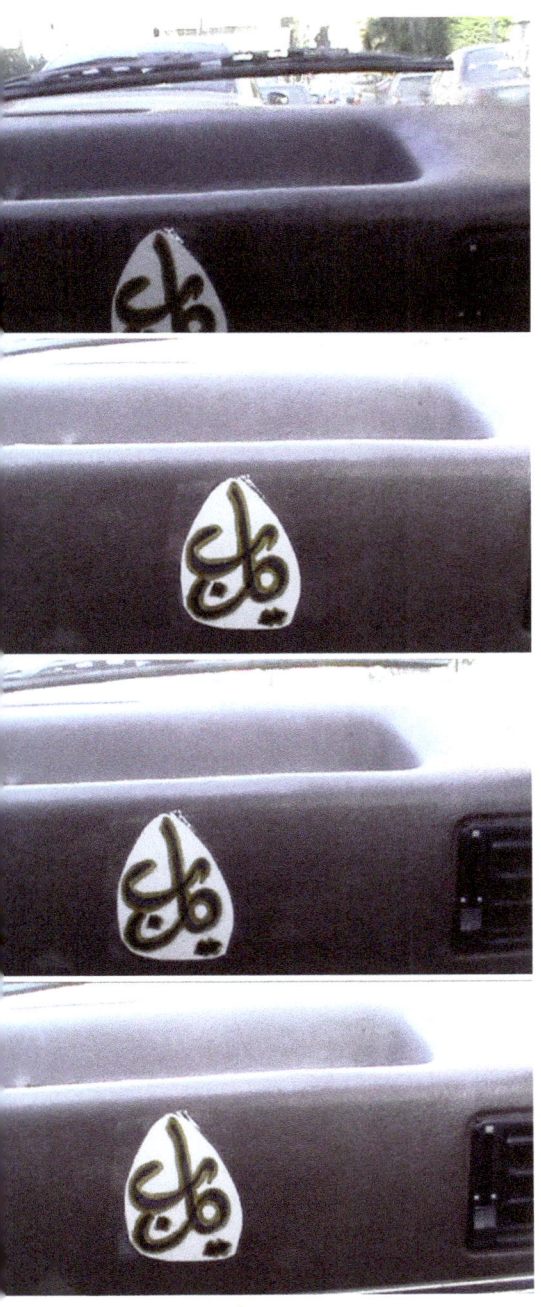

The choice of recording I made in the type of space I was in (whether inside the taxis or outside on the streets) related to, or was forced by, the type of control operating in that space. The assumption or hypothesis I followed in my recording method implies that political control privileges seeing over hearing, in that security personnel do not allow video recording in public spaces, whereas I assumed sound recording would more likely go unnoticed. Thus, my method connects hearing with exterior spaces, and seeing/hearing with interior spaces. However, in what follows, my research demonstrates that the control exerted by conflict extends to the interiority of the car space, thereby breaking the hearing/seeing connection practised in and from that space.

More importantly, the practice-led method I have used was one that capitalized on my spontaneous encounter with H.H. and developed this into a planned exercise that challenged the surveillance 'strategies' adopted by the militia in a 'tactical' manner. Consequently, I shifted from the note-writing technique that I used in the first exercise into video and audio recording in the second exercise, in an attempt to document – to chase and capture – the invisibility, ephemerality and immateriality of the sonic borders that one encounters in everyday urban life.

The second exercise was a tactical one that took place in 'the space of the other';[33] it was, as de Certeau puts it, through 'the art of the weak' that I responded to the urban practices used to dominate by 'others' who seek to control through security and surveillance. In differentiating between the processes of hearing and listening, 'hearing represents a passive experience, listening an active one'.[34] In my method, I used recording to transform the passivity of 'hearing' in urban space into the active practice of 'listening'; in doing so, I aimed to formalize or formulate the heard and overheard through the act of listening to the actual voices when recording, and then later to the recordings obtained.

Sound recording technology has been criticized by researcher Murray Schafer, in his work on soundscape, for the way it separates sound from its natural context through the use of recording techniques and devices.[35] Schafer uses the term 'schizophonia' to describe the experience of taking recorded sound out of its natural context.[36] On the other hand, recording techniques are considered in the planning of art performances that will be recorded, which means that the kind of recordings used, even if schizophonic, will influence the production of original works.[37] In the case of my research project, the type of recording I applied relates to the political context and security level that have forced the schizophonic experience by splitting between sound and image recording. Schizophonia may also apply to the activities of political control that interfere between individuals and their contexts. These activities constitute a bordering practice that disconnects the senses (hearing and seeing); spaces (exterior and interior); modes of recording (audio and video); and representations (sound and image).

In sound studies, anthropologists, geographers and musicologists, among other scholars, have argued for the value of hearing and the audible in studying the social world, and they have criticized the privileging of vision and images over hearing that has been argued as essential to modern thought, modernity and visual culture studies.[38] From a different perspective, however, the privileging of hearing over seeing has, as Sterne argues, come under heavy criticism from theorists, including Jacques Derrida, whose theory of deconstruction 'inverts, inhabits and reanimates the sound/vision binary, privileging writing over speech and refusing both speech-based metaphysics and presence-based positive assertions'.[39] The principles and problems concerning the relationship between hearing and seeing, and between sound and sight, remain unsettled, despite the extensive literature across various disciplines, each of which defines that relationship for its own particular purposes. Steven Connor, for example, has argued:

> In our culture, and perhaps others besides, the relations between sound and sight may be said to be largely indexical, by which I mean that the evidence of sight often acts to interpret, fix, limit, and complete the evidence of sound. Seeing may then appear as the destination or terminus of sound – 'oh, now I see what you mean' … As the two senses on which human beings seem most to rely, hearing and sight are closely interwoven but not necessarily synchronized. Though light moves faster than sound, these relations are reversed in the logic of human perception; it is sound that seems to be immediate, and sight, as the sense with which we achieve balance and understanding, that follows after. Hearing proposes; sight disposes.[40]

The phrase 'Hearing proposes; sight disposes' captures how the relationship between the sonic and its translation into written material – as images – operates as the basis for this research project. W.J.T. Mitchell has examined the differences between words and images in terms of how imagery includes the graphic, optical, perceptual, mental, and verbal.[41] Although words and images are from the same family, Mitchell notes that each is distinct and used differently by the many disciplines that refer to these definitions. Mitchell refers to both words and images as signs. For example, a diagram of a picture of a man (presenting a real man), the pictogram of a man, and the phonetic sign for the word 'man', and presents a tableau that can be read 'not as movement from world to mind to language, but from one kind of sign to another'.[42] The relationship between different kinds of signs is, according to Mitchell, dialectical, and hence involves a struggle between the signs:

> The dialectic of word and image seems to be a constant in the fabric of signs that a culture weaves

around itself. What varies is the precise nature of
the weave, the relation of warp and woof ... The
history of culture is in part the story of a protracted
struggle for dominance between pictorial and
linguistic signs ... At some moments this struggle
seems to settle into a relationship of free exchange
along open borders; at other times the borders are
closed and a separate peace is declared.[43]

Ludwig Wittgenstein argued that mental images – provoked by speech and
thoughts – and real (physical) images belong to the same category: 'Mental
images of colours, shapes, sounds, etc., etc., which play a role in communication
by means of language we put in the same category with patches of color actually
seen, sounds heard.'[44] In Wittgenstein's argument, both mental and real images
need the mind in order for them to exist; whether images are 'there' (in real
life) or 'not there' (in the mind), they need to be consciously acknowledged as
images and they need language rooted in a particular cultural/historic tradition
to understand and express what they stand for as images/signs.[45]

The writing of words – in the manner of *Presence and Absence* and *Look,
Someone is Filming* – does not depict the mental images provoked by speech or
thought, but it makes material and visual words from the immaterial and spoken
words, thereby making absence present. However, the reading of the writing may
provoke mental or verbal images in the reader's mind. Writing here is a process
that operates within and across the differences and relationships that exist
between signs – between the immateriality of words as mental images and the
materiality of words as real images. As such, it constitutes a bordering practice.

The multiple recorded journeys that I took through the sites reveal a subtler form
of interest in politics on the part of taxi drivers. This was evident in how the focus
on personal and religious memorabilia differed from the political-sectarian visual
displays prominent in taxis in earlier periods of political unrest, and exemplified
in H.H.'s use of visuals and political music. This suggests that, on the one hand,
the need to generate income might supersede political affiliation during a period
of unrest, and, on the other, that the participants in these journeys may have
been less politically involved than H.H. However, what became more evident
during my journeys was the interference of people who decided to comment
on my video recording from spaces outside the taxi: 'Look, someone is filming'.
Despite my having devised what I thought would be a safe method, this did
not stop the state's internal security forces from interrupting my taxi journey to
investigate the intention behind my choice to video record the interior of a taxi.
This produced a moment in the research when I had no choice but to turn off
the camera, and to record listening rather than seeing (Fig. 61). Thus, listening
rather than seeing is the result of turning off the camera, and the act of turning
off the camera places emphasis on one sense. This demonstrates what I have
previously suggested: the spatial experience of each type of recording may be a

practical, and not merely a methodological and conceptual, matter, depending on the type of control operating in the space where the recording is being made.

The video footage and sound recordings I obtained from the different taxis and walking journeys provide the material for the film *Look, Someone is Filming*. The film is constructed of two adjacent screens, right and left, and of three consecutive scenes. The choice of two adjacent screens was made in order to establish visually and pragmatically a number of different borders and negotiations that the work explores: first, the political and spatial division between the two areas where the research took place; second, the divisions between inside the taxi and outside on the street; and third, the conceptual boundary between hearing and seeing – and between sound and image. Having established these opposites/negotiations on the screen, the structure of three scenes comes to negotiate the borders of these binary oppositions. The tripartite structure follows the three types of journey taken and the type of recording used in each: in the car, using video recording; in walking, using audio recording; then back to the car, using audio recording. The choice in the third journey of returning to the car to use audio recording rather than video recording was made to complicate the idea that hearing belongs to the exterior and seeing to the interior, and to explore the spatial experience provided by hearing in the car interior while crossing geographic borders.

The film starts with the left screen showing the footage of the video camera scanning the interior of the three taxis in which I took three journeys in search of political and sectarian visual evidence. The evidence I noticed is annotated in English on a white box located at the bottom left of the screen. The left screen is also used to present in words, translated from spoken Arabic into written English, my conversations with the drivers that took place inside the taxis, as well as the comments I heard, which came from outside. These last comments are transcribed in Arabic and then translated into English. The English and Arabic words are both in white on a black background and replace the footage of the interior space of the car dashboard. This is to present the spoken words as important material occupying the interior of the car space and functioning as a border, in a similar way to the political-sectarian visual evidence that the camera was scanning (or searching for). Simultaneously, the right screen scans the outside area as the taxi passes by. It aims to relate the interior space of the taxi to the area, in order to study the border being negotiated between these two spaces. The second scene is taken from my walking journey in both areas using sound recording only. The sonic material heard and overheard in Mazraa (Barbour) is captured on the right screen, and that from Tarik al-Jdide on the left. Again, the material I heard is transcribed into Arabic and translated into English. The third scene returns to the interior of the taxi recorded while crossing from one area to the other. Each screen follows one journey and translates the sonic Arabic into written English, presenting the conversation with the drivers on a black background. The visual evidence noticed inside the cars is annotated in English on white boxes at the bottom left of the two screens.

BARBOUR WALKING JOURNEY

S1 From shop [Unidentified TV channel]

Unidentified politician's voice
… I think that all parties will participate in the parliamentary consultation, because we don't want to oppose the state or the norms. But I believe that …

ص١ من المحل [اذاعة تلفزيونية غير محددة]

صوت سياسي غير محدد
... أعتقد بأن الجميع سيشارك في الاستشارات النيابية، لأننا لا نريد مقاطعة الدولة، و لا نريد مقاطعة الأصول و الأعراف .إنما أعتقد...

S2 From shop [Radio Sawt Libnan 93.3 FM]

Musical news intermission
[music]

ص٢ من المحل [راديو صوت لبنان ٩٣.٣ اف.ام]

فاصل موسيقي اخباري
[موسيقى أخبار]

S3 From pavement [Voice]

Man
Salam alaykum, how are you?

ص٣ من الرصيف [صوت]

رجل
السلام عليكم، كيفك؟

S4 From shop [Radio Liban Libre 102.3 FM]

News presenter
… the newly appointed prime minister started today …

ص٤ من المحل [راديو لبنان الحر ١٠٢.٣ اف.ام]

مذيع اخباري
... بدأ الرئيس المكلف اليوم ...

S5 From shop [Unidentified TV channel]

First unidentified politician's voice
… he declined to extend the term of president Lahoud, but upon his return from Syria he extended it.

Second unidentified politician's voice
I am talking about president Al Hrawi

First unidentified politician's voice
also for president Al Hrawi it's the same story, he was adapting

صه من المحل [اذاعة تلفزيونية غير محددة]

صوت سياسي غير محدد ١
... يرفض التمديد للرئيس لحود، راح عالشام و رجع و مدد للرئيس لحود.

صوت سياسي غير محدد ٢
أنا عم بحكي عن الرئيس الهراوي.

صوت سياسي غير محدد ١
كمان وقت الرئيس الهراوي زات الخبرية، إذاً كان يتأقلم.

S6 From pavement [Voice]

Woman 1
The kids were sent home from school today

Man
No, not all of them. The Makassid school sent their's home

Woman 1
I'll tell you why - they were worried about the children being stranded there.
And then the poor children would get frightened.

Girl
Who designed this?

Woman 1
Uncle Mannas

Woman 2
What did they design?

Man
They drink tea everyday, and hang the teabags on the tree.

ص٦ من الرصيف [صوت]

امراة ١
الأولاد راحوا و رجعوهن

رجل
لأ، ما الكل، المقاصد رجعوهن

مراة ١
حقلك ليش. مش مشان شي. خوفة ما يصير شي و يعلقوا الأولاد.

فتاة
مين عمل هالديزاين؟

امراة ١
هيدا عمو مناس

امراة ٢
شو عاملين؟

رجل
بيشربوا شاي كل يوم هو والشباب، و بعلقوا الكياس عالشجرة

TARIK AL-JDIDE WALKING JOURNEY

S7 From pavement [Voice]

Man
Hajjeh, what did I do wrong?

Woman
Nothing, but you are looking and I told you this parking space is taken. Tell Abu Bassam to move his car, so people can park on either side.

ص٧ من الرصيف [صوت]

رجل
حجة شو عملت أنا؟

امراة
ما عملت شي، بس أنت عم تتطلع و أنا عم بحكي معك انو الموقف مأخوذ.

S8 From pavement [Voice]

Boy
Yes, I knew it was you who ate it. No one leaves the crust except you. I knew

ص٨ من الرصيف [صوت]

صبي
انت ياللي آكلها، ما حدا بيترك الأطراف إلا انت، أنا عرفت.

S9 From shop entrance [Voice]

Man 1
What's wrong with you brother?

Man 2
It was I who advised him

Man 3
So now this will happen at the Martyr square every evening at six? What is it for?

Man2
Now no one will go down to pray there, to avoid any trouble

ص٩ من مدخل المحل [صوت]

رجل ١
شو إشبك خيي؟

رجل ٢
هيدا أنا نصحته

رجل ٣
هلأ كل يوم الساعة ستة عشية بدو يصير هيك بساحة الشهدا! لشو هالشي كلّه؟

رجل ٢
هلأ خلص ما حدا بينزل يصلي اذا صار إشكال أو صار شي.

S10 From pavement [Voice]
Man
Was it you setting those tyres on fire yesterday?

ص۱۰ من الرصيف [صوت]
رجل
أنت كنت عم بتولع دواليب مبارح؟

Fig.61
Map of the sounds recorded in the walking journey.

The conceptual decision behind the use of language, transcription and translation in the film will be discussed in the next section on 'Translating'. The loss of visual reference in the scenes of the audio recording will also be referred to later, where the type of spatial experience and bordering practice that is produced in relation to time/history will be analysed.

The recorded journeys collectively examine how people transmit political sonic material from their spaces (shops and cars) while listening to formal media through television and radio stations. Through the processes of 'listening to' and 'reading' these sonic releases in the documented work (the film and this essay), another form of live media of an informal nature is proposed. This everyday-life media crosses borders, as it is channelled from one person's space to another, such as from cars, or shops relaying television and radio content to the street, or between people chatting on pavements and balconies. Although the process of overhearing happens unintentionally while wandering the city, it provides a clear example of how people build up their own information about political events even if they are not politically interested or involved. It also provides an examination of that overheard sonic material, which reveals how politically charged our everyday sonic material 'told and heard' is, and how normalized and unnoticed it has become by local residents.

It is tempting to suppose that overhearing is an inescapable act. However, as Schafer argues, listening is a choice: 'We have no ear lids. We are condemned to listen. But this does not mean our ears are always open.'[46] Listening is not only a practical biological process; it is also a controlled process. Schafer differentiates between those who listen and those who decide not to listen, and he provides the example of dictatorships that fell because the dictators did not listen to the sound of revolutions on the way.[47] Within the realm of listening and the audible there are sounds that are unheard and silenced, despite the fact that they vibrate or materially exist in the world. The overheard is not any sound; it is in some ways the opposite of sounds that are not heard, since overheard sounds are heard when they are not meant to be. The practice of overhearing sounds in Beirut can be a way of exerting control over senses, practices and spaces. Overhearing can be understood as 'the auditory "colonization" of the "site" of experience'.[48] The process of overhearing is a socio-spatial dialectic in which the overheard becomes part of residents' audible material and lived experience. *Look, Someone is Filming* emphasizes how the process of overhearing can be understood as an invasive and controlling act that occurs across the borders between physical and mental spaces.

TRANSLATING

In 'The Task of the Translator', Walter Benjamin argues how the process of translating from one language into another exposes the nature of both languages involved. He explains the role of translation in relation to the kinship, as well as the foreignness, between languages. According to Benjamin, languages may not have the same origin, but they are nevertheless related by the fact that they all intend to express meaning: 'Languages are not strangers to one another, but are, a priori and apart from all historical relationships, interrelated in what they want to express.'[49] Their foreignness is revealed, however, in the untranslatability of certain words and contexts from one language to another, specifically when the context in which a word or a sentence is used in one culture differs from, or is of no or little relevance to, the culture into which it is to be translated. Hence: 'translation is only a somewhat provisional way of coming to terms with the foreignness of languages.'[50]

The original text and the translation are important to each other not simply because the latter issues from the former. As Benjamin notes, they are independent of one another and continue to develop separately, with each language developing in a dynamic process over time – through changes in words, sentences and structure, and in relation to the historical/cultural context where this development takes place. Translation eliminates the superiority of one language over another, and translation can be understood as a critical practice that reveals the interdependency of languages, as well as the way in which they supplement each other.

Drawing on Benjamin's ideas in relation to postcolonial theory, Homi Bhabha has discussed translation not as a literary process but as a means of revealing cultural differences between colonizers and colonized. Bhabha comments on the impossibility of achieving total translation from one culture to the other – that is, the impossibility for the colonizer to control the colonized and to totally eliminate difference between the two cultures.[51] Modes of translation may include, for example, the translation of language, customs, culture and architecture from the colonizer's homeland into the colony, as well as the use of translation to educate colonized subjects in the hope of influencing their minds. It is through untranslatability, according to Bhabha's postcolonial critique, that cultural difference maintains itself and by which the colonized resist the colonizer: for Bhabha, 'the production of cultural meaning [is located] in the realm of the untranslatable, the interstices between languages and cultures.'[52]

Thus, translation is a bordering practice between cultures that marks difference, but it also offers a space of possibilities generated out of that difference. It is because of this twofold role – the ability to examine and challenge the original work through its translation and vice versa, and the potential new space offered by that process – that I take translation to play a critical spatial practice in my work. Specifically, this occurs through the different techniques I use to record sound and to translate sound into images and written material in both Arabic and English.

Linguistic translation, from Arabic to English, is at the heart of my work, for although I am an Arabic-speaking citizen and the empirical research was conducted in Lebanon with Arabic-speaking participants, my research is delivered in

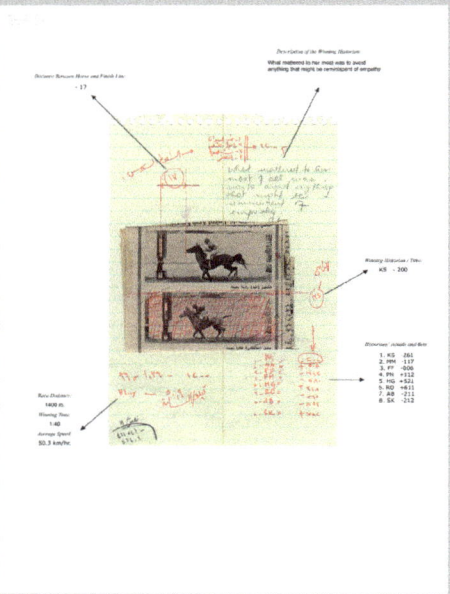

Fig. 62
The Atlas Group in collaboration with Walid Raad. *Missing Lebanese Wars*,
1996-2002, plate 134.

the form of a written document in the English language and my work is exhibited outside Lebanon. Translation and working across languages are common practices in research disciplines specifically concerned with translation as a subject matter, and this is also the case when the creation of artwork includes language in its production. The presentation of work in different cultural and linguistic contexts involves moving from translation as a linguistic form of explanation in the form of, for example, subtitles, to translation itself as a mode of production that does not exclude confrontation or alienation.

Through my work, I have been interested in how other Lebanese artists work with language and translation, whether in the form of writing or speech – in visual arts, films and performances – and how they have taken different approaches to the translation of their works (or the use of language) and the presentation of their work in international multilingual contexts. For example, Walid Raad's art practice comprises mainly lecture performances and gallery installations that exhibit visuals and videos of his lectures. Raad always performs his lectures in the English language, whether the lecture takes place in an Arab city such as Beirut or in a Western one such as London. In *The Atlas Group* (1989–2004), a fictional archival project that researched and documented the Lebanese civil war from 1975 to 1990, Raad refers to documents that he claims were given to the group by individuals and institutions, and others which were created by the group, to archive the history of the civil war.[53] Raad treats these documents

Fig. 63
Akram Zaatari, still from *In This House*, 2005.

in his practice as pieces of historic evidence to study and to be used in constructing his narratives about the history of war. As part of his artistic language, Raad translates the text in these documents into English in the form of notes and annotations (Fig. 62).

Raad uses Arabic text to give credibility and a historical and contextual dimension to the documents he uses, in order to indicate that they are 'original' documents and not created by the artist, whereas the English text functions as another layer belonging to the formal, even institutional, language of documentation and study of the historic archive. The foreignness (for an international and non-domestic audience) of the subject of the Lebanese war is highlighted by the use of foreign languages in the work; this foreignness gives the artist a free space and a control tool to construct his version or his own reading of history. Raad's use of language is highly controlled: it sets positions between the artist and his artwork by questioning the nature/source of that art, and between the historical and the fictional.

For the film maker Akram Zaatari, the priority seems to be to produce a work that communicates with an international art audience who mainly understand the English language, and this includes the Lebanese art audience. In this respect, Zaatari is clear about the cultural background of his audience. In his documentary *In This House* (2005) (Fig. 63), Zaatari mixes Arabic with English so that both languages contribute to the making of the work; however, Arabic operates as the spoken 'everyday' and empirical, while English takes the position of the written, and analytical, on the screen. In other works, such as *Letter to a Refusing Pilot* (2013), English is used as the language of the narrator (that is, the artist) himself.

A common strand in relation to translation, which appears in the works by Raad and Zaatari, is the seemingly practical use of translation to overcome linguistic barriers in order to present their works at international art institutions and venues where the work has to be translated or subtitled in English for it to be shared. But this 'practical use' is nothing other than an indication of the artists' respective political and cultural positions across countries and languages. The different modes of translation used by them begin to unfold the complexity of their position, the problematical nature of language, the many interplays of translation in the production of artworks, and the ways in which different audiences perceive and experience these works differently. Translation becomes questioned as a potential tool of control and as an artistic language in the hands of these artists, perhaps because it has been forced upon them through the cross-cultural position they hold in the international art scene. The different modes of translation create the possibility of production generated across languages and through the communication and mis-communication offered by cross-cultural encounters. This echoes Bhabha's notion that cultural difference is, on the one hand, a space for communication and a site of production of the new, and, on the other hand, a space of mis-communication and a site of resistance.

Look, Someone is Filming uses translation in a number of ways, but mainly to point to the immateriality of the sounds heard every day in Beirut. Translation can be summarized through two interrelated modes: first, linguistic translation and transcription; and second, material translation. In the first mode, the spoken Arabic and sounds heard in the film are translated into written English on the screen – this involves a translation of one language into another – but before the linguistic translation occurs, the spoken and heard Arabic has been translated into written Arabic text, in a process usually called transcription. In a much looser use of the term 'translation', the material objects and visual evidence noticed in the taxis are also 'translated' into written English annotations on the screen. Readability and see-ability are at the heart of the process of translating the immateriality of sound into the materiality of images. The use of the different modes of translation aims to question the prevalence of everyday sonic material, such as daily conversations and the sounds we overhear and encounter, which are usually assumed to be ordinary and, at times, hidden or unnoticed. By employing translation, and following Benjamin's conceptual work, my research and practice aim to expose and unsettle the original sonic material by translating it into text. The process of translation is more complex than this, however, as it includes not only the material translation of sounds into images but also the translation of Arabic into English – that is, cultural translation.

The aim in the film is to set the English language at the start of the taxi scene as the only text that appears on the screen. English acts as a language of subtitles that is usually used in foreign films, and English also acts through the annotations to highlight material objects and visuals of political-sectarian relevance in the film, such as religious calligraphy that might be familiar to a Lebanese audience but requires translation for a foreign audience. In so doing, the annotations also work as visual signs to which the local audience need to pay attention, even when the signified is familiar in a scene that might otherwise go unnoticed. However, the work places the English text in the middle of the screen, rather than at the bottom where subtitles usually appear. This shift in location marks language as a key conceptual and aesthetic element in constructing the work for the audience. The film then shifts in the walking scene to include an Arabic transcription – in addition to the English translation – of the sounds heard. If one examines the transcription from spoken to written Arabic, one attains a closer and more detailed examination of the original context of the sonic material of the street sounds heard in the film.

My work deals, therefore, with 'translatability'. According to Benjamin, translatability is a sign of significance in a literary work:

> Translatability is an essential quality of certain works, which is not to say that it is essential that they be translated; it means rather that a specific significance inherent in the original manifests itself in its translatability.[54]

Through the decisions I took about what to translate and what not to translate, the importance of the film's sonic subject matter is highlighted: English translation is employed as a signifier – as a visual sign of sonic borders – and to expose the Arabic content of the sonic material.

This works in line with Jane Rendell's use of psychoanalyst Jean Laplanche's concept of the 'enigmatic signifier' as that which is 'a signifier *to someone* rather than a signifier *of something*'.[55] Rendell uses Laplanche's understanding of psychic translation '"as the passage from a message to its understanding," an act that is not necessarily only interlingual, operating between languages, but intersemiotic, working between sign systems'.[56] Rendell discusses the role of translation performed through speech in her cross-cultural encounters with 'others', 'where experiences of foreign-ness or alien-ness produced aleatory trajectories'.[57] Alien-ness is manifested in translation performed through speaking a foreign language, as well as through the foreign existence of a person in a different culture/land, or outside his/her cultural context. Rendell shows that the foreignness of languages and places allows for the occurrence of human encounters and spatial experiences of a contradictory nature and for the production of aleatory trajectories produced through misunderstandings – one misunderstanding that leads to a dead end but the discovery of a new place nonetheless, and another that leads to the transgressive crossing of a border.

In *Look, Someone is Filming*, the issue of readership and language competency across Arabic and English-speaking audiences – in terms of location and linguistic ability – is important. The decision of what to translate and for whom aligns with Rendell's concepts of alien-ness and aleatory trajectories created through the different readings and experiences offered by translation and the foreignness experienced at the border between languages. The experience and communication lived through the work are not parallel or fixed among the whole audience. But this is to remind us that language is only one of many elements that influence the extent to which an artwork communicates with its audience: the cultural and educational background of each member of the audience, and how familiar he/she is with the artistic language and references that the work employs, also need to be considered.

Christopher Johnson, in a discussion of dubbing and subtitles in relation to language and difference, has highlighted the creative potential of subtitles not to explain but to produce parallel meanings (in an argument similar to that of Benjamin in 'The Task of the Translator'). It is this existence of the English and Arabic text, seen as words on the same screen and accompanying audible Arabic voices, that allows for the creation of a space of difference across languages to be put into play. In this way, the process of translating can be understood as a practice that borders cultural difference and takes place across the immateriality of sound and the materiality of image. One set of linguistic sonic borders is translated into another set of spatial borders which can be listened to, and which can be seen, read, and experienced in different ways.

Language is not only temporal; it is also spatial: 'The deferral of meaning, the undecidability of language, seems to come not from its temporal development or deployment but from its spatial constitution.'[58] It is important, therefore, to consider how different audiences from different political affiliations and cultural backgrounds might experience and read the sonic borders translated/transcribed. Thus, the work proposes that language can change in meaning even between speakers of the same language.

The temporal and spatial aspects of sound recordings, in comparison to those of images, could be explained in the transitory nature of sound with respect to the permanency of image:

> Sound recording allows for the temporal dislocation of a sound from its time and place of origin, but does not facilitate the ability to do the auditory equivalent of sustaining the gaze on an image for as long or as short as one desires.[59]

The film employs the difference in the experience of sound recording and image. Through transcribing and translating sounds that are dislocated from their context, the reading of a written text while listening to the sound itself operates along the lines of the interrelation that 'Hearing proposes; sight disposes.'[60] Here, the sound heard – its meaning and the way it might be experienced – can be negotiated by reading (and seeing) its translation and transcription on the screen. The process of translating sound into images allows for the acts of hearing and seeing the same subject matter to operate simultaneously yet distinctively, as neither process replaces the other, but rather each supplements the other, especially as a new spatial/temporal experience in the gallery space that provides a context which differs from the original. Thus, transcription and translation act together to move sonic borders into a different relation to one another in the gallery space, where the loss of the visual references associated with the original context is compensated by written annotations that describe the sound and its source (where it comes from, such as the space, the device, or the person).

Sterne notes the different types of historical experience lived through sonic recordings:

> History is nothing but exteriorities. We make our past out of the artifacts, documents, memories, and other traces left behind. We can listen to recorded traces of past history, but we cannot presume to know exactly what it was like to hear at a particular time or place in the past. In the age of technological reproduction, we can sometimes experience an audible past, but we can do no more than presume the existence of an auditory past.[61]

In *Look, Someone is Filming*, removal of the visual references relating to the original context from which the recorded sound was taken is a bordering practice that collapses the geographic distance and timespan between spaces, events and people's voices. This bordering practice of collapsing time and space, and the loss of one set of spatial references and their replacement by another, is a critical spatial practice offering a new spatial construction that changes the relation of past and present, since all the actors' voices are brought into the present time. Historical and relatively old (or at least older) political events and news broadcast by media outlets, such as stories of Lebanon sending students back home for security reasons, and discussions of political figures who were involved in the civil war, and are still in power, mix with current issues and with people's conversations on the streets. The content of this news is similar to that aired during the civil war; therefore, the interpretation of the sonic material – recorded, listened to and read – during the walking journey establishes a set of relations between time and space, and between past and present. These relations are sequential – whereby one sonic event occurs after the other – and simultaneous – whereby the past (of the civil war) is brought into the current time. The result is that past and present are allowed to coincide and to differ.

In the first exercise, H.H. tells his story directly in his taxi, a space where I (the researcher) listened, and where the story of this research project and methodology begins. In the second exercise, the process of overhearing, experienced in three other taxis and during a walking journey, occurs across spaces that

Fig.64
This is How Stories of Conflict Circulate and Resonate gallery installation
at Cities Methodologies exhibition, UCL, London, 2011.

border and cross one another. The act of transferring a sound from one space to another is an act that creates not only a potential invasion but also a possible connection. Through narration, the divisions that exist between physical spaces can be transgressed and, sometimes, connected.

Presence and Absence and *Look, Someone is Filming* are examples of critical bordering practice. In both, listening, hearing and overhearing are variously focused, layered and diffused. The interactions of these auditory practices create personal borders that interpret the meaning of the sounds in relation to the political position of the recipients. The sonic practices I mentioned at the start of this chapter – the overhearing of news, the songs people play and listen to, the media stations they tune in to, the content of their conversations, and the stories they tell – alter people's spatial experience and perception of city spaces. The interrelated processes that occur between the immateriality of sonic borders and 'material' reality might be understood in terms of the socio-spatial dialectic posited by Soja. While sonic borders, as this chapter has shown, translate into the materiality of everyday space through their impact on other types of practices/spaces, they nevertheless maintain the integrity of their immaterial nature by being ephemeral.

It is perhaps a personal process when sonic recipients or passers-by – those who listen acutely, or those who overhear indirectly – construct their own invisible borders, controlling and censoring their mobility and spatial practices, by, for example, avoiding certain parts of the city in their daily journeys. Such personal borders, although they cannot be seen, overlap with and add to the physical divisions existing in the city – and the personal borders may even overcome the physical divisions through the processes of negotiating and narrating.

The 'overhearing' of the informal media that is created through the transmission of sonic material from someone else's space surpasses the limits and borders of the geography of formal media. Instead, the overhearing bridges spaces that are porous in quality and politicized by the nature of the sonic material infiltrating them.

Bordering
Practice 04

MATCHING

DISPLACEMENT

The Twin Sisters are 'About to' Swap Houses

Fig.65
Map of the geographic location of R.G. and L.G. houses.

Could you draw the route map to your twin's house?

Twin sisters whom I have known since childhood decided
to swap their houses, respectively in Tarik al-Jdide and the
adjacent Mazraa areas separated by the Mazraa Main Road.
They were married to men of different political allegiances,
and their husbands were living in the wrong areas. The sisters
thought that by swapping houses they could ensure that the
geography of their residence would be in line with the political
allegiances of their husbands. At least, this was their intention
in the wake of the armed clashes of May 2008 between
Hezbollah and the Mustaqbal movement in Beirut and the
street harassment their husbands experienced. However, due
to more recent changes in the political situation in Lebanon at
the time when I worked with them between 2010 and 2012,
this swapping had not yet taken place. I was nevertheless
intrigued by the idea that one might alleviate political tension
by swapping residence, and so provide a safer home and
protection for one's family. The proximity of the houses the
sisters wished to swap, and their state of being 'about to'
swap, are parameters integral to the definition of new forms of
displacement in Lebanon. I wanted to investigate and to image
(as well as imagine) the field where this displacement would
take place, and to perform the process that would be involved in
the swap. So I asked each sister to draw a map of the route from
her residence to her sister's, and to track this route on the city
skyline with a video camera.

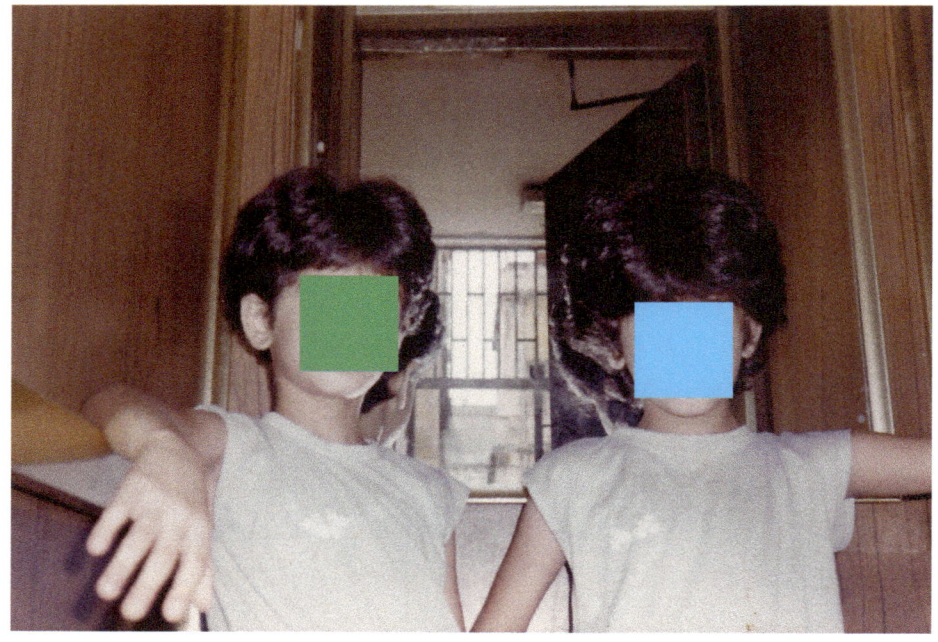

Fig.66 (Above)
Photograph I taken in the lift of the twin's
childhood house, summer 1986, Beirut.

L. was born on
October 12 1978,
at 09:10 am
ل. ولدت في ١٢
تشرين أول ١٩٧٨
عند ٩:١٠ صباحاً

R. was born on
October 12 1978,
at 09:12 am
ر. ولدت في ١٢
تشرين أول ١٩٧٨
عند ٩:١٢ صباحاً

Fig.67 (Overleaf)
Photographic survey of the floor and ceiling
plan of R.G and L.G. houses.

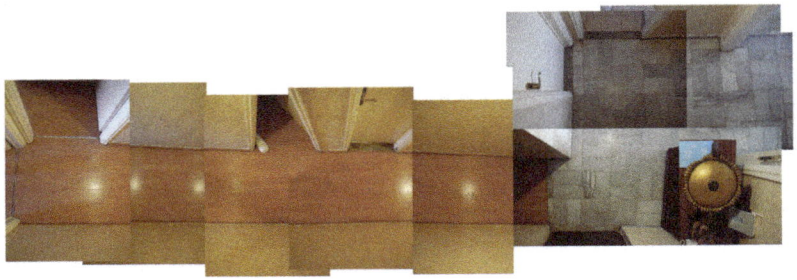

L. House in Tarik Al-Jdide: Corridor

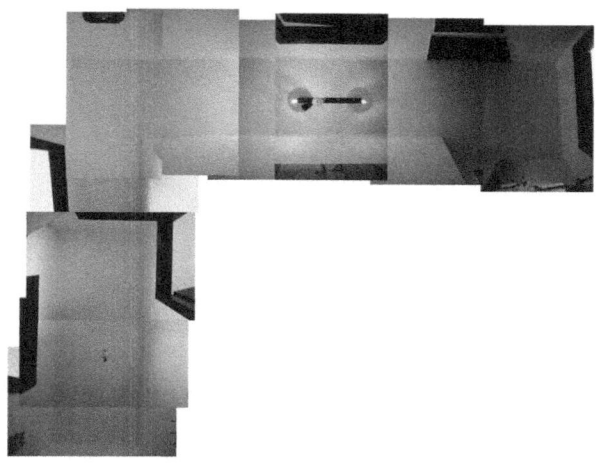

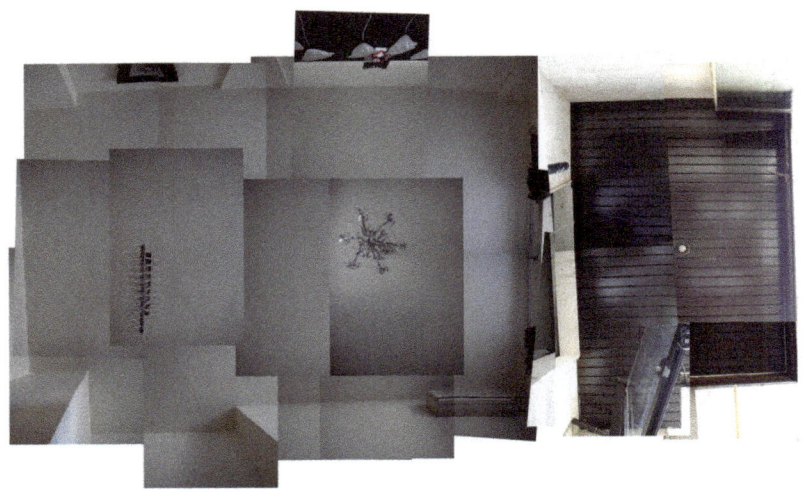

■ L. House in Tarik Al-Jdide: Living Room

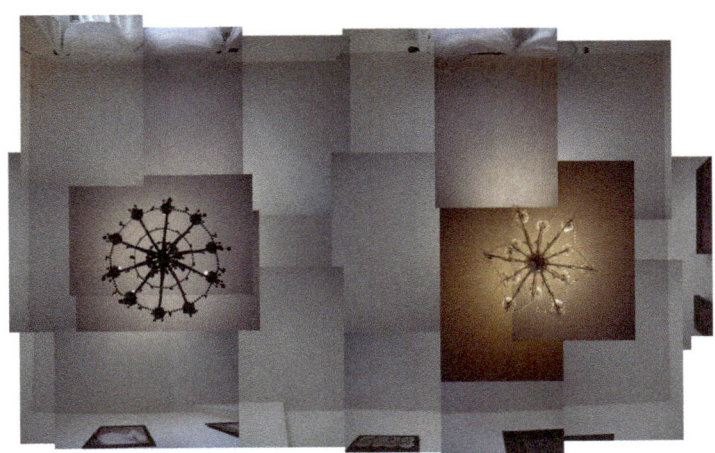

■ R. House in Mazraa: Living Room

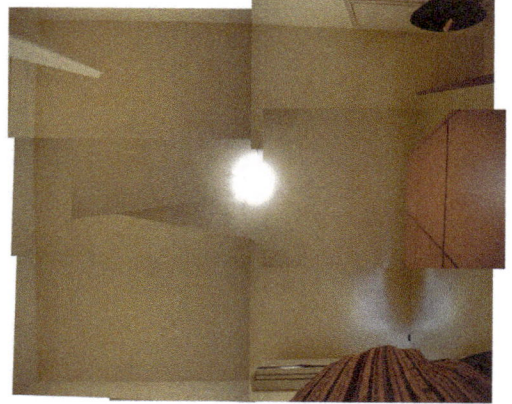

L. House in Tarik Al-Jdide: Master Bedroom

R. House in Mazraa: Master Bedroom

■ L. House in Tarik Al-Jdide: Children's Bedroom

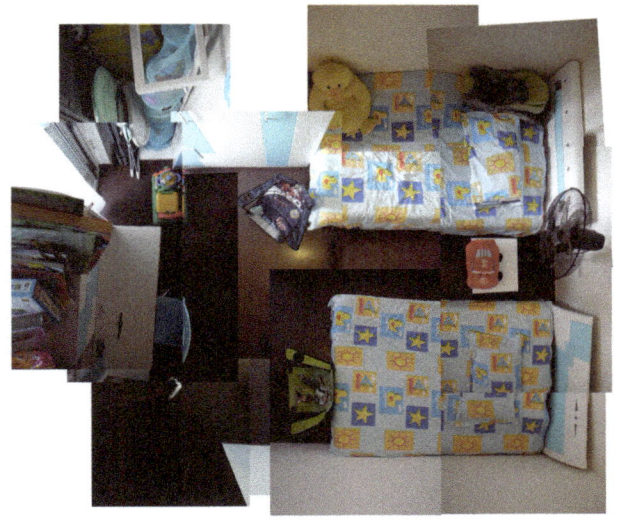

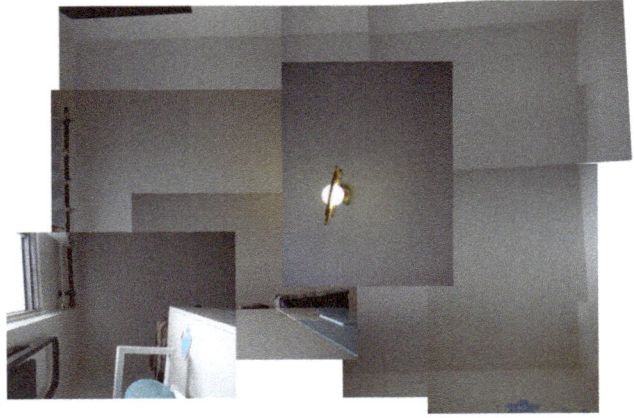

R. House in Mazraa: Children's Bedroom

■ L. House in Tarik Al-Jdide: Overview

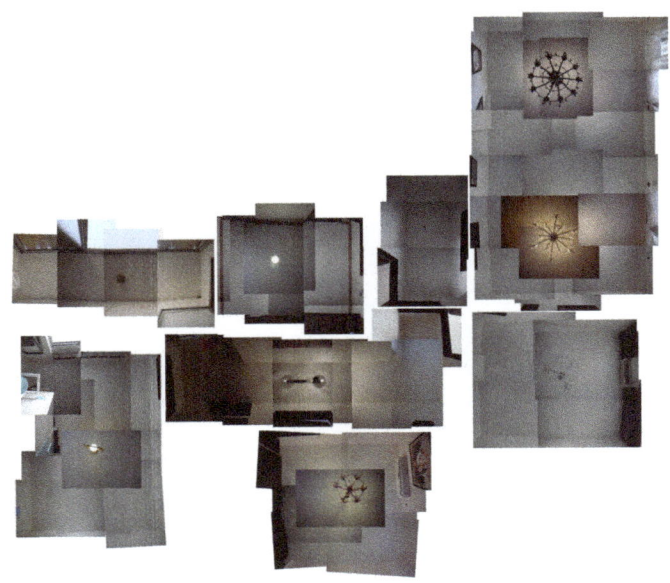

R. House in Mazraa: Overview

INTRODUCTION

The Twin Sisters are 'About to' Swap Houses introduces *swapping* as a voluntary and non-violent act of (self-)displacement. It is a bordering practice that takes place across geographies divided along sectarian and political lines, is specific to this particular moment of time in Beirut, and is a variant of the forced violent displacement by armed conflict that marked Lebanon's earlier civil war. The research project with the twins echoes the current subtle and invisible movements of residents and the demographic change currently occurring in the city and its peripheries, which has prompted residents to prefer living either in areas of a homogeneous sectarian nature in order to avoid the possible clashes that might arise from mixing, or in totally heterogeneous mixed areas where no political party dominates. These movements are not publicly announced and they happen through normal real estate market exchange in the country. This chapter looks at how these types of movements are self-displacements that operate as a social and spatial arrangement; it examines how people organize themselves in relation to their belongings, homes and lives. I use the term 'arrangement' when talking about displacement to imply an element of agency on the part of residents who perform such a move, and who, in their desire to decrease tension, normalize displacement so that it becomes – through 'arrangement' – an everyday practice.

In this chapter, mobility is considered in relation to bordering practices – a negotiation process between crossing borders and making borders. It concerns the movements not only of people and of objects but also of ideas and considerations about the future on the part of residents – considerations which include the movement of their bodies in that future.[1] Tim Cresswell has written:

> the act[s] of moving, whether at a micro scale or across continents, are tied into sets of meanings that go on to play a role in the production of future mobilities. Moving, meaning and bodily practice are entwined in ways that travel through history.[2]

Displacement, immigration, emigration and the movement of refugees are all spatial practices involving mobility and the relocation of people from one place to another within or across nation-state borders. These different movements include the self and the urban space as locations, and individuals and groups as operators. 'Some movements are forced; others are a product of socioeconomic position and the privilege of a passport',[3] writes Julie Peteet of the various politics of movements in the age of capitalism and globalization. According to Peteet, each of these movement practices has its own social, political, legal and theoretical specificity that should not be confused with the others, especially when we talk about the forced displacement of people by conflict and war. Describing the shift from and in place caused by displacement as the shift and split between location and identity, Peteet notes how displaced people struggle to maintain their former ties in a new place:

Refugees and migrants put into relief both the fragility and the strength of ties between people and territory, and also how these complex links can encompass and travel through multiple time-space zones. In other words, identity is spatialized and place remains critical, but in ways that can incorporate high levels of mobility, attachments to points of departure, and multiple meanings of place ... If culture was becoming unhinged from place and territory, nowhere should this be more apparent than among the displaced.[4]

Rosi Braidotti has differentiated between the nomadic subject as a figuration who relinquishes fixity and for whom 'identity [is] made of transitions',[5] and exiles and migrants who are motivated by 'the politics of location' and economic structures. She maintains that these political movements should not be 'met-aphorized into a new ideal' or figure such as the nomad.[6] Noting the privileged position of the polyglot nomadic intellectual, Braidotti argues for the displaced person's choice of the nomad 'as a form of political resistance to hegemonic and exclusionary views of subjectivity'.[7] In this respect, displacement is not always negative; indeed, it may often be understood as a positive choice. Certainly, this is what the cultural critic Homi Bhabha sees in the condition of migrants who, he suggests, offer a hybrid space, constructed at the meeting between departure (the place of origin) and arrival (the place of destination).[8]

In Lebanon's civil war (1975–90), displacement was mainly a forced violent act practised by armed militias.[9] It took place predominantly across the religious lines that had already divided the country into two separate geographies, and it forced Muslims and Christians to move in accordance with these lines of division. However, the demographic rearrangement of the two sides, each comprising a homogeneous religious population, is in actuality made up of more complex clusters of sectarian, political and class entities, where the mode of mixing and interaction varies (and is based not only on sectarian affiliation). The civil war displacement has created different spatial and social arrangements of the communities amounting to what is called 'Lebanese coexistence'. In this respect, coexistence manifests itself both in the spatial movement of different sectarian groups from one area (or side) to another in the country, and in the groups' social and political interactions within the borders of the country. In addition, those displaced by war in Lebanon have always been associated with the status of *muhajar* ('war-displaced'), a term which denotes a person of 'lesser value', sometimes a lesser citizen, or even, as the anthropologist Aseel Sawalha notes, a *muhtal* ('an occupier'). Long-term residents – of Beirut, for example – use this discourse to describe the war-displaced as outsiders and usurpers on account of their having 'illegally' occupied properties.[10]

With the memory of forced displacement, and a country geographically segregated during the civil war, the twin sisters wished to swap houses in order to align their husbands' political allegiances with the politics of their domestic locations. In their swapping plan, they sought to avoid violent acts of disruption or being forced into a sudden move by war or armed conflict. One sister's husband was a member of the Shiite Amal movement, but the couple lived in Tarik al-Jdide, an area under the political power of the Sunni Mustaqbal movement (the political rival to Amal and Hezbollah). The other sister's husband worked for Mustaqbal, while the couple lived in Mazraa (Burj Abi Haidar), an area under the political power of Amal and Hezbollah. The sisters' projected move across the two areas – in contrast to the movements of other more obvious, forced displacements – was a silent, invisible movement. Through their decision to swap, the sisters have opted not to assume the status of the 'war-displaced'.

This chapter provides, therefore, an example of the strategies practised by political parties today to achieve division and social segregation across sectarian lines by creating the conditions from which displacement emerges as a response rather than as the 'forceful' movement of people by the military. It is based on a research project and its associated gallery installation that look into and construct the sites of potential displacement as an extended spatial and social arrangement, spanning from the interior spaces inhabited by the twins to the urban context in which both houses are located. My research in this chapter is concerned with the proximity of the twins' dual acts of intended displacement, acts which are poised on the cusp of 'about to', the moment before something occurs – in this case, the act of swapping – and which lend an elongated temporal state of 'on hold' to the practice of displacement.

Throughout the period of my research, I visited the twin sisters at their houses several times – in the winter of 2010, and in the summers of 2011 and 2012 – and each time I carried out photographic documentation and other research exercises, including drawing and video recording. These exercises related to a series of movements connected to the sisters' own lives, to their husbands on the streets, to the personal memorabilia scattered between them and their husbands inside their houses, and to the imagined movements that are yet to take place across the city during the anticipated swapping. I present this visual material here and I position the different movements of the two couples against the background of demographic change and displacement that have taken place in the history of modern Lebanon. The series of movements tracked in this chapter are specific to the sisters, but they also relate more generally to Lebanon's present and past. In the process, I embed the present (swapping) in the past (armed displacement), and I seek to understand the social and spatial geography of political division and how this has caused other modes of displacement within Lebanon following marriage laws and the narrative of 'Lebanese coexistence'.

I propose and discuss how displacement has the intention of *matching*: of moving in order to make the same. This is the bordering practice I project in the installation, one which suggests the creation of spatial moments and movements of twinning and matching urban spaces across visual horizons and through lines drawn on maps, captured at a moment of time which is 'about to' swap. My practice in this chapter is a critical bordering practice that aims to visualize and construct what the sisters wished to avoid in their chosen type of silent and invisible displacement, to perform their intended displacements, and to examine the spatial and visual potentials of such displacements.

After a general overview of displacement and the different socioeconomic and political factors related to spatial practices around movement and mobility, the rest of the chapter is structured according to seven titles that consider different forms of displacement. Under the first title, 'Displacement as Swapping', I define swapping as a form of displacement particular to the twins' narrative; then, in 'The Mobility of Displacement', I discuss how the mobility of the sisters' swapping differs in both its invisibility and its voluntary choice from the visibility and involuntary nature of forced displacement. I go on to show, in 'The Space of Displacement and the Time of "About to"', the temporal and spatial parameters integral to the bordering practice of swapping. I link displacement as a movement in urban space to social and religious movements in Lebanon in 'Displacement in Marriage'. Then, in 'Displacement as Lebanese Coexistence', I situate the sisters' displacement choice as a reaction to Lebanon's history of displacements and wars, and I consider the different spatial arrangements and social geography manifested by these displacements as part of the country's political narrative of coexistence. I present the physical and imagined movements of the sisters and their husbands as I documented them in 'Displacement as Imagined Experience and as Daily Movement', and, through presentation of the gallery installation in 'Displacement as Matching', I propose the bordering practice of *matching*.

DISPLACEMENT AS SWAPPING

To 'displace' is to 'remove or shift [something] from its place; to put out of the proper or usual place'; to 'oust (something) from its place and occupy it instead'.[11] It is important to consider the places from and to which something or someone is displaced, for displacement causes changes on both sides – at the point of departure (or place of origin) as well as at the destination. In displacement, specifically when caused by war, a place is most often emptied of a particular group of people to be filled by another group; in this regard, a 'balance' between the three places of displacement – the site from which one group is removed, the site to which the group is removed, and the site from which the replacement group comes – is not necessarily achieved. Such displacement creates, therefore, a change and 'imbalance' in the three places involved. The imbalance relates to Peteet's observation that displacement causes a split between place and identity.

A swap is 'an act, or the action, of "swapping" or exchanging; (an) exchange'.[12] Swapping entails an exchange between two entities. Usually, two subjects exchange objects, but here I suggest that two subjects exchange places rather than objects, with the result that one comes to occupy the space of the other. This space is not merely geographical; it has also been intentionally chosen to 'match' the political position of that space.

Hostages are often swapped for money, and soldiers are swapped between fighting groups or countries. Swapping usually takes place as part of the negotiation process between two contested groups to solve a conflict or reach a political agreement. The rules of the exchange are based on the power relationship and the type of contract or agreement between the two groups involved. For example, in 2011, a total of 1,027 Palestinian prisoners were swapped for one Israeli soldier,[13] an illustration of how the 'value system' in the 'exchange' process is not based simply on equality or balance of numbers.

In relation to displacement, the sisters' intention to swap is an act with agency: it is a chosen re-arranging to achieve order and 'balance', and it is an alternative to the chaos and imbalance of forced displacement. The sisters aim to make two distinct spaces, with each filling the space of the other through the exchange process they propose. This type of swapping creates a sectarian and political homogeneity of the population in each of the two respective urban areas involved. Their swapping is a form of control that they decide to perform on their own lives as a response to the political situation forced upon them by the country; it is an act of swapping which aims to solve a problem and to prevent an anticipated clash that could occur as a result of their husbands mixing with people from opposing political backgrounds in the area. The sisters could be said to be seeking to achieve normality in an abnormal everyday life. The need to match politics with geography within Lebanon is a response to the specificity of conditions in present-day Beirut; this matching is a border crossing of the social geography at times of conflict.

The social structure of families – and, in this narrative, specifically of sibling relations – enables the swapping process to take place. The psychoanalyst Juliet Mitchell explains that the relationship of sisters in a family structure is horizontal, in comparison to the vertical and hierarchical relationship between parents and children.[14] The swapping of spaces takes place across that horizontal social structure, and it can be connected to the horizontal spatial structure that exists in urban space between the two houses and their areas. The sisters' decision to match geography with politics is also a spatial manifestation in urban space of their biological and familial twinning.

THE MOBILITY OF DISPLACEMENT

The mobility of the twin sisters' intended acts of swapping is invisible and by choice, unlike that of other acts of displacement – for example, as experienced by refugees. In this respect, it is worth noting the dichotomy integral to mobility in general and to border control, for on the one side there is the privilege of passport and socioeconomic position, and on the other there is the 'choice' forced on the displaced and those who are not citizens. Refugees are marked by their bodily mobility and their legal status in relation to the state: through these nexuses they are visible, controlled and differentiated as 'others'. Alison Mountz has commented that 'refugees are always othered legally ... They are sighted, marked, coded, and forced to move in ways that become encoded in law.'[15] Legalized movement may give certain rights to the displaced to move and work, depending on the regulations of the host country, yet this legal status is a form of control over the social and political status of the displaced individual as a 'non-citizen' or a 'lesser citizen' in relation to the state and to other citizens. Furthermore, and in relation to the mobility of subjects and border control, Mountz shows how the regulation of nation-state borders has migrated 'into the discourse of daily life where the identity of the alien subject is constructed'.[16] She describes how the control of borders transcends the monitoring of a country's material or formal border by spreading narratives that mobilize in general against those, such as migrants and refugees, who are on the move outside the border:

> The meaning of border shifts spatially and conceptually and is called upon to perform many tasks. One function is to link the regulation of mobility to identity and territory: to link who one is to location, and in so doing policing national borders around identities.[17]

Mobility is also a form of spatial practice, as Tim Cresswell and Peter Merriman have argued:

> Mobility is practised, and practice is often conflated with mobility. To move is to do something. Moving involves making a choice within, despite the constraints of society and geography. It is no surprise, therefore, that in Michel de Certeau's oft-cited classic *The Practice of Everyday Life* ... he focuses on the act of walking in the city in order to elucidate the tactical practices of the weak.[18]

Hence, although the mobility of the displaced is a forced movement, this movement alters a certain political condition that existed at the place of origin (departure) and could be dangerous. Thus, movement involves a change both of location and of personal conditions.

THE SPACE OF DISPLACEMENT AND THE TIME OF 'ABOUT TO'

The key spatial and temporal parameters of the swapping displacement are the proximity of the sisters' displacement across the two adjacent areas, and the time of this intended displacement – the time of 'about to' swap, this time being 'on hold' as the sisters wait to displace themselves. Both the spatial proximity, and the time of waiting for displacement, can be related to mobility, a key term in studies about borders and bordering practices.[19] According to Jørgen Ole Bær-enholdt, mobility is 'associated with flow and freedom, as opposed to territorial fixity by bonds and borders'.[20] This flow occurs as a response to communication and travel technology in the age of globalization, where openness and the per-meability of borders contrast with situations of extreme securitization used to control mobility,[21] and where the apprehension of proximity is complicated and defined as 'a lived relation of nearness and farness'.[22] With mobility and the flow of information across the globe, proximity and distances are negotiated: the far is brought closer whereas the near may become distant. While some scholars are concerned with discussing proximity at a large distance – for example, in relation to the crossing of nation-states' borders and to technological progress – the sociologist David Bissell has concentrated on the study of power and politics in small-scale mobilities. Bissell argues that 'the neighbourhood and the neighbour are distinct in that they put the concept of proximity to centre-stage', and that the neighbourhood proposes the social bonds and interaction of neighbours and their corporal movements.[23]

In the case of the two areas under discussion here, the small-scale mobilities intersect with politics on both a local and a global scale, thereby providing an example of how the politics of mobility operate. According to Bærenholdt, 'mo-bility may be governed … [but] it is first and foremost … a political technology' used to govern societies, an act that he calls 'governmobility', or 'ruling through connections'.[24] Governmobility combines mobility with Foucault's concept of governmentality, which is the 'self-government of a population' through which citizens 'have been institutionalised with certain understanding and routines … to exercise various forms of governing practices on various occasions'.[25] Foucault shows how territory is used to govern society and how, in modernity, governing happens when the population internalizes systems of power.[26] The 'self-displacing' that the twin sisters perform can be thought of as the self-gov-erning of mobility. In their case, the self-governing of their mobility implies the self-governing of their territory, the limiting of their movement within specific geographic borders, and, accordingly, the limiting of the movement of their future plans and even their imagination of that future.

Mobility and borders also have temporality. Moments of stillness and 'stuckness' – which should not be taken as boundedness or rootedness – are part of mobility practices. According to Tim Cresswell: 'One place where kinds of stillness [wait-ing, for example] happen, for some more than others, is at borders.'[27] However, when the border is not merely a physical entity or space but is practised and dispersed as part of the everyday, stillness – or what I call here the time of 'about to' – it becomes an elongated state that is 'thoroughly incorporated into practices of moving'.[28] Such displacement becomes, therefore, an everyday practice that operates on different scales (as I show below in the discussion of 'Daily Movement').

Thus, the spatial, physical proximity between the two areas of the twin sisters' respective residences, and the temporal state of 'about to', effect the swap and offer a new way of understanding civil conflict and the production of geopolitical and social borders within the border of one country. In this paradigm, the kind of displacement that occurs across this close proximity is mobilized (or indirectly suggested) by political parties – those who have the power to undertake potential violent clashes – and it is applied by residents – those who wish to undertake movement, even displacement, as a precautionary move practised as an everyday activity in that continuous time of 'about to' move or divide.

DISPLACEMENT IN MARRIAGE

When considering displacement and sectarian segregation at a social and urban level in a country like Lebanon, we cannot escape discussing marriage as a social contract that facilitates the mixing/movement of a couple from different backgrounds within the borders of the same home. The home is a place of intersection between an external conflict occurring in an urban place and an internal site where conflict may be transformed, persist, or play out differently.

Claude Lévi-Strauss described marriage as the exchange of women between men, whether daughter (from father to husband) or sister (from brother to husband). Marriage exists in order:

> to ensure the permanency of the social group by means of intertwining consanguineous and affinal ties. They may be considered as the blueprint of a mechanism which 'pumps' women out of their consanguineous families to redistribute them in affinal groups.[29]

In the case of Lebanon, marriages may occur to establish alliances between different social, political or sectarian groups.

The twin sisters' marriages are not ones that occurred across religion (Christian–Muslim), nor across sects (Sunni–Shiite). Both sisters are Sunni and both are married to Sunni men; however, the political allegiance of one of their husbands is to the Amal and Hezbollah Shiite parties, while the political affiliation of both sisters and the other husband is to the Sunni Mustaqbal movement. This situation might appear complex, but it is a good example of how politics, and not only sectarian or religious affiliation, plays a role in the social and political geography of Lebanon.

The husband who resides in Tarik al-Jdide and works for Amal and Hezbollah is from the Kurdish (Sunni) community. The Lebanese Kurds are a minority group who fled to Lebanon in 1924 from Turkey; at that time, some of them were given Lebanese nationality, but their citizenship, identity, social status and integration in the country are subject to ongoing struggle.[30] Lebanese Kurds are not officially represented in parliamentary and state institutions, but their electoral votes count and thus they play a role in political life and alliances. Currently their political loyalty is divided in line with the division in the country; perhaps in pursuit of the status such an alliance might bring them, one of their factions supports Hezbollah while the other supports Mustaqbal, among other parties.

The other husband, who resides in Mazraa (Burj Abi Haidar), works for the Mustaqbal security. Thus, the relation of both men to their respective political parties is not only an affiliation based on religion or politics; it is also an economic relation based on employment. Because of their employment, any political turmoil or street clashes involving their parties also involves and affects them, threatening the security of the areas where they live and creating tension inside their houses.

The twin sisters' marriages cut across the sectarian and political divisions. In contrast to Lévi-Strauss's definition of marriage as the exchange of women between men, the twin sisters' role as wives involves the wish to exchange houses and to undertake this act of exchange as women in order to engender a different situation for their husbands. Rather than the wife being contained within the home as a passive object, exchanged by a man, here the wife has spatial agency, and wishes – by swapping her home – to potentially transform the life of her husband.

Cross-marriage (or mixed-faith marriage; *zawaj al-mukhtalat*) in Lebanon mainly refers to marriage across religions, between Christians and Muslims, but it is also used to refer to marriage across sects within the same religion, such as those between Sunni and Shiite. Cross-marriages between Christians and Muslims have always been the most problematic marriages in the country, and such couples are often considered controversial. Given that civil marriage does not exist in Lebanon, and that the marriage has to be performed following religious rules, one of the partners has to follow the other's religious procedures, which represents a form of displacement from one's own community. In general, both Islam and Christianity allow a man to marry a woman from a different religion without the need for the woman to convert, while neither religion permits the marriage of a woman to a man from outside her religion.[31] There are, therefore, two forms of displacement if the marriage is to follow religious rules: one of rejecting, the other of following.

As an alternative to religious marriage procedures, many mixed-faith couples have opted to travel outside the country – for example, to Cyprus – to undertake a civil marriage, which they later register in Lebanon.[32] In this case both a man and a woman displace themselves into a third place, dropping the religious rules they have previously followed and which their families still follow. Though the marriage can be registered, any children the couple have must follow their father's faith and the personal code (concerning inheritance, election, death, etc.) of his religion. Hence the current laws that follow religious rules in Lebanon force the woman, through her children, to follow her husband.

Despite various efforts by activists and lawyers who have called for civil marriage to be legalized, it is still not allowed under Lebanese law.[33] Civic organizations and activists see civil marriage as the entry point for a secular or non-sectarian state – and thus a solution to the deadlock the country has reached with its current constitution.[34] More recently, the issue of civil marriage has entered political manoeuvring through Saad Hariri, Mustaqbal's leader, who in his 2013 parliamentary electoral campaign announced his support for civil marriage and the civil state, and in so doing distinguished his position from that of other Sunni religious leaders. A political reading of this situation suggests that his intention is to meet his Christian allies in the country on a 'moderate' Sunni basis as opposed to that of the more religious Shiite (Hezbollah) in Lebanon and the rising Muslim Sunni extremists in other parts of the Arab world.[35]

In the context of the social division that Lebanon has reached during the current period of unrest, the journalist and writer Bilal Khbeiz has commented that what has been deconstructed cannot be rebuilt, either by cross-marriage or by free commerce – with the implication that cross-marriage has been regarded as a sign of assimilation across religious borders in the wake of the civil war.[36] An advertisement by the Chamber of Commerce, Industry and Agriculture promoting civil peace and encouraging people to 'support the economy, against civil war' states that 750,000 Lebanese, out of a total population of approximately 4 million, are the offspring of cross-marriages: 350,000 from Christian–Muslim marriages, and 400,000 from Sunni–Shiite. Writing about this advert, Sahar Mandour comments that the language of the advert to mobilize against a 'sectarian war' uses 'sectarian identity' to identify citizens (offspring of cross-marriage) and classifies the population into blocs – a Sunni–Shiite bloc and a Christian–Muslim bloc, as well as those who are not from cross-marriage.[37] However, the advert presents a picture of the complexity of the social and religious structure of families; and it clearly shows the shift in the public representation of the Lebanese political-sectarian conflict, from the border between Christian and Muslim that marked the civil war, to the border between Sunni and Shiite that marks the current period of unrest. Cross-marriage, whether Christian–Muslim or Sunni–Shiite, is a form of border crossing, as it involves the exchange of both women and men across religious and sectarian divides.

DISPLACEMENT AS LEBANESE COEXISTENCE

Lebanon is a culture that has seen many forms of displacement. It is worth considering the sisters' decision of swapping in relation to their memory and experience of the displacement that took place during the Lebanese civil war period when they were children. The definition of Lebanese 'coexistence', according to the country's official political system and narrative, is the existence of different sects in one country under a democratic 'confessional power-sharing formula'.[89] Farid El-Khazen, a politics scholar and a Lebanese member of parliament, defines three patterns for the concept of coexistence. The first is an imposed state of coexistence, whereby communities mix together unwillingly and their interaction is based on inequality. The second is based on the desire of people to interact on an equal footing. And the third is a spontaneous coexistence that 'doesn't imply any political or other controversy since it has become a natural state of living'. He notes that Lebanon was closer to the second pattern before the civil war and moved to the first during the war.[39] For El-Khazen, coexistence concerns the politics that govern the type of interactions which take place between different communities. However, coexistence has also taken different spatial arrangements at each new period of the country's history of conflict, forming the social geography where residents' movements, forced or suggested, have adopted a socio-spatial practice of matching, crossing and swapping geographic and political borders to achieve either a homogeneous or heterogeneous arrangement.

The country has experienced the displacement of various communities within and across its borders as a result of wars, including the civil conflict and wars between Lebanon and other countries. It is worth here briefly summarizing people's movements in such displacements along four main intersecting trajectories that have shaped the country's social and political geography: the Palestinian diaspora (1948); the civil war (1975–90); the reconstruction period that followed the civil war (1990–present); and the Israeli occupation of the south (1978–2000) and their series of wars and invasions of Lebanon (1978, 1982, 1996, 2006).[40]

PALESTINIAN DIASPORA

In 1948, five years after the independence of Lebanon, the country witnessed the influx of Palestinian refugees expelled from their homeland in what was called *Al-nakbah* (the disaster) at the outbreak of the Arab-Israeli war and the subsequent Arab defeat, following the British Balfour Declaration that led to the United Nations partitioning Palestine in 1947 and the emergence of the state of Israel.[41] Palestinians resided in refugee camps across the country. Those able to integrate into Lebanese communities settled in towns and cities;[42] however, those who did not have the financial means settled in camps. Today, there are 12 Palestinian refugee camps in Lebanon, and around 444,500 registered refugees,[43] of whom approximately 220,000 reside in camps.[44]

CIVIL WAR

The Lebanese civil war, which began in 1975 and lasted until 1990, created major internal displacement and demographic changes, with around 28 per cent of the population (an estimated 800,000) being temporarily or permanently forced to flee. This led to the violent imposition of religious affiliation throughout much of the country and to the division of Beirut into Christian and Muslim sectors.[45] In Beirut, Muslim and Christian zones were divided by a militarized ten-mile-long 'green line'.[46] In creating this divided city, the destruction and emptying of Beirut's central district, which was a shared commercial, financial and social area, produced a situation engendering an 'impossibility for it to be a meeting place between people'.[47] Christians and Muslims, including the Sunni Palestinians, moved across that line of religious and political division from both sides of the city. In addition, Druze and Christians from the Chouf district were displaced to villages and cities, including Beirut, following the line of division of the country's geography.[48] The civil war displacement process was led by militias, who used brutal and organized 'cleansing' operations that forced the minorities who had stayed on each side to leave at a later stage.[49] Thus, the war intensified the ties and the need 'to match' religious and sectarian affiliation across geographical borders.

ISRAELI WARS AND OCCUPATION

The Israeli occupation of south Lebanon from 1978 to 2000 forced the Shiite community, who constitute the majority population of the south, as well as other sects and the Palestinians, to move to other villages in the south and to Beirut. It also forced some to squat in war-ravaged and abandoned buildings, creating informal settlements on the edges of the city and its centre during the civil war.[50] The consecutive Israeli wars and invasions of 1982, 1996 and 2006 caused further temporary and permanent displacements in the areas they targeted.[51]

RECONSTRUCTION PERIOD

During the post-war period, the reconstruction plan spearheaded by the state, which aimed to rebuild the destroyed city centre and return the displaced, mainly gave financial compensation to those displaced by the war.[52] This created another set of displacements and informal settlement in new places, by relocating the war-displaced to other areas in and around Beirut, rather than returning them to their homes and villages. The return of the displaced to their homes was not fully completed or even possible as an ambition, whether for economic reasons – since there was no work in their home villages – or because some villages were still occupied – as was the case in south Lebanon until 2000. Some feared mixing with people who had fought against them during the war, while for others the long period of civil war had produced a new generation of displaced people who had turned into urbanites.[53] Sawalha has commented on the consequences of the reconstruction plan:

> Rather than return to their villages, the war-displaced, evicted under the conditions of postwar reconstruction, have relocated to squatter suburbs on the city's periphery. In other words, the launching of a vast project for modern reconstruction has produced the very symptoms it was designed to eliminate: informality, illegality, visual blight, patched together services.[54]

My research focuses on the period following the assassination of the Sunni prime minister, Hariri, in 2005, which led to the withdrawal of the Syrian army from the country and the political division between the Sunni and Shiite communities. Since 2005, political and civil turmoil has been extensive, with political assassinations, sporadic bombings, an Israeli war in 2006, another war between the Lebanese army and Fatah al-Islam militants in the Nahr el-Bared Palestinian refugee camp in the north in 2007, sectarian armed clashes mainly in May 2008, and continuous tension in areas at the northern border with Syria that has intensified since the outbreak of the Syrian civil war in 2011. The Israeli war in 2006 mainly targeted the Shiite community in south Lebanon and the southern suburbs of Beirut, under the pretext that these were the areas where supporters of Hezbollah resided. The deliberate destruction of the suburbs (the military zone of Hezbollah) resulted in the displacement of around a million of the country's population.[55] The newcomers from the suburbs were mainly Shiites heading to various parts of Beirut, predominantly to mixed areas that include both Sunnis and Shiites, and even to Christian areas.

According to the Norwegian Refugee Council's report (2010) on displacement in Lebanon, there are 'no new displacements [in Lebanon] but causes of past conflicts [are] unresolved', with 17,000 people remaining displaced; however, there are 'no remaining IDPs [internally displaced people] from the 2006 [Israeli] conflict [and] no information was found on IDPs who might have sought settlement options other than return'.[56] The report thus indicates the possibility of those displaced in 2006 having found long-term residence in areas other than those from which they were displaced. This suggests that the social geography has been affected by the war even if there are no longer officially displaced people. In addition, the report mentions that the May 2008 clashes caused significant temporary displacement of around 6,000 Sunni families in north Lebanon.[57]

Nevertheless, the varied unrest since 2005, accompanied with new security measures and rising political tensions between Sunnis and Shiites, has established a new demographic movement and social geography of residents in Beirut that is less mobilized and visible than those displacements mentioned above.

As a result of instability and the fear of clashes, people prefer to live in areas that are either of a homogeneous sectarian nature, or which are totally mixed, creating anxiety among the Christian community in these areas. Frank Mermier describes how the fear of violence has defined the social geography and the movements of residents in Beirut since 2005:

> urban mobility and the distribution of real estate investments are also linked to various forms of psychosis engendered by fear or the actual outbreak of violence, to the perception of a communitarian 'us' and the fear of its desecration, all this in tandem with the vagaries of regional tensions and a more or less embryonic war with Israel.[58]

The post-war period has been marked by territorial conflict that has adopted real estate and the buying of land as its main territorial strategy to claim space. Hiba Bou Akar has researched two peripheral areas of Beirut, the Christian and Shiite area of Chiyah, and the Druze and Shiite area of Choueifat:

> during 'times of peace' conflict has continued, yet it has less to do with military maneuver and positioning than with the production of a spatial order of sectarian and political difference... through such mechanisms as land and housing markets, urban planning, and zoning regulations.[59]

The movement of residents and the buying and selling of land and properties between Sunni and Shiite in Beirut does not enter politicians' or media debates. However, in 2010 Boutros Harb, a government minister, proposed a law that summarized the degree of division among the sectarian communities and high-lighted the Christian anxiety in the country over the Islamic dominance in areas of Christian presence. The 'Harb' draft law prohibited the buying and selling of land between individuals not belonging to the same religion (namely, between Christians and Muslims) for a period of 15 years.[60] Harb explained that his pro-posed law was intended to protect 'coexistence' and to prevent segregation. He added that Lebanon was witnessing an organized buying-up of land on the part of individuals and companies from one sect by another. The Harb law was support-ed by several newspaper articles reflecting Christian fear of Islamic dominance through land-owning, and naming factors behind this: mainly the money coming from rich and mainly Sunni Arabs from the Gulf, and also the money of real estate developers and sectarian organizations linked to Hezbollah and Iran.[61] The Harb law was not the first to attempt to prevent the exchange of land ownership across religions: a similar law had been proposed by Raymond Edde at the beginning of the civil war in 1975, and another by Harb himself in 1984, while a 1984 fatwa (religious judgment) by the head of the Shiite council, Mohamad Mahdi Shams E'ddine, declared a prohibition (tu'harrim) on the selling of Muslims' land to non-Muslims. Shams E'ddine explained that the buying of land was not for commercial and economic reasons but rather for a political one: it aimed to destroy the principle of coexistence in Lebanon. Hence, to protect coexistence, so that no community could take over the place of the other and own more land, he proposed a ban on the sale or purchase of land across religions.[62] Both Shams' and Harb's propositions demonstrate the fragility of Lebanese coexistence: first, by exposing a narrative that presents Lebanon as a country of different sects living together; and second, by exposing the practice of coexistence as a struggle over land ownership among the different sectarian communities.

The displacements caused by the civil war aimed to produce homogeneous sectarian communities across two separate geographies (two Beiruts). The reconstruction period that followed resulted in class homogeneity rather than religious homogeneity, specifically in the destroyed centre of Beirut, re-launching the city as a commercial and economic centre based on the interests of capital (although we can read a sectarian affiliation with capital).[63] The reconstruction period also witnessed a tendency of people to live in areas of religious heterogeneity. The civil unrest since 2005 – which is still part of the post-war period and the consequences of the civil war – is causing new and further displacement of communities from the relatively mixed heterogeneous Beirut and its surroundings into homogeneous clusters living 'next to each other' rather than 'with each other', where one sect pushes the other outside the cluster. The displacements at different periods of the country's conflict form, therefore, different spatial arrangements of Lebanese coexistence.

HETEROGENEITY AND COEXISTENCE

Coexistence as a political narrative has been used heavily by Lebanese officials to celebrate the Lebanese sectarian mosaic, but the term 'coexistence' only serves to remind us that, if it means heterogeneity, then 'existence' means only homogeneity. This operates in a similar fashion to the difference between marriage and cross-marriage according to religious rules: to have the word 'cross' attached to marriage serves to remind us that marriage – without the 'cross' – is pure.

Heterogeneity – the mixing of sects within the same space – is always at stake in sectarian and ethnic conflicts. Martin Coward use the term 'urbicide' to describe the killing of buildings and possible heterogeneity in the case of Mostar in the Bosnian war:

> buildings, as that which constitute the world as a shared/public, spatial experience, are the condition of possibility of an essential heterogeneity. Urbicide refers to the killing (by destroying its conditions of

> possibility) of that which characterizes urbanity: heterogeneity. Since buildings constitute the spatiality of existence as fundamentally shared/public, ... destroying the buildings that make up the urban fabric is essentially a destruction of the conditions of possibility of heterogeneity.[64]

Heterogeneity offers the possibility of a politics that exists through difference, since, as Coward comments, 'politics is comprised of antagonistic relations of identity/difference'.[65] However, the term 'urbicide' concerns the direct destruction of buildings to achieve a homogeneity of urbanity, and thus a homogeneity of politics. This concept can be applied to the destruction of Beirut's central district (downtown) during the Lebanese civil war. The area was a shared space among different sects and classes; destroying it prevented the mixing of people in that space. Beirut's 'war' today can be thought of in this new language of destruction, for the city is subject to urbicide, albeit a slower and more silent one that does not include the attacking of buildings as such but the voiding or emptying of buildings by their own occupants through acts of self-displacement – practised decisions to avoid conflict, and taken as precautionary measures. The twin sisters' wish to swap is a very particular case, but it is part of a broader pattern that is taking place where new displacements aim to 'match' politics and geography and to attain homogeneity – the opposite of 'coexistence'.

DISPLACEMENT AS IMAGINED EXPERIENCE
AND AS DAILY MOVEMENT

Those who have experienced wars, internal civil wars or wars between countries, are familiar with both long-term displacement and the short-term or temporary displacements that occur in response to an emerging crisis. Examples of short-term displacements include seeking protection in the basement of a building, or leaving home for a more secure neighbourhood, village or city. These short-term displacements end when the family returns home. The period might vary from a few hours to several months. However, in many cases, what is planned to be short term becomes long term. The state of displacement generally involves moving necessities and choosing objects depending on the criticality or urgency of the situation and the amount of time available to prepare and pack.

Many Lebanese artists working in different media have taken the state of displacement produced by war as their subject matter. The image of the war-displaced moving along the roads with their domestic belongings, such as mattresses and suitcases, is vivid in people's memories and imaginations, and appears in the work of several key artists. In the 2006 Israeli war against Lebanon, when the memories of the civil war were re-lived and experienced again, some Lebanese artists featured the displacement kits that the Lebanese

Fig.68
Mazen Kerbaj, *My Life in a Bag*, 2006.

Fig.69
Ayman Baalbaki, *Bonjour Wadi Abu Jamil*, 2006.

put together. For example, Mazen Kerbaj's *My Life in a Bag* (2006)[66] illustrates what the artist carried in his bag each time he left his flat; among its contents were his passport and that of his son, carried in anticipation of a sudden need to use them (Fig. 68). Ayman Baalbaki's sculptural series depicts displaced people and their possessions, mainly moving from villages to the city; these works include a car with a pile of mattresses, suitcases, and household utensils on top, in *Destination X* (2010), and a rooster on top of a wrapped-up mattress with household utensils, in *Bonjour Wadi Abu Jamil* (2006) (Fig. 69).[67] And Palestinian artist Mona Hatoum's installation, *Mobile Home* (2005) features domestic objects moving slowly back and forth on wire that is stretched between two barricades (Fig. 70). These works express people on the move; and they also express the mobility of homes that are deprived of their architectural framework. Without this framework, the homes are displaced as fragments of objects and furniture, arranged in different ways to construct a situation representing both an unsettled present and an uncertain future.

When I spoke to the twin sisters in 2012, their displacement across the areas had not yet occurred, but street clashes had meant that the sister from Tarik al-Jdide had twice had to move temporarily to her sister's house in Mazraa, once for one night and once for a few hours. And the other sister had to leave to go to her husband's village house outside Beirut. Thus, both sisters had experienced

Fig.70
Mona Hatoum, *Mobile Home*, 2005.

short-term displacements. Moreover, the sisters and their husbands practised other types of displacement on a daily basis, which included the movement of memorabilia (such as photographs) scattered between them within the parameters of their houses, and the mobility of the husbands outside on the streets. The sisters are not aware of this type of displacement when they describe their everyday life, since they regard it as part of normal daily activity.

There are two types of anticipated displacement at work for the twins: the plan of their own making – to swap houses – which is a long-term displacement; and their constant fear that something will occur and force them to move suddenly against their will, and this includes short-term displacements. All these displacements include the movement of objects, people, and spaces. I surveyed and documented these different movements and types of displacement as I observed them from 2010 to 2012. Some of these movements are symmetrical in the relation they create between the two sisters, their husbands and houses, and others are asymmetrical, that is, they occur only in one house or are practised by only one sister or only one couple. In parallel to this photographic documentation of movements, I carried out a photographic survey of the floors and ceilings of their houses (presented at the beginning of this chapter) in order to continue my investigation into the space or sites of the displacements that span from the interiors to the exteriors. This photographic construction presents the houses as fixed structures, locations, and departure and destination points for the various movements (Fig. 67).

Preparations to Swap – The Twin Sisters and their Husbands

In anticipation of the swap, the sisters and their husbands undertook work to prepare the houses, and personal objects had been moved inside and between the parameters of the two houses.

■ Tarik al-Jdide: the husband in Tarik al-Jdide had painted a room in the house in Mazraa in a pink colour for his daughter, and he had installed washing lines on the kitchen's balcony.

■ Mazraa: no changes or preparations had been carried out by the Mazraa couple in the Tarik al-Jdide house.

Fig.71

Escape Kits – The Twin Sisters

In the two houses, each twin sister had her escape kit ready at a convenient location in anticipation of an emergency and a sudden move.

■ Tarik al-Jdide: one sister had a beach bag hanging on a door handle, which was also used in emergencies for packing the newborn baby's necessities.

■ Mazraa: one sister had a handbag stored on top of a closet in the children's room. It contained mainly clothing, nappies and food for her newborn baby.

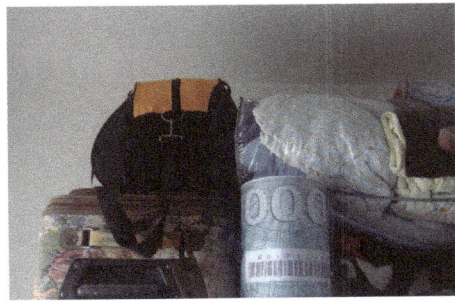 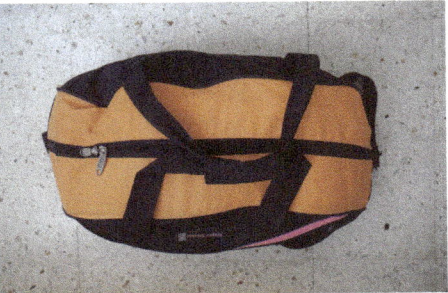

Fig.72

Photographs of Political Leaders – The Twin Sisters and their Husbands

In the two houses there were photographs of political leaders, framed and displayed among the family photographs. These photographs were put there by both sisters and their husbands.

■ Tarik al-Jdide: there was a photograph of Hariri in the formal living room, printed on a clear-glass frame and placed on the side table. He represents the wife's political affiliation. A photograph of the current Shiite Speaker of Parliament, Nabih Berri, was in a wooden frame on the wall in the living room. He represents the husband's political affiliation.

■ Mazraa: husband and wife supported the assassinated Sunni prime minister, Hariri, and had his framed photograph in the living room on the wooden shelf with other displays.

Fig.73

In 2011, a year after I first documented the photographs, both had been removed from their places and moved inside the house.

In 2011, a year after I first documented the photograph, the Hariri photograph was still in its place in the living room, but it was concealed among the baby accessories, notebooks and household gadgets.

Mobility on the Street – Husbands

Each husband walked from his house down the street in the opposite direction from the other to the Mazraa Main Road that separates them, and from there each continued his daily journey by car.

■ Tarik al-Jdide: the husband drove his car, which he parked on the main road. He worried that his car might be attacked if it were parked in the neighbourhood. By walking he could also more easily escape a physical attack.

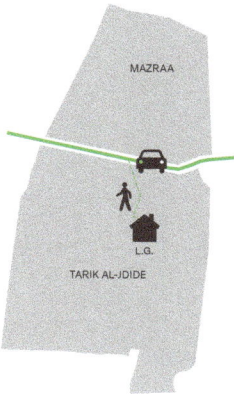

■ Mazraa: the husband waited on the Mazraa Main Road for his work car to pick him up. By walking to the road, he aimed to avoid a possible street confrontation with men from the neighbourhood on the streets, which could be generated by the political connotations of his work car if it were to enter the neighbourhood.

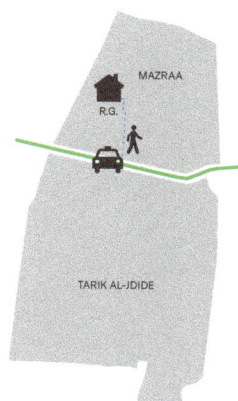

Fig.74

Iconic Views – The Twin Sisters and their Husbands

Each twin sister looked out of her window. Outside, each could see, framed by her window, a scene where violent clashes had taken place. From the windows, the city's streets and buildings that the sisters encountered on a daily basis were the backdrops to the violent events of the recent past. These urban scenes appear as iconic views in the sisters' description of them and the events they hosted.

■ Tarik al-Jdide: one twin sister looked down from her balcony to see the car park where her husband was chased. She looked in the opposite direction towards her sister's neighbourhood, and talked about the clashes – events from the recent past that took place in this urban setting.

■ Mazraa: one twin sister looked down from her high window to the streets where army personnel stand and their jeeps are parked to separate contested groups. These are signs of the violent clashes that occurred in the area.

Fig.75

The bag (the escape kit) that is ready to go, and which has already experienced displacement; the photographs that move around inside the house and get divided between husbands and wives; the husbands who walk outside the neighbourhoods to gain free mobility; the city's iconic views experienced as a daily visual journey of past violent events: these are narratives about movements that the sisters expressed, and they are also practices of physical movement. They are in fact movements of daily displacements that are practised on several levels, and in anticipation of the full displacement – the swapping – that is 'about to' happen. The time of 'about to' is not merely a waiting time in anticipation of displacement; this 'on hold' time is also an elongated state of daily displacements of the self in the time and space of the present.

DISPLACEMENT AS MATCHING

In *The Migrant Image*, T.J. Demos presents modernity through the lens of exile, echoing Walter Benjamin's and Edward Said's views on the age of modernity as 'the age of the refugee, the displaced person', and of 'mass immigration'. According to Demos: 'such is modernity-as-exile, a characterization defined by the dislocating ravages and alienating effects of capitalism and nationalism'. If the twentieth century is the age of nation-states with defined territorial borders and the mobilization of nationalism, then refugees and migrants present us with a counter-narrative of identity politics that exposes the cost of the national and capitalist project manifested by the expulsion of some groups and the domination and fixity of others.[68]

More specifically, Demos discusses the age of global crisis through the work of artists who have dealt with the issues of refuge and migration, and who have changed and challenged the condition of moving images in the documentary art of films and photography.[69] By 'mobilizing the image as much as imaging mobility', Demos suggests that such artists have invented representation strategies that adopt displacement as a language and

> disrupt the purity of film and language alike. As a result, the categories of the visual, the auditory, and the scriptural are rendered insufficient on their own, as necessarily dialogical and stranded in their incompleteness and therefore contingent on contextual determinations for their meanings.[70]

What results, he argues, is the subjectivity of displacement and of mobility; the refusal of one hegemony, purity, and a single national identity; the diversity, heterogeneity, and the differences (both positive and negative) in and through which the displaced live; the privileged crossing of artists between cultures and media – all of which contribute to the new aesthetic and politics of the exper-imental art of migration that is 'always on the move'.[71] In this respect, Demos suggests that displacement in art is one of potentialities.

The mobility involved in the twin sisters' plan to swap suggests the need for a mobile investigation of the sites where the displacement is to take place. This is an investigation that concerns proximity and explores how the displacement across this close distance may solve a potential disaster. The interiors of both houses and the streets outside them are where the twins' swapping is planned to take place, and where trials and small-scale displacements have already oc-curred. At their houses, I asked each of the sisters individually to draw the route map from one house to the other, and I video-recorded the drawing process. I also asked each sister to locate the other sister's house from her high-level balcony, using a small video camera. These simple mapping exercises aimed to mobilize and visualize what the sisters wanted to avoid in their chosen type of displacement, a displacement that is invisible and silent. The exercises enable them to perform this act of swapping, and to investigate the possibilities that might be generated out of the action.

One sister drew a route map that is very faithful to the actual urban plan, with a grid of building lots and roads – it reflected her technical training in interior design (Fig. 76). The other sister drew a route map as she experienced and imagined her journey to her sister's house (Fig. 77). Her drawing was a continuous but deviating route that connected the two houses: a tunnel-like passage with no interruption, she eliminated all the side roads and buildings. After she finished drawing the route, she added street names, reference points and landmarks. On both maps, the sisters identified the Abdel Nasser mosque as a reference point that is located on the Mazraa Main Road, which is almost halfway between the two houses and separates the two areas. Strikingly, they both drew the mosque simultaneously at exactly the same point in the respec-tive video footage documenting the drawing process: after one minute and 10 seconds. While one sister drew the mosque, the other wrote 'mosque' on her map and then drew it. The mosque has no direct religious significance for either of them, since neither are religious, but they refer to it as a major landmark in the area, for the part of the Mazraa Main Road where the mosque is located is called by its name.

The drawing of the route map is important for two reasons: it shows the proximity of the displacement scenario and the locations where the twin sisters' move-ments may take place, and it gives a topographic overview of the geographic image of the site. However, the drawing of the routes eliminates and conceals any evidence of conflict or segregation between the two areas, and it shows both the two areas as a normal urban extension of each other and the twin sisters as belonging to that urban extension. The drawing is also a speculative process (from memory and imagination) that relates to past, and possibly future, experience, whereas the photography and video recording used in this project are documentations and evidence of present time and space.

Fig.76
The route map drawn by R.G.

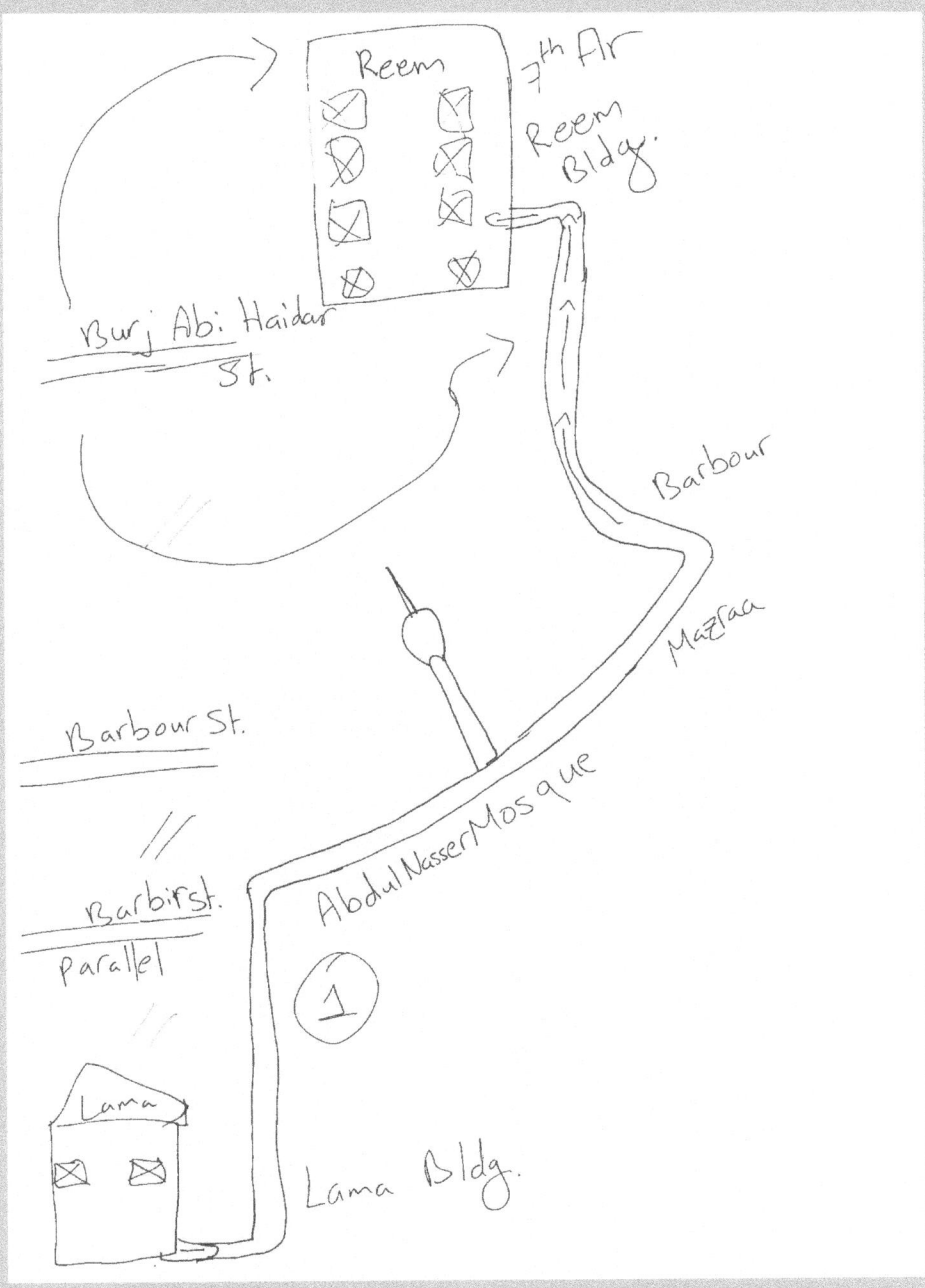

Fig.77
The route map drawn by L.G.

Fig.78
Stills from 'Finding Houses', *The Twin Sisters are 'About to'*
Swap Houses, 2012.

The two pieces of video footage obtained from the balconies show a dense urban space, filled with a succession of buildings that conceal the streets in between – a landscape of buildings, rooftops and sky. That the video camera could act as a place finder and binoculars to see the buildings closely intrigued both sisters, who decided to use the 'zoom' option. One sister claimed that she had identified her sister's building from the water tanks located on the roof. The other sister said it was impossible to find her sister's building, since it was concealed behind buildings; however, she was able to estimate the location of the building without actually being able to see it, and she moved the camera along the buildings' façades as if she were walking the streets to reach her sister's house.

In each of the sisters' footage, the movement of the camera recording the urban space embodies their movement as they search for the other's house. The two scenes navigate the urban space by zooming in and out, moving left to right, up and down, trying to find the other building. The sisters applied a control to the urban space footage, similar to the control they have applied to their lives by deciding to swap house; they wish to (re)arrange the urban geography of both areas by moving things around.

In the gallery installation, I responded to their bordering practice of matching politics and geography through my own critical bordering practice – that is, a bordering practice and a critical spatial practice. This practice involves finding moments of matching and twinning in the footage obtained from the two exercises performed with the sisters. The pieces of footage that track the façades of each area are matched: one is flipped and positioned below the other across a horizontal line, in an attempt to match the urban scenes and to connect the geography of the two areas (Fig. 78). The scene is slowed to intensify the searching quality embedded in each of the sisters' camera movements, one sister looking for the other in the landscape of buildings. Her search is at once poetic and violent, and it is reminiscent of the targeting of buildings in the footage of snipers and airspace army machinery. I project the scene onto the wall in the gallery space.

The two pieces of footage from the exercise of drawing the routes are overlaid on one another in the direction following the houses' geographic location in the site of the Mazraa district; that is, one sister's drawing starts from one side of the footage (north), and the other's starts from the opposite side (south) (Fig. 80). The resulting scene matches that moment in time in each piece of footage when one sister drew a mosque and the other sister simultaneously wrote the word 'mosque'. This scene is projected onto the floor. The viewer engages with the work by looking down at the drawing scene on the floor, where one sister draws her journey to the other sister's house, while facing the projection on the wall of the visual search one sister makes for the other sister's home using a video camera (Fig. 79, 81). The viewer is located, therefore, in a space of swapping, one which crosses borders through the practice of matching. In this space, there is a negotiation of continuous matching that aligns geographies across the visual horizon and through lines drawn while narrating a journey on a map.

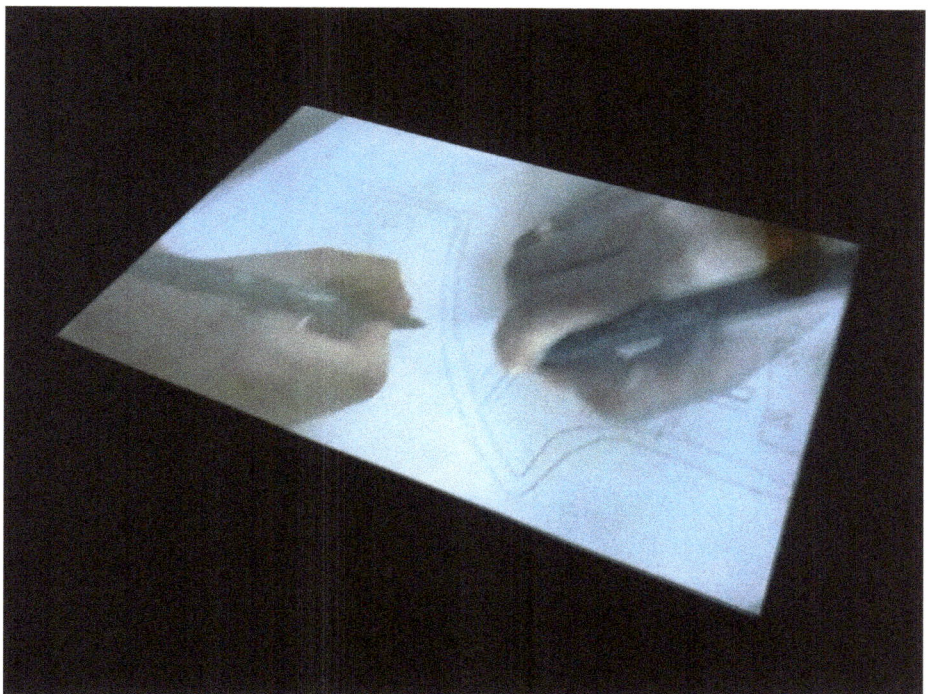

Fig.79
The Twin Sisters are 'About to' Swap Houses, gallery installation at Cities
Methodologies exhibition, UCL, London, 2012.

Displacement is not understood here only as the geographic movement from one space to another. Instead, I suggest it is a process of negotiation: an elongated state of displacing the self, creating the split in the connection between location and identity on a daily basis and on different scales, while waiting for the full displacement to occur across geographic lines. The bordering practice of daily displacement that I have highlighted here, and its correlate in the wish to swap in order to match, are features of the current conflict. They propose the narrative of Lebanese coexistence as a condition in which different communities arrange their geographic location in line with the sectarian and political affiliations of a place and the contemporary political situation. Although these are movements of displacement which appear voluntary and non-violent, and which occur within 'normal' real estate exchanges and family structure, they still result from bordering practices that are violent and relate to the bordering practices of securitization and surveillance. All the bordering practices applied by political parties indicate that displacement is the ultimate form of division of people and geography. Displacement and the physical and social divisions that follow from it are the opposite of negotiation: the emptying of buildings by their occupants reflects the voiding both of heterogeneity from social life and of the possibilities that are generated from mixing, difference, and 'politics'.

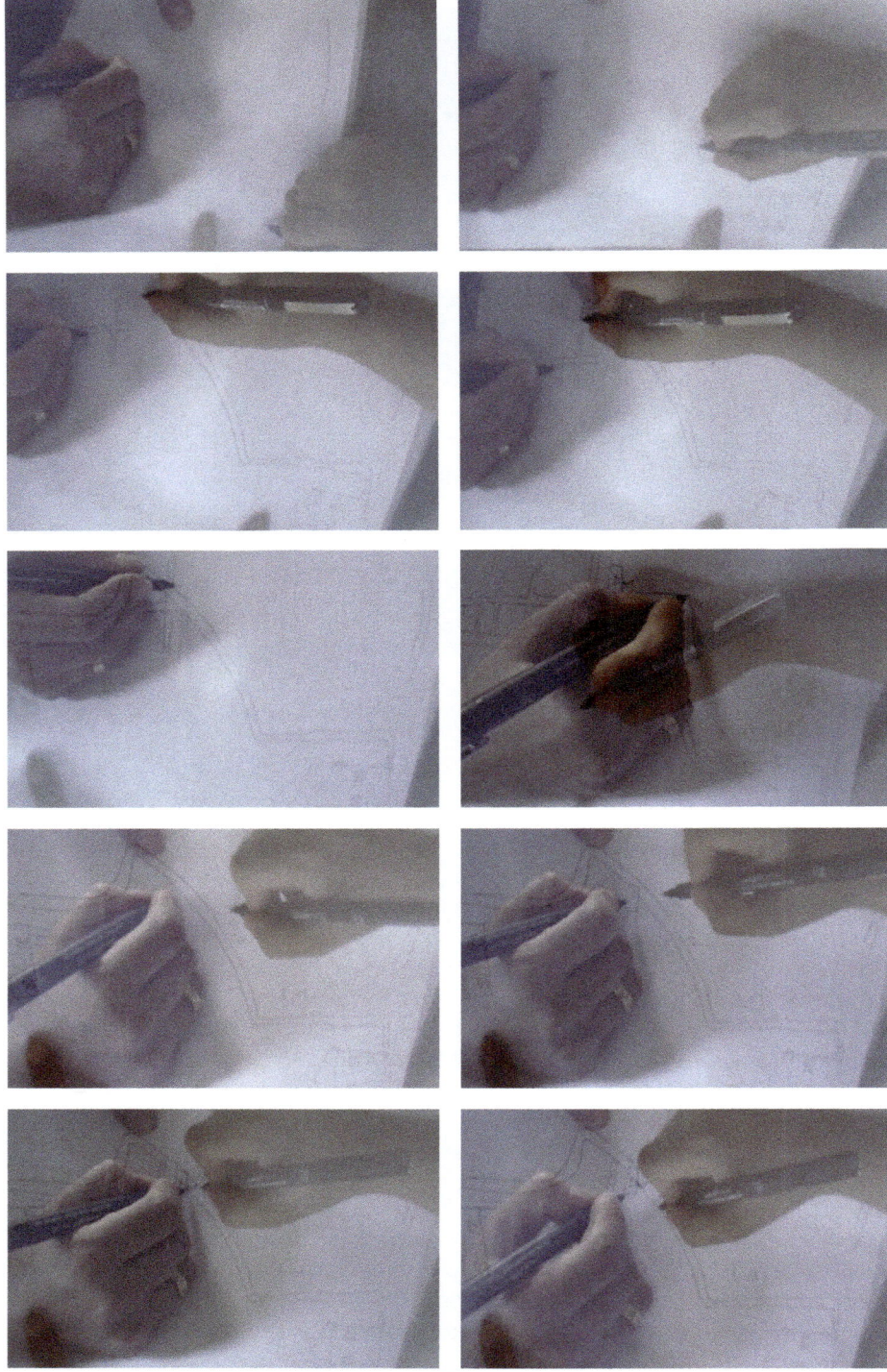

Fig. 80 (Opposite)
Stills from 'Drawing the route map', *The Twin Sisters are 'About to' Swap Houses*, 2012.

Fig. 81 (Above)
The Twin Sisters are 'About to' Swap Houses, gallery installation at Cities Methodologies exhibition, UCL, London, 2012.

Epilogue:
Temporal Bordering Practices
of Resistance

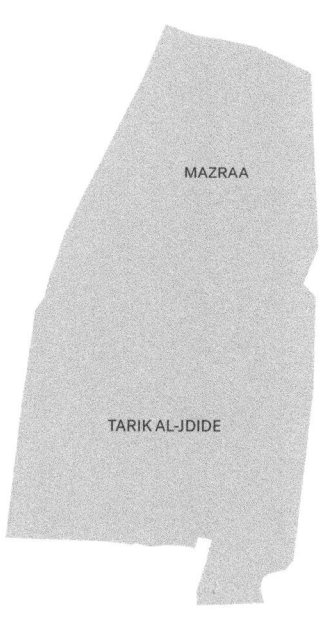

Fig. 82
Map of Mazraa and Tarik al-Jdide.

INTRODUCTION

In *Negotiating Conflict in Lebanon*, I have explored the bordering practice of political–sectarian conflict as a tactic and strategy in everyday life, and the bordering practice of research and art as a form of critical spatial practice. Bringing the discussion of critical spatial practice into the study of borders provides a certain destabilization and scrutiny of existing border conditions and positions. This includes the artist's own position, method used, and narratives produced in and about urban sites. In this epilogue I reflect on my own position in the making processes of this project's method and narratives. I focus on the temporal aspect of my engagements with the research topic and the urban site. In particular, I focus on the capacity of art practices to provide different forms of resistance at varying degrees of conflict, practices that mobilize an active role for residents in claiming city spaces.

Tactics of resistance depend on time, as they do not have a proper place in the way that strategies do.[1] They are in constant search for opportunities to turn them into future potentialities. Their temporal mode of occupying the present time – their contemporariness – is different from that of the conflict strategies: because they are at a critical distance from their own time, they never coincide with it fully, and whatever they win they do not hold on to without it evolving – otherwise tactics turn into strategies.[2] I make, therefore, a contrast between the temporal bordering practices of conflict's strategies and those of art and research as tactics to project onto future possibilities that transcend the limits of time and space and transform certain border conditions – border conditions that are past, present and potentially future.

The exploration of the temporal aspects of borders is twofold. First, it provides an extension in time to the understanding of borders as spatial constructions inscribed in material space and manifested through representations of space, such as maps and political procedures. In addition, it forces a historical consideration of borders that are often thought of in current political debates and media as ahistorical, and it positions them within a continuous timeline from past to present that implicates different cultures and political powers, such as East and West. Second, the temporal is a propositional tool to negotiate the conflict's strategic borders, using site actions, multimedia representations and gallery art installations to activate them in time and expose the processes of constructing narratives of borders and divisions.

TIME: PAST CONTEXT

Each chapter in this book highlights the role of borders not only in relation to space but also in relation to time. Bordering practices are spatial practices, certainly, but they are also temporal processes. Focusing on the temporal aspect of bordering practices, as I explain in the Introduction, shows how violence gradually intensifies, how long it takes to build a border, and the way a border's spatial qualities change over time. I have also considered diachronicity: how, as an element of confrontation and occupation, time is deployed in the bordering practices associated with the current conflict.

In general, two temporal aspects related to bordering practices are worth highlighting: the recurrence of conflict practices from the civil war period, and the prolonged time of living in conflict or, as I have described it, the long time of waiting for a trouble that is 'about to' happen while still engaging in daily activities. In other words, recurrence and the state of being on hold characterize how bordering practices associated with conflict play out in present time.

In 'Bordering Practice 01: Hiding', the mukhtars tell, from their offices, stories of conflict that connect events across a period of around 30 years, as if there had been no interruptions or temporal distances between the pre-war, civil war and the post-war periods. The mukhtars' narratives describe how old and new political leaders and alliances can repeat practices and confrontations along the lines of old and new borders and demarcations. The presence of surveillance surrounding the women at their balconies, in 'Bordering Practice 02: Crossing', shows how the practice of surveillance in neighbourhoods by militia members goes back to the civil war period (1975–90) and has gradually resurfaced with some modifications, alongside new practices, since the events of 2005. The political sounds played in the city soundscape, in 'Bordering Practice 03: Translating', also collapse timespans between present and past and bring the sound of old events into the present moment. Finally, in 'Bordering Practice 04: Matching', the twin sisters experience daily displacement within their houses and across the city; their 'swapping houses' plan is continually postponed and is always 'about to' happen. Their plan comes out of the experience of the violent displacements that the country witnessed in the civil war, and their aim is to prevent this from recurring.

Klas Borell has used the concept of 'bracketing' in relation to Beirut's conflict: residents open parentheses in time and/or space, and they make use of the periods and spaces of released tension. Bracketing, which I would consider to be a bordering practice that takes place in time and space, is a method for renormalization; as Borell writes, it is an attempt 'to return to the previous state of "normality"'.[3] However, for Borell, this bracketing and renormalizing is concerned with the present time only; it does not take into account time as an extension from the past.

According to Bruno Latour, 'we have shifted from the time of Time to the *time of Simultaneity*' – that is, to the time of space, where no one is interested in history or the future, but rather in 'cohabiting' the space of the present simultaneously and in contradiction. Latour maintains that time in relation to succession still exists, but that it is no longer important, particularly in relation to progress.[4]

In the case of Lebanon, the evident recurrence of civil war practices does not imply, as one might expect, that there has been any process of learning from, or reflection on, the past. This is tied to a state of collective amnesia, as Fawwaz Traboulsi argues, which facilitates this repetition through a kind of refusal to analyse the past in which these events originated.[5] On the other hand, living in a state of 'about to' happen prolongs the present in a way that is not synchronized with space – as demonstrated in the state of waiting while engaging in other activities. 'Everything has become contemporary',[6] to use Latour's words; it has become elongated in the present and detached from the past.

There is a contemporariness to the Lebanese conflict practices that is concerned with occupying the present time and coinciding with it fully. It is opposite to the conceptual definition of Giorgio Agamben's contemporariness that entails a distance and disjunction from the present time and allows for a critical per-ception and assessment of ones' own time.[7] Indeed, the Lebanese conflict is 'chronic' yet always contemporary: it produces temporal bordering practices that are positioned in the present and are concerned neither with looking back at history nor thinking of the future as a better space for 'cohabitation' or even for contradiction; rather, the temporal border practices practise division as an ongoing living condition, day by day.

NARRATIVE: PRESENT RESPONSE

The question arising from engagement in such a research project is whether the narrative I have presented on the political–sectarian conflict, and its manifes-tation in spatial practices, is in itself another bordering practice that reinforces the existing social division, rather than an attempt to analyse and elucidate, or even 'solve', it. Because Sunni, Shiite, Druze and Orthodox Christian identities structure my investigation into borders, I have introduced the research project and the site of the Mazraa district along these sectarian lines.

Narrative is expressive and allows the communication and development of ideas. Narrative is also contagious in spreading and exaggerating existing worries and prejudices that are not necessarily innate.[8] This is evident in the political narrative in Lebanon that emphasizes the importance of the sectarian identity of individuals, promoting this ahead of all other social concerns. In this respect, the narrative of this research project is to some extent shaped and led by what is propagated in media reports and politicians' speeches, which typically precede the religious and sectarian logic in any discussion about politics and the possibilities for a political life outside these religious constraints in Lebanon.

It is essential to highlight the impact of existing political narratives, and how such discourse can dominate the everyday life of Lebanese residents. The possibilities for operating outside these existing narrative structures, and the modes of negotiating them, should be considered.[9] We might think of the role of the research and art projects in sites of conflict as 'critical spatial practices' that, as I have argued in this book, are able to transform borders' narratives and to affirm existing ones.

The narrative I put forward in this book is not a re-production of the 'chronic' sectarian narrative over time. Instead, I dissect the political–sectarian narrative and show the layers that intertwine with the social, political and economic domains of residents, and I explore the narrative as a practice, lived and con-structed over time and able to change.

More importantly, I employ spatial strategies and representation techniques, in and off the urban site, through site actions, multimedia representations and gallery art installations to intervene in the space between, and to produce alter-native narratives to, borders. The four bordering practices I invented of *hiding* in 'Administration', *crossing* in 'Surveillance', *translating* in 'Sound', and *matching* in 'Displacement' are critical spatial practices that displace and transform bor-ders in time and space. They are able to work across time and shuffle temporal relationships and construct associations between past, present and future that are restricted, possibly deliberately, in the current politics.

What is the nature of the borders at stake in the gallery situation? The works might not provide direct answers, but they question the possibility of imagining the world and constructing artworks and situations without borders and hierar-chies. As such, the artworks question the material definition of borders as solid, permeable, or ephemeral, and the assessment of the role of borders as active or passive, tactical or strategic, and necessary or redundant.

RESISTANCE: FUTURE POTENTIALITIES

The method I carried out in the urban sites from residents' spaces positioned my research (and myself) in-between places. This position of an in-between, offered through trust, sets up the possibility for alternative practices in urban public spaces and creates new spatial possibilities through art practices at times of conflict. This suggestion of an alternative 'in-between place' can operate in two different directions as resistance tactics: either as a passive place of resistance into which to retreat, or as an active place of resistance from which to negotiate through politics and claim a position for democratic practices and rights in the public arena.

I developed the method of working with other people, especially in contest-ed spaces, through my work at Febrik. Febrik is a collaborative platform that primarily works in Palestinian refugee camps in the Middle East; it employs participatory art and architecture research processes to propose site-specific interventions (of different forms and scales) that aim for social change in the direct environment of the participants.[10] At the outset of my research on the project in this book, I thought that my interventions had to be located in the site of Mazraa itself, to have impact there and to change something in the site; however, I found myself quite intuitively drawn to propose interventions 'off-site', or in what Robert Smithson would call the 'non-site',[11] in the form of installations in the gallery space. This is because the gallery provided me with a space to experiment and to test ideas that did not necessarily take into account those people included in the research's empirical process; it also enabled me to pro-duce works that do not give back directly to the community. The gallery provided me with a space where the political sensitivities and constraints experienced at the sites I was researching were not the only concerns, and where ideas and constructions could be played out confrontationally with no consideration for censorship. In the gallery space, I was able to retreat from the politics outdoors – and I felt safe.[12]

So, is it the pressure of the conflict that has pushed me inside the space of the gallery? Perhaps yes. Certainly, this is not the only possible way to react. Between the intellectual and personal safety I felt in the gallery space, and the urgency of the political situation outside in the site, there is a site of negotia-tion and a range of sites for producing and presenting work, including urban interventions, publications, events, and the Internet. Hence, there is no rigid separation or border between the site of the research and the site of the gallery and all the other sites in between. In my case, I have considered these sites of negotiation to be part of a bordering practice that borrows from one site and delivers in another; it is a practice that entails materially, spatially and temporally transforming borders.

An example on the bordering practice of resistance is the practices of civil society in Lebanon. Although I focused in this book on bordering practices that emerged in the wake of the political–sectarian conflict that resurfaced in 2005, since 2011 the country has been affected by the political turmoil in the Arab world and particularly the outbreak of the Syrian war, a conflict in which Hezbollah plays an active role. At the same time, the deterioration of governance and state institutions in Lebanon persists. As a response, civil society initiated a series of practices, including protests, neighbourhood initiatives and organized political campaigns, to address the worsening living conditions and the political deadlock in the country. The concerns and battles of civil society include corruption, the electoral law, women's citizenship rights, violence against women, LGBTQ rights, refugee rights, foreign/domestic worker rights, rent law, privatization of public spaces, public protection of the coastline, waste management and environmental concerns. These are hopeful tactical practices. They are also bordering practices that deal with particular conditions of borders (past, present and potentially future), and they are critical spatial practices in their conscious aim to transform the 'chronic' (recurring and on-hold) status quo and to gain a position of power in everyday life. They aim to change space and, consequently, time. The tactics of resistance of such urban practices and of art practices in and about urban space are very much interrelated in their aims and processes. Yet the challenge for the success and continuity of the current tactics of resistance in Lebanon, such as those of civil society, is to aim, by focusing on their temporal bordering practice potential, for evolution and to seize space as a dynamic domain contrary to place acquisition and the logic of border.

It is necessary to start considering degrees of conflict, threat and urgency experienced in a place of conflict and social change and to suggest works as responses that vary in their processes and spatial forms and that move across a wide spectrum between sites and off-sites. In other words, works can and do operate in multiple sites of existence and resistance. One can ask in response to the dangers threatening the existence of cities and countries: How can the ongoing political–sectarian conflict be challenged and what are the possibilities for operating outside (or escaping) existing narratives and the forced borders of politics? Is it possible not to lag behind the imposed strategies of control and instead to gain control over one's time, space, and future? What is the nature of the next practices of resistance?

ENDNOTES

Introduction: Bordering Practices

1   Michel de Certeau, *The Practice of Everyday Life,* trans. Steven Rendall (Berkeley, CA: University of California Press, 1988); Henri Lefebvre, *The Production of Space,* trans. Donald Nicholson-Smith (Oxford: Blackwell, 1991); Jane Rendell, *Art and Architecture: A Place Between* (London: I.B. Tauris, 2006).

2   Alexander C. Diener and Joshua Hagen, *Borders: A Very Short Introduction* (New York: Oxford University Press, 2012).

3   Lana Asfour, 'Lebanon and the Syrian Refugee Crisis,' Open Democracy, 13 March 2014. Accessed 7 July 2014, http://www.opendemocracy.net/opensecurity/lana-asfour/lebanon-and-syrian-refugee-crisis.

4   Samir Khalaf, *Heart of Beirut: Reclaiming the Bourj* (London: Saqi, 2006), pp. 13-8.

5   Cornelia Zeineddine, 'Transformation and Challenges of the Lebanese Political Parties,' *Middle East Political and Economic Institute,* 15 December 2013. Accessed 7 July 2014, mepei.com/in-focus/5419-transformation-and-challenges-of-the-lebanese-political-parties.

6   Ussama Makdisi, 'Reconstructing the Nation-State: The Modernity of Sectarianism in Lebanon,' *Middle East Report,* no. 200 (1996): pp. 23-6.

7   Ibid., p. 25.

8   Ibid., p. 26.

9   Certeau, p. xix.

10 Lefebvre, pp. 55-6.

11 Rendell, p. 8.

12 Ibid., pp. 6-12.

13 Mona Fawaz, Mona Harb, and Ahmad Gharbieh, 'Living Beirut's Security Zones: An Investigation of the Modalities and Practice of Urban Security,' *City & Society* 24, no. 2 (2012).

14 Ibid., p. 182.

15 Certeau, p. xix.

16 Ibid.

17 Ibid., p. xx.

18 Ibid., p. xix.

19 Ibid., p. xvii.

20 Ibid., p. 117.

21 Ibid., p. 117.

22 Ibid., p. 116.

23 Ibid., pp. xx, 116.

24 Ibid., pp. xix, 117.

25 Ibid., pp. xix.

26 Lefebvre, p. 33.

27 Ibid.

28 Ibid., pp. 38-40.

29 Ibid., pp. 33, 38-9.

30 Ibid., p. 38.

31 Ibid.

32 Ibid., p. 39.

33 Ibid., pp. 33, 38-9.

34 Edward W. Soja, *Postmodern Geographies: The Reassertion of Space in Critical Social Theory* (London: Verso, 1989), p. 77.

35 Certeau, pp. xix, 36.

36 Etienne Balibar, 'The Borders of Europe,' in *Cosmopolitics: Thinking and Feeling Beyond the Nation,* ed. Pheng Cheah and Bruce Robbins (Minneapolis: University of Minnesota Press, 1998), pp. 217-20.

37 Parker and Vaughan-Williams, 'Lines in the Sand? Towards an Agenda for Critical Border Studies,' *Geopolitics* 14, no. 3 (2009): p. 586.

38 Diener and Hagen, p. 59.

39 Parker and Vaughan-Williams, p. 583.

40 N. Vaughan-Williams, 'The UK Border Security Continuum: Virtual Biopolitics and the Simulation of the Sovereign Ban,' *Environment and Planning D: Society and Space* 28, no. 6 (2010): pp. 1071-83. Quoted in James D. Sidaway, 'The Return and Eclipse of Border Studies? Charting Agendas 1,' *Geopolitics* 16, no. 4 (2011): p. 973.

41 Steve Pile and N. J. Thrift, *Mapping the Subject: Geographies of Cultural Transformation,* (London: Routledge, 1995), p.3.

42 Ibid., p.13.

43 Mike Crang and N. J. Thrift, *Thinking Space* (London: Routledge, 2000), pp. 9-10.

44 Daniel Meier, 'Borders, Boundaries and Identity Building in Lebanon: An Introduction,' *Mediterranean Politics* 18, no. 3 (2013): pp. 352.

45 *Oxford English Dictionary,* Oxford University Press. Accessed 19 March 2014, www.oed.com.

46 Nicholas Bourriaud, 'Relational Aesthetics,' in *Participation,* ed. Claire Bishop (London: Cambridge, 2006), pp. 160-1.

47 Ibid.

48 Susan Stanford Friedman, *Mappings: Feminism and the Cultural Geographies of Encounter,* (Princeton, NJ: Princeton University Press, 1998), p. 153.

49 Teresa Pires do Rio Caldeira, *City of Walls: Crime, Segregation, and Citizenship in Sao Paulo* (Berkeley: University of California Press, 2000), p. 19.

50 Certeau, p. 125.

51 Ibid., p. 123.

52 Ibid., p. 129.

53 Keith Jenkins, *Re-Thinking History* (London: Routledge Classics, 2003), p. 38.

54 Ibid., p. 39.

55 Ibid., p. 8.

56 Pile and Thrift, p. 17.

57   Hal Foster, *The Return of the Real: The Avant-Garde at the End of the Century* (Cambridge, MA: MIT Press, 1996), p. 180.

Bordering Practice 01: Hiding

1   W.J.T. Mitchell, 'Representation,' in *Critical Terms for Literary Study*, ed. Frank Lentricchia and Thomas McLaughlin (Chicago: University of Chicago Press, 1990), p. 11.

2   Ibid.

3   Ibid., p. 12.

4   Ibid., p. 21.

5   Henri Lefebvre, *The Production of Space*, trans. Donald Nicholson-Smith (Oxford: Blackwell, 1991), pp. 38–9.

6   Ibid.

7   Keith Jenkins, *Re-Thinking History* (London: Routledge Classics, 2003).

8   Edward Hallett Carr, *What Is History?* (Basingstoke: Palgrave, 2001).

9   Ibid., p. 24.

10   Quoted in Rima Maktabi, 'Lebanon's Missing History: Why School Books Ignore the Past', *CNN*, 8 June 2012. Accessed 7 July 2014, edition.cnn.com/2012/06/08/world/meast/lebanon-civil-war-history/index.html.

11   Hassan Krayem, 'The Lebanese Civil War and the Taif Agreement,' *AUB*. Accessed 15 March 2014, ddc.aub.edu.lb/projects/pspa/conflict-resolution.html.

12   Ibid., p. 6.

13   Arda Arsenian Ekmekji, 'Confessionalism and Electoral Reform in Lebanon,' *The Aspen Institute*, 19 July 2012. Accessed 15 March 2014, www.aspeninstitute.org/publications/confessionalism-electoral-reform-lebanon/, pp. 2–4.

14   Krayem, 'The Lebanese Civil War and the Taif Agreement,' p. 6.

15   Ibid.

16   Arnold Hottinger, 'Zu'ama in Historical Perspective', in Leonard Binder (ed.), *Politics in Lebanon* (New York: Wiley, 1996).

17   Hassan Krayem, 'Reading in the Meaning and the Results of Municipal Elections: Representation, Participation, and the Role of Social and Political Powers [in Arabic] قراءة في معنى الإنتخابات البلدية و نتائجها: التمثيل والمشاركة ودور القوى الأجتماعية والسياسية,' in *Municipal Elections in Lebanon in 1998: The Birth of Democracy in Civil Society* [in Arabic] [الانتخابات البلدية في لبنان ١٩٩٨، مخاض الديمقراطية في بنى المجتمعات] (Beirut: Al-Markaz Al-Lobnani Li'Dirasat, 1999), pp. 587–606.

18   Historically, the mukhtar played a reconciliatory role in their local communities. The root of reconciliation (*soloh*) as part of the mukhtar's duties goes back to the years between 1861 and 1864 under Ottoman rule when the Lebanese protocol was issued and declared the formation of 'Mount Lebanon'. At that time, the 'sheikh' was the local elected administrator who managed the villages, in parallel with *qadi el soloh*, who was a judge playing the reconciliatory role between residents. Both positions were replaced by that of the mukhtar in 1864.

19   Hoda Rizk, 'Beirut Mukhtar Elections in Light of Its Municipal Elections [in Arabic] انتخابات بيروت الاختيارية في [، ضوء انتخاباتهاالبلدية],' in *Municipal Elections in Lebanon in 1998: The Birth of Democracy in Civil Society* [in Arabic] [الانتخابات البلدية في لبنان ١٩٩٨، مخاض الديمقراطية في بنى المجتمعات] (Beirut: Al-Markaz Al-Lobnani Li'Dirasat, 1999), p. 269.

20   Firas El-Shoufi, 'Son of the Beik Is Beik and the Son of the Emir Is Emir [in Arabic] ابن البيك بيك وابن المير [ميّر،],' *Al-Akhbar*, 9 July 2013. Accessed 7 July 2014, Al-Akhbar.com/node/186743. See also Hani Fahs, 'Political Inheritance in Lebanon between Muslims and Christians [in Arabic] من حلو إلى حلو: الوراثة السياسية في [لبنان بين المسلمين والمسيحيين],' *Al-Mustaqbal*, 16 September 2003. Accessed 7 July 2014, www.almustaqbal.com/v4/Article.aspx?Type=np&Articleid=29391.

21   Samir Khalaf, 'Primordial Ties and Politics in Lebanon,' *Middle Eastern Studies* 4, no. 3 (1968): p. 247.

22   Ibid., pp. 253–4, 260. See also Fawwaz Traboulsi, *A History of Modern Lebanon* (London: Pluto Press, 2007), p. 43.

23   Krayem, 'Reading in the Meaning and the Results of Municipal Elections,' pp. 593–6.

24   Najwa Bassil, 'The Mukhtars' State and Their Role in Civil Peace in Lebanon [in Arabic] واقع المختارين [ودورهم في إرساء السلم الأهلي في لبنان],' (UNDP, 2012), p. 11.

25   Charles Adwan, 'Municipal Elections of 1998 in Comparison to the Elections of 1963 [in Arabic] [الانتخابات البلدية عام ١٩٩٨ في مرآة انتخابات عام ١٩٦٣],' in *Municipal Elections in Lebanon in 1998: The Birth of Democracy in Civil Society* [in Arabic] الانتخابات [البلدية في لبنان ١٩٩٨، مخاض الديمقراطية في بنى المجتمعات] (Beirut: Al-Markaz Al-Lobnani Li'Dirasat, 1999), pp. 583–5.

26   *Guide De La Ville De Beyrouth* (Beirut: Conseil Municipal de la Ville de Beyrout; AZ Societe d'Edition & Production, 2009–2010), p. 4.

27   Ibid.

28   Krayem, 'Reading in the Meaning and the Results of Municipal Elections,' p. 588.

29   Arsenian Ekmekji, p. 7.

30   This was the case in the municipal/mukhtar elections in 1998 (see Krayem, 'Reading in the Meaning and the Results of Municipal Elections,' p. 603) and in the elections of 2010. See Sarkis Naoum, 'The Position This Day [in Arabic] الموقف اليوم، [دققوا جيدا في تدني نسبة المقترعين],' *An-Nahar*, 11 May 2010.

31   Paul Salem, 'Electoral Law Reform in Lebanon, the Experience and Recommendations of the National Commission,' *Arab Reform Initiative*, 27 July 2006. Accessed 15 March 2014, www.arab-reform.net/en/node/343, p. 2.

32   Abed Ghalayini, one of the 24 members of Beirut's municipal council elected in 2010 (Beirut, 16 January 2012).

33   Mukhtar Salim al-Madhoun (Beirut, January 2012).

34   Krayem, 'The Lebanese Civil War and the Taif Agreement' p. 5.

35   Bassel F. Salloukh, 'The Limits of Electoral Engineering in Divided Societies: Elections in Postwar Lebanon,' *Canadian Journal of Political Science / Revue canadienne de science politique* 39, no. 3 (2006): pp. 642–50. The importance of these electoral borders relates to the election of the 19 parliamentary members for Beirut alone – ten Christians and nine Muslims – out of the total

of 128 members of parliament for the whole country. (Parliamentary seats set for Beirut are distributed as follows: six Sunni, two Shiite, one Druze, one Maronite, one Greek Orthodox, one Greek Catholic, three Armenian Orthodox, one Armenian Catholic, one Protestant and one other Christian.)

36   Ibid., pp. 637–8.

37   This is explained by mukhtar al-Madhoun, as well as by mukhtar Razzouq.

38   Rola Mouawad, 'Beirut the Two District, between Municipal Boycott and Consensus on Mukhtars Led to Low Voter Turn out Second [in Arabic] بيروت الثانية بين المقاطعة البلدية والتوافق على المختارين انخفضت الحماسة [ونسبة المشاركة]', An-Nahar, 10 May 2010.

39   Rizk, pp. 269–70.

40   On this, see Michael Johnson, Class & Client in Beirut: The Sunni Muslim Community and the Lebanese State, 1840-1985 (University of Michigan, Michigan: Ithaca Press, 1986), pp. 123-7.

41   Usama Al-Aref, The Memory of the Sand [in Arabic] [ذاكرة الرمل] (Zalka: Mukhtarat, 2005), p. 72.

42   Samir Kassir, The History of Beirut [in Arabic] [تاريخ بيروت] (Beirut: Dar An-nahar, 2006), p. 535.

43   Frank Mermier, 'The Frontiers of Beirut: Some Anthropological Observations,' Mediterranean Politics 18, no. 3 (2013): p. 377.

44   Ibid.

45   Salim Nasr and Diane James, 'Roots of the Shi'i Movement,' MERIP Reports, no. 133 (1985): pp. 11–12. Quoted in Mermier, p. 377.

46   Salim Nasr, 'New Social Realities and Post-War Lebanon,' in Recovering Beirut: Urban Design and Post-War Reconstruction, ed. Samir Khalaf and Philip S. Khouri (Leiden: Brill, 1993). For further discussion of the Israeli occupation and wars, see Chapter 4.

47   Mukhtar Ghareib Hassan was elected for Minet el-Hosn district, but his office was in Mazraa district; he is an example of those mukhtars who work outside their electoral district, a practice that al-Madhoun considered to be illegal.

48   Pierre Atallah, 'Harb's Suggestion against Cantonizations and Sectarian Segregation [in Arabic] [اقتراح حرب للتصدي للكانتونات ومنع الفرز بين الطوائف]', An-Nahar, 5 January 2011.

49   Writer Khaled Saghieh (Beirut, January 2010).

50   Rizk, p. 270.

51   Hassan Krayem, 'Reading in the Meaning and the Results of Municipal Elections,' p. 606.

52   Elizabeth Picard, 'Beyrouth : La Gestion Nationale D'enjeux Locaux,' in Municipalités Et Pouvoirs Locaux Au Liban, ed. Agnès Favier (Cahiers du Cermoc, Beyrouth, Cermoc, 2001), p. 289.

53   Mermier, p. 380.

54   Arsenian Ekmekji, p. 15.

55   Krayem, 'The Lebanese Civil War and the Taif Agreement,' p. 6.

56   Naoum, 'The Position This Day.'

57   'Conflict in Cities.' Accessed 15 March 2014, conflictincities.org/. Pullan said this in a lecture at London Metropolitan University in 2012 on the Conflict in Cities and the Contested State project, a research project on divided cities, including Beirut.

58   'Map of Beirut by Julius Loytved, Danish Vice-Consul' (1876).

59   Bureau Topographique de L'Arinee Francaise du Levant, 'Beyrouth' (February 1922).

60   Bureau Topographique des Troupes Françaises du Levant (T.F.L.), 'Beyrouth' (Service Géographique de l'Armée, 1936).

61   Annexe de l'Institut Geographique National au Levant, 'Beyrouth' (June 1941).

62   Service Geographique, 'Beyrouth Ville' (December 1959).

63   As-Safir, 'Beirut after Dahyeh under Shelling and Armed Battles [in Arabic] بيروت بعدالضاحية تحت القصف] والعمليات الحربية]', As-Safir, 7 February 1984.

64   An-Nahar, 'Violent Clashes Centred in Corniche Mazraa, Al-Mat'haf Area Bring Back the Memories of Demarcation Lines [in Arabic] [مواجهات دامية محورها كورنيش المزرعة، المتحف استعاد أجواء خطوط التماس]', An-Nahar, 28 January 2007.

65   Naji Shamil (Beirut, December 2013).

66   Ibid.

67   Ibid.

68   Farouq Al-Jamal, That's Life [in Arabic] [الدنيا هيك] (Beirut: Dar El-Elm Lil'Malayeen, 1997), p. 252.

69   Mitchell, p. 21.

70   Picard, 'Beyrouth : La Gestion Nationale D'enjeux Locaux,' p. 289.

71   Walter Benjamin, Illuminations, edited with an introduction by Hannah Arendt; trans. Harry Zohn (London: Fontana, 1970), pp. 72–5.

Bordering Practice 02: Crossing

1   Katrin Kaschadt, 'Of the Power of the Gaze,' in Ctrl Space: Rhetorics of Surveillance from Bentham to Big Brother, ed. Thomas Y. Levin, Ursula Frohne and Peter Weibel (Karlsruhe and London: ZKM and MIT, 2002), p. 118.

2   Allan Sekula, 'Photography between Labour and Capital,' in Leslie Shedden et al., Mining Photographs and Other Pictures, 1948–1968: A Selection from the Negative Archives of Shedden Studio, Glace Bay, Cape Breton, Nova Scotia Series: Source Materials of the Contemporary Arts (Halifax, NS: Press of the Nova Scotia College of Art and Design/University College of Cape Breton Press, 1983). Quoted in Geoffrey Batchen, 'Guilty Pleasures,' in Ctrl Space, p. 447.

3   David Lyon, 'Technology Vs. "Terrorism": Circuits of City Surveillance since September 11, 2001,' in Cities, War, and Terrorism: Towards an Urban Geopolitics, ed. Stephen Graham (Malden, MA: Blackwell, 2004), p. 308.

4   David Lyon, Theorizing Surveillance: The Panopticon and Beyond (Cullompton, Devon: Willan Publishing, 2006), pp. 4–5.

5   Mona Fawaz, Mona Harb and Ahmad Gharbieh, 'Living Beirut's Security Zones: An Investigation of the Modalities and Practice of Urban Security,' City & Society 24, no. 2 (2012): p. 181.

6   Bernard Comment, The Panorama (London: Reaktion, 1999), p. 7.

7   Ibid., p. 8.

8   Ibid., pp. 134–8.

9   Fawaz, Harb and Gharbieh, p. 185.

10 Suad Joseph, 'The Public/Private: The Imagined Boundary in the Imagined Nation/State/Community: The Lebanese Case,' *Feminist Review*, 57 (1997): pp. 87–9.

11 Kaja Silverman, *The Threshold of the Visible World* (New York: Routledge, 1996), pp. 124–47.

12 Ibid., p. 167.

13 From the film synopsis, *Je Veux Voir* (2007), Joana Hadjithomas and Khalil Joreige. Accessed 17 July 2018, http://hadjithomasjoreige.com/i-want-to-see/.

14 Kathleen Lennon and Margaret Whitford, *Knowing the Difference: Feminist Perspectives in Epistemology* (London and New York: Routledge, 1994), p. 5.

15 Wilhelm S. Wurzer, *Panorama: Philosophies of the Visible* (London: Continuum, 2002), p. vii.

16 Kristin Monroe, 'Being Mobile in Beirut,' *City & Society* 23, no. 1 (2011): p. 96.

17 Fawaz, Harb and Gharbieh, p. 189.

18 And more recently in line with the war in Syria.

19 Jon Coaffee, 'Recasting the "Ring Steel": Designing out Terrorism in the City of London?' in *Cities, War and Terrorism*, p. 277.

20 Fawaz, Harb and Gharbieh, p. 189.

21 Denis Wood and John Fels, *The Power of Maps* (New York: Guilford Press, 1992).

22 It is worth noting here that the Amal leader, Nabih Berri, has been the Speaker of the House since he was first elected at the end of the civil war in 1992. Berri was a resident in Barbour during the civil war before he moved outside the area after the end of the war.

23 Mustaqbal (Future Movement), was originally founded informally in 1992 after the end of the civil war; it was officially registered as a political party in 2007 after the assassination of Prime Minister Rafic Hariri in 2005.

24 Balconies in Lebanon, and specifically in Beirut, used to be places of habitation for outdoor social activities, as in various other Mediterranean cities. This has dramatically changed in the past ten years, especially with the introduction of curtain glass as part of the building materials permitted by building law in Lebanon to cover balconies, in order to gain more space and to protect from the weather due to global warming and pollution. Most recently this has included the desire to be enclosed and retreat from the outside noise of politics.

25 Samir Khalaf, 'Urban Design and the Recovery of Beirut,' in *Recovering Beirut: Urban Design and Post-War Reconstruction*, ed. Samir Khalaf and Philip S. Khouri (Leiden: Brill, 1993), p. 27.

26 Kaschadt, pp. 114–19.

27 Michel Foucault, *Panopticism* (Harmondsworth: Penguin, 1979), pp. 195–228.

28 Kevin D. Haggerty and Richard V. Ericson, 'The Surveillant Assemblage,' *The British Journal of Sociology* 51, no. 4 (2000): p. 605.

29 Gilles Deleuze, *Negotiations*, 1972–1990 (New York: Columbia University Press, 1995), pp. 177–82.

30 Walter Benjamin, *Charles Baudelaire: A Lyric Poet in the Era of High Capitalism*, trans. by Harry Zohn (London: Verso, 1997).

31 Haggerty and Ericson, p. 607.

32 Iain Borden, 'Thick Edge,' in *Intersections: Architectural Histories and Critical Theories*, ed. Iain Borden and Jane Rendell (London: Routledge, 2000), p. 228.

33 Ibid., p. 233.

34 Mazen Kerbaj and Jana Traboulsi, *You Here* (2009), in *Beirut: Mapping Security*, ed. Mona Fawaz, Mona Harb and Ahmed Gharbieh (Rotterdam: IBAR, 2009).

35 Judith Squires, 'Private Lives, Secluded Places: Privacy as Political Possibility,' *Environment and Planning D: Society and Space* 12, no. 4 (1994): p. 387.

36 Ibid., p. 395.

37 Ibid., p. 399. (My emphasis.)

38 Lennon and Whitford, p. 14.

39 Ibid., p. 10.

40 Edward W. Said, *Orientalism* (London: Penguin, 1995).

41 Derek Gregory, *The Colonial Present: Afghanistan, Palestine, and Iraq* (Malden, MA: Blackwell, 2004), p. 13.

42 Ibid., p. 17.

43 Displacement and social geography are discussed in more detail in *Bordering Practice 04*.

44 Gregory, p. 18.

45 For example, Michael Auon, who fought the Syrian army in Lebanon in the 1980s, is now an ally with Hezbollah and the Syrian (Assad) regime. Also, the Sunni community in Beirut are now allies with the Lebanese Forces, a Christian militia which was involved in battles against Muslim communities during the civil war period.

46 Daniel Meier, 'Borders, Boundaries and Identity Building in Lebanon: An Introduction,' *Mediterranean Politics* 18, no. 3 (2013): p. 353.

47 Judith Butler, 'Giving an Account of Oneself,' *Diacritics* 31, no. 4 (2001): p. 37.

48 Ibid., pp. 22, 24.

49 An-Nahar, 'Violent Clashes Centred in Corniche Mazraa, Al-Mat'haf Area Bring Back the Memories of Demarcation Lines' [in Arabic] [مواجهات دامية محورها كورنيش المزرعة، المتحف استعاد أجواء خطوط التماس ,' *An-Nahar*, 28 January 2007.

50 Over intimate images of her naked mother, the artist layers a letter in Arabic from her mother. The work explores the distance imposed by the displacement of the artist's family from Palestine to Beirut and the distance created by the artist's further displacement from Beirut to London.

51 Batchen, p. 459.

52 Ibid., p. 451.

53 Live/Taped Video Corridor, installation, 1969–70. Dorte Zbikowski, 'Bruce Nauman,' in *Ctrl Space*, pp. 64–7.

54 Harun Farocki, 'Harun Farocki,' in *Ctrl Space*, p. 422.

55 Klaus Theweleit, *Lettre International* no. 12 (1991). Quoted in Farocki, p. 423.

Bordering Practice 03: Translating

1   Joachim Ernst Berendt, *The Third Ear: On Listening to the World* (New York: Henry Holt, 1985), p. 32. Quoted in Michael Bull and Les Back, 'Introduction: Into Sound', in *The Auditory Culture Reader*, ed. Michael Bull and Les Back (Oxford: Berg, 2003), p. 2.

2   Bull and Back, p. 2.

3   Michel de Certeau, *The Practice of Everyday Life*, trans. Steven Rendall (Berkeley, CA: University of California Press, 1988), p. 129.

4   Brandon LaBelle, *Acoustic Territories: Sound Culture and Everyday Life* (London: Continuum, 2010), p. xvii.

5   Bull and Back, p. 8.

6   Steve Goodman, *Sonic Warfare: Sound, Affect, and the Ecology of Fear* (Cambridge, MA, and London: MIT, 2009), p. xiv.

7   Paul Moore, 'Sectarian Sound and Cultural Identity in Northern Ireland,' in *The Auditory Culture Reader*, p. 267.

8   Marleen De Witte, 'Accra's Sounds and Sacred Spaces,' *International Journal of Urban and Regional Research* 32, no. 3 (2008): p. 697.

9   Jonathan Sterne, *The Audible Past: Cultural Origins of Sound Reproduction* (Durham: Duke University Press, 2003), p. 11.

10 Ibid., pp. 10–13.

11 Edward W. Soja, *Postmodern Geographies: The Reassertion of Space in Critical Social Theory* (London: Verso, 1989), p. 78.

12 At the time of this research, Tarik al-Jdide had a Sunni majority and was under the political power of the Sunni Mustaqbal movement, whereas Mazraa was mixed between Sunni, Shiite and minority Christian but was under the political power of the Shiite Amal movement and Hezbollah.

13 See Introduction to this book, section 'Bordering as a Political–Sectarian Practice.'

14 Michael Bull, 'Soundscapes of the Car: A Critical Study of Automobile Habitation,' in *The Auditory Culture Reader*, p. 371.

15 Stanley Cohen and Laurie Taylor, *Escape Attempts: The Theory and Practice of Resistance to Everyday Life* (London: Routledge, 1976), p. 50. Quoted in Bull, p. 371.

16 Bull, p. 358.

17 Theodor W. Adorno and J. M. Bernstein, *The Culture Industry: Selected Essays on Mass Culture* (London: Routledge, 1991), p. 16. Quoted in Bull, pp. 371–2.

18 Charles Hirschkind, *The Ethical Soundscape: Cassette Sermons and Islamic Counterpublics* (New York: Columbia University Press, 2009), p. 6.

19 Ibid., p. 110.

20 Ibid., p. 106.

21 Jacques Attali et al., *Noise: The Political Economy of Music* (Minneapolis: University of Minnesota Press, 1985), p. 3.

22 C. Gurney (1999), 'Rattle and Hum: Gendered Accounts of Noise as a Pollutant: an Aural Sociology of Work and Home'. Paper presented to the Health and Safety Authority Conference, York, April. Quoted in Rowland Atkinson, 'Ecology of Sound: The Sonic Order of Urban Space,' *Urban Studies* 44, no. 10: p. 1905.

23 Ibid.

24 Bull and Back, p. 9.

25 Certeau, p. 37.

26 Sterne, p. 19.

27 Michael Gallagher and Jonathan Prior, 'Sonic Geographies: Exploring Phonographic Methods,' *Progress in Human Geography* 38, no. 2 (2013): p. 5.

28 Ibid.

29 Martin Chulov, 'Lebanon Protesters Clash with Army over New Hezbollah-Backed PM,' *Guardian*, 25 January 2011. Accessed 7 April 2014, www.theguardian.com/world/2011/jan/25/lebanon-protest-hezbollah-pm.

30 It is important to note that both the taxis and the street are controlled spaces. In the taxis, it is possible to see who controls the space and to engage with them directly – and they are not armed. In the street, however, it is not possible to see who is watching or on whose behalf they are operating – and in many cases they are armed.

31 Bull and Back, p. 9.

32 Sterne, pp. 14–15.

33 Ibid., p. 15. This litany is 'most clearly elaborated in Walter Ong *the presence of the word…*' among other writers. See ibid., p. 352.

34 Certeau, p. 37.

35 Paul Rodaway, *Sensuous Geographies: Body, Sense, and Place* (London: Routledge, 1994), p. 84.

36 Murray Schafer, *New Soundscape: A Handbook for the Modern Music Teacher* (London: Universal Edition, 1974).

37 A discussion of Schafer's work is in David W. Samuels et al., 'Soundscapes: Toward a Sounded Anthropology,' *Annual Review of Anthropology* 39 (2010): p. 333.

38 Sterne, p. 26.

39 For discussion on modernity in relation to vision, see *The Auditory Culture Reader* and also *The Audible Past*.

40 Sterne, p. 18. See also Samuels et al., p. 331.

41 Steven Connor, 'Edison's Teeth: Touching Hearing,' in *Hearing Cultures: Essays on Sound, Listening, and Modernity*, ed. Veit Erlmann (Oxford: Berg, 2004), p. 154.

42 W.J.T. Mitchell, *Iconology: Image, Text, Ideology* (Chicago: University of Chicago Press, 1986), p. 10.

43 Ibid., p. 27.

44 Ibid., p. 43.

45 Ludwig Wittgenstein, *The Blue and Brown Books* (New York: Harper, 1958), p. 89. Quoted in Mitchell, p. 15.

46 Mitchell, pp. 46–7.

47 Murray Schafer, 'Open Ears,' in *The Auditory Culture Reader*, p. 25.

48 Ibid.

49 Bull, pp. 371–2.

50 Walter Benjamin, *Illuminations*, edited and with an Introduction by Hannah Arendt; trans. Harry Zohn (London: Fontana, 1970), p. 72.

51 Ibid., p. 75.

52 Homi K. Bhabha, *The Location of Culture* (London: Routledge, 1994).

53 Felipe Hernández, *Bhabha for Architects* (London: Routledge, 2009), p. 36.

54 Achim Borchardt-Hume et al., *Walid Raad: Miraculous Beginnings* (London: Whitechapel Gallery, 2010), p. 23.

55 Benjamin, p. 71.

56 Jane Rendell, *Site-Writing: The Architecture of Art Criticism* (London: I.B. Tauris, 2010), p. 198.

57 Ibid., p. 203.

58 Ibid., p. 200.

59 Mike Crang and N. J. Thrift, *Thinking Space* (London: Routledge, 2000), p. 5.

60 Samuels et al., p. 338.

61 Connor, p. 154.

62 Sterne, p. 19.

Bordering Practice 04: Matching

1   Tim Cresswell, 'Mobilities II: Still,' *Progress in Human Geography* 36, no. 5 (2012): p. 651.

2   Ibid., p. 646.

3   Julie Peteet, *Landscape of Hope and Dispair: Palestinian Refugee Camps* (Philadelphia, PA: University of Pennsylvania Press, 2005), p. 24.

4   Ibid., p. 26.

5   Rosi Braidotti, *Nomadic Subjects: Embodiment and Sexual Difference in Contemporary Feminist Theory* (New York: Columbia University Press, 1994), p. 22.

6   Ibid., p. 21.

7   Ibid., p. 23.

8   Homi Bhabha, *The Location of Culture* (London: Routledge, 1994), pp. 158–60.

9   Fawwaz Traboulsi, *A History of Modern Lebanon* (London: Pluto Press, 2007), p. 192.

10 Aseel Sawalha, 'Healing the Wounds of the War: Placing the War-Displaced in Postwar Beirut', in *Wounded Cities: Destruction and Reconstruction in a Globalized World*, ed. Jane Schneider and Ida Susser (Oxford: Berg, 2003), p. 278.

11 *Oxford English Dictionary*, Oxford University Press. Accessed 19 March 2014, http://www.oed.com.

12 Ibid.

13 *Guardian* editorial, 'Gilad Shalit Exchange for Palestinian Prisoners – as It Happened,' *Guardian*, 18 October 2011. Accessed 14 November 2013, http://www.theguardian.com/world/blog/2011/oct/18/gilad-shalit-release-palestinians-live.

14 Juliet Mitchell, *Psychoanalysis and Feminism* (London: Penguin, 2000), pp. 375–6.

15 Alison Mountz, 'Refugees – Performing Distinction: Paradoxical Positionings of the Displaced,' in *Geographies of Mobilities: Practices, Spaces, Subjects*, ed. Tim Cresswell and Peter Merriman (Farnham: Ashgate, 2013), p. 255.

16 Ibid.

17 Ibid., p. 256.

18 Tim Cresswell and Peter Merriman, *Geographies of Mobilities: Practices, Spaces, Subjects* (Farnham: Ashgate, 2013), p. 5.

19 Tim Richardson, 'Borders and Mobilities: Introduction to the Special Issue,' *Mobilities* 8, no. 1 (2013): p. 1.

20 Jørgen Ole Bærenholdt, 'Governmobility: The Powers of Mobility,' *Mobilities* 8, no. 1 (2013): p. 20.

21 Richardson, p. 3.

22 David Bissell, 'Pointless Mobilities: Rethinking Proximity through the Loops of Neighbourhood,' *Mobilities* 8, no. 3 (2012): p. 351.

23 Ibid., pp. 349, 351.

24 Bærenholdt, pp. 20, 31.

25 Ibid., p. 25.

26 Ibid., p. 23.

27 Cresswell, pp. 648, 649.

28 Ibid., p. 648.

29 Claude Lévi-Strauss, *Structural Anthropology*, trans. Monique Layton (Chicago: University of Chicago Press, 1983), pp. 302–3.

30 Dana Mazraani, 'On Hay El Krad: A Kurdish Sunni Neighborhood in Bourj El Barajneh,' in *Narrating Beirut from Its Borderlines*, ed. Hiba Bou Akar and Mohamed Hafeda (Lebanon: Heinrich Böll Stiftung Middle East, 2011), pp. 58–85.

31 An exception is Greek Orthodoxy, in which both partners have to be Christians; see Joana Khoury, 'Mixed Marriage ... Love Transcends Sectarian Barriers [in Arabic] [الزواج المختلط حب يتخطى قيود الطوائف]', *An-Nahar*, 5 July 2007.

32 Layal Keiwan, 'Same Sect Partners. Why Are They Choosing Civil Marriage [in Arabic] [...أبناء الطائفة نفسها فلماذا يتزوجون مدنيا]', *An-Nahar*, 23 August 2011.

33 On 18 January 2013 the first civil marriage took place in Lebanon; the interesting thing about it is that it was not between a Christian and a Muslim but between a Sunni Muslim woman and a Shiite Muslim man. There is still no statute law, but the lawyer who prepared the marriage draft found an interpretation of the Lebanese decree; see Arwa Al-Husseini, 'Lebanon's First Civil Marriage,' *Now* (2013). Accessesd 14 July 2014, http://now.mmedia.me/lb/en/reportsfeatures/lebanons_first_civil_marriage. Civil marriage law proposals go back to the years 1910, 1926, 1951 and 1998, and each time they have faced opposition from the religious leaders of all sects. Layal Hadad, 'Optional Civil Marriage through the Power of Internet [in Arabic] [الزواج المدني الاختياري بقوة الآنترنت]', *Al-Akhbar*, 27 July 2007.

34 Keiwan.

35 Hassan Illeik, 'Hariri Unveils Future's New Slogans Via the Big Screen,' *Al-Akhbar*, 15 February 2013. Accessed 15 May 2014, english.Al-Akhbar.com/node/14985.

36 Bilal Khbeiz, 'The Excitement in Asking for Loss [in Arabic] [الحماسة في طلب الخسارة]', *An-Nahar*, 7 September 2007.

37 Sahar Mandour, '750 Thousand [in Arabic] [ألفا ٧٥٠]', *As-Safir*, 19 August 2013.

38 Hassan Krayem, 'The Lebanese Civil War and the Taif Agreement' (undated). Accessed 15 March 2014, ddc.aub.edu.lb/projects/pspa/conflict-resolution.html.

39 Farid El-Khazen, 'Coexistence: The Lebanese Experience.' *Opuslibani*. Accessed 17 March 2014, opuslibani.org.lb/Lebanon/coexistence.html.

40 There have been other displacements of communities to the country, such as those of Armenians and Kurds, and, since 2011, of Syrians.

41 Peteet, pp. 2–3.

42 Ibid., p. 6.

43 United Nations Relief and Works Agency for Palestine Refugees in the Near East, UNRWA. Accessed 17 May 2014, www.unrwa.org/where-we-work/lebanon.

44 Peteet, p. 6.

45 Georges Assaf and Rana El-Fil, 'Resolving the Issue of War Displacement in Lebanon,' *Forced Migration Review* no. 7 (7 April 2000). Accessed 15 December 2013, http://www.fmreview.org/FMRpdfs/FMR07/fmr7.10.pdf.

46 Sawalha, p. 271.

47 Samir Kassir, *The History of Beirut* [in Arabic] [تاريخ بيروت] (Beirut: Dar An-nahar, 2006), pp. 252–60.

48 Assaf and El-Fil, p. 31.

49 Nasser Yassin, 'Wp/18 Violent Urbanization and Homogenization of Space and Place: Reconstructing the Story of Sectarian Violence in Beirut,' *UNU-WIDER*, no. 2010/18 (2010): p. 1.

50 Sawalha, p. 276.

51 Internal Displacement Monitoring Centre, *Lebanon: No New Displacement but Causes of Past Conflicts Unresolved* (Geneva: Norwegian Refugee Council, 2010), p. 3.

52 Sawalha, p. 276.

53 Ibid., pp. 282–3.

54 Ibid., p. 288.

55 Internal Displacement Monitoring Centre, *Lebanon: No New Displacement but Causes of Past Conflicts Unresolved*, p. 5. See also 'The Reconstruction of Haret Hreik: Design Options for Improving the Livability of the Neighborhood,' ed. Mona Fawaz and Marwan Ghandour (Beirut: American University of Beirut – Reconstruction Unit at ARD, 2007), p. 1.

56 Ibid., p. 1.

57 Ibid., p. 8.

58 Franck Mermier, 'The Frontiers of Beirut: Some Anthropological Observations,' *Mediterranean Politics* 18, no. 3 (2013): p. 377.

59 Hiba Bou Akar, 'Contesting Beirut's Frontiers,' *City & Society* 24, no. 2 (2012): p. 150.

60 Pierre Atallah, 'The Maronite Council Expresses Concerns Regarding the Land and Identity [in Arabic] [الرابطة المارونية قلقة على الأرض والهوية: وزيرا الداخلية والعدل] ومصرف لبنان مسؤولون,' *An-Nahar*, 13 January 2011.

61 'Harb's Suggestion against Cantonizations and Sectarian Segregation [in Arabic] [اقتراح حرب للتصدي للكانتونات ومنع الفرز بين الطوائف],' *An-Nahar*, 5 January 2011.

62 Abass Assabagh, 'A Fatwa by Imam Shams E'ddine Issued 27 Years Ago Prohibiting Muslims from Selling Muslims' Lands to Non-Muslims Is Revived in Minister Boutrous Harb's Draft Law Aiming for Coexistence [in Arabic] [سبقت مشروع الوزير بطرس حرب وهدفها التعايش فتوى للإمام شمس الدين قبل ٢٧ عاما تحرم بيع الأراضي لغير المسلمين],' *An-Nahar*, 4 January 2011.

63 Hiba Bou Akar, 'Displacement, Politics, and Governance: Access to Low-Income Housing in a Beirut Suburb,' unpublished Master's thesis, MIT, 2005.

64 Martin Coward, 'Community as Heterogeneous Ensemble: Mostar and Multiculturalism,' *Alternatives: Global, Local, Political* 27, no. 1 (2002), p. 49.

65 Ibid., p. 37.

66 Mazen Kerbaj, 'Kerblog.' Accessed 19 March 2014, http://mazenkerblog.blogspot.co.uk/2006_07_01_archive.html.

67 See, for example, a description of these works in Rose Issa, *Ayman Baalbaki: Beirut Again and Again* (London: Beyond Art Production, 2011), pp. 70–81.

68 Edward W. Said, 'Reflections on Exile,' *Granta*, 13 (Autumn 1984), p. 159. Quoted in T. J. Demos, *The Migrant Image: The Art and Politics of Documentary During Global Crisis* (Durham: Duke University Press, 2013), p. 1.

69 Demos, *The Migrant Image*, p. 255.

70 Ibid., p. xv.

71 Ibid.

Epilogue: Temporal Bordering Practices of Resistance

1 Michel de Certeau, *The Practice of Everyday Life*, trans. Steven Rendall (Berkeley, CA: University of California Press, 1988), pp. xix, 36.

2 Ibid., p. xix.

3 Klas Borell, 'Terrorism and Everyday Life in Beirut 2005: Mental Reconstructions, Precautions and Normalization,' *Acta Sociologica 51*, no. 1 (2008): p. 67.

4 Bruno Latour, 'From Realpolitik to Dingopolitik,' in *Making Things Public: Atmospheres of Democracy*, ed. Bruno Latour and Peter Weibel (Cambridge, MA, and London: MIT, 2005), p. 40.

5 Fawwaz Traboulsi, 'Posters as Weapons,' in *Off the Wall: Political Posters of the Lebanese Civil War*, ed. Zeina Maasri (London: I.B. Tauris, 2009).

6 Latour, p. 40.

7 Giorgio Agamben, *What is An Apparatus? And Other Essays*, trans. David Kishik and Stefan Pedatella (California: Stanford University Press, 2009), pp. 41–5.

8 Teresa Pires do Rio Caldeira, *City of Walls: Crime, Segregation, and Citizenship in Sao Paulo* (Berkeley, CA: University of California Press, 2000), p. 19.

9 Noel Parker and Nick Vaughan-Williams, 'Lines in the Sand? Towards an Agenda for Critical Border Studies,' *Geopolitics* 14, no. 3 (2009): p. 583.

10 Joumana Al-Jabri, Reem Charif and Mohamad Hafeda, *Creative Refuge: Art-Based Research Workshops with Children in Palestinian Refugee Camps* (Beirut: Tadween Publishing, 2010).

11 Robert Smithson, 'The Spiral Jetty (1972),' in *Robert Smithson: The Collected Writings*, ed. Jack Flam (Berkeley, CA: University of California Press, 1996), pp. 143–53.

12 It is interesting to compare my movement to the gallery space to the movement of artists in the 1960s who shifted their site of work from the white gallery space to the outside world as an act of resistance and to rebel against the art world.

BIBLIOGRAPHY

Books and Journal Articles

Adorno, Theodor W. and J. M. Bernstein. *The Culture Industry: Selected Essays on Mass Culture.* London: Routledge, 1991.

Adwan, Charles. 'Municipal Elections of 1998 in Comparison to the Elections of 1963' [in Arabic] [الإنتخابات ١٩٦٣ عام انتخابات مرآة في ١٩٩٨ عام البلدية .] In *Municipal Elections in Lebanon in 1998: The Birth of Democracy in Civil Society* [in Arabic [لبنان في البلدية الانتخابات `١٩٩٨، مخاض الديمقراطية في بنى المجتمعات] Beirut: Al-Markaz Al-Lobnani Li'Dirasat, 1999.

Agamben, Giorgio. *State of Exception.* Chicago: University of Chicago Press, 2005.

Agamben, Giorgio. 'Security and Terror.' *Theory and Event* 5, no. 4, 2002.

Al-Aref, Usama. *The Memory of the Sand* [in Arabic] [الرمل ذاكرة]. Zalka: Mukhtarat, 2005.

Al-Jabri, Joumana, Reem Charif and Mohamad Hafeda. *Creative Refuge.* Beirut: Tadween Publishing, 2014.

Al-Jamal, Farouq. *That's Life* [in Arabic] [هيك الدنيا]. Beirut: Dar El-Elm Lil'Malayeen, 1997.

Atkinson, Rowland. 'Ecology of Sound: The Sonic Order of Urban Space.' *Urban Studies* 44, no. 10 (1 September 2007): 1905–17.

Attali, Jacques, Brian Massumi, Fredric Jameson and Susan McClary. *Noise: The Political Economy of Music.* Theory and History of Literature. Minneapolis: University of Minnesota Press, 1985.

Awan, Nishat, Tatjana Schneider and Jeremy Till. *Spatial Agency: Other Ways of Doing Architecture.* London: Routledge, 2013.

Bærenholdt, Jørgen Ole. 'Governmobility: The Powers of Mobility.' *Mobilities* 8, no. 1 (December 2013): 20-34.

Balibar, Etienne. 'The Border of Europe.' In Cosmopolitics: Thinking and Feeling beyond the Nation. Edited by Pheng Cheah and Bruce Robins. Minneapolis: University of Minnesota Press, 1998.

Batchen, Geoffrey. 'Guilty Pleasures.' In *Ctrl Space: Rhetorics of Surveillance from Bentham to Big Brother.* Edited by Thomas Y. Levin, Ursula Frohne and Peter Weibel, 447–59. Karlsruhe and London: ZKM and MIT, 2002.

Benjamin, Walter. *Illuminations.* Edited and with an introduction by Hannah Arendt. Translated by Harry Zohn. London: Fontana, 1970.

Benjamin, Walter. *Charles Baudelaire: A Lyric Poet in the Era of High Capitalism.* Translated by Harry Zohn. London: Verso, 1997.

Berendt, Joachim Ernst. *The Third Ear: On Listening to the World.* New York: Henry Holt, 1985.

Bhabha, Homi K. *The Location of Culture.* London: Routledge, 1994.

Bissell, David. 'Pointless Mobilities: Rethinking Proximity through the Loops of Neighbourhood.' *Mobilities* 8, no. 3 (2012): 349–67.

Borchardt-Hume, Achim, Zürich Kunsthalle, Paris Festival d'Automne à, and Gallery Whitechapel Art. *Walid Raad: Miraculous Beginnings.* London: Whitechapel Gallery, 2010.

Borden, Iain. 'Thick Edge.' In *Intersections: Architectural Histories and Critical Theories.* Edited by Iain Borden and Jane Rendell. London: Routledge, 2000.

Borell, Klas. 'Terrorism and Everyday Life in Beirut 2005: Mental Reconstructions, Precautions and Normalization.' *Acta Sociologica* 51, no. 1 (2008): 55-70.

Bou Akar, Hiba. 'Contesting Beirut's Frontiers.' *City & Society* 24, no. 2 (2012): 150–72.

Bou Akar, Hiba. 'Displacement, Politics, and Governance: Access to Low-Income Housing in a Beirut Suburb.' Unpublished Master's thesis, MIT, 2005.

Bou Akar, Hiba and Mohamad Hafeda. *Narrating Beirut from Its Borderlines.* Edited by Hiba Bou Akar and Mohamed Hafeda. Lebanon: Heinrich Böll Stiftung Middle East, 2011.

Bourriaud, Nicholas. 'Relational Aesthetics.' In *Participation.* Edited by Claire Bishop, London, 2006.

Braidotti, Rosi. *Nomadic Subjects: Embodiment and Sexual Difference in Contemporary Feminist Theory.* New York: Columbia University Press, 1994.

Brandell, Inga. *State Frontiers: Borders and Boundaries in the Middle East.* London: I.B. Tauris, 2006.

Bull, Michael. 'Soundscapes of the Car: A Critical Study of Automobile Habitation.' In *The Auditory Culture Reader.* Edited by Michael Bull and Les Back. Oxford: Berg, 2003.

Bull, Michael and Les Back. 'Introduction: Into Sound.' In *The Auditory Culture Reader.* Edited by Michael Bull and Les Back. Oxford: Berg, 2003.

Butler, Judith. 'Giving an Account of Oneself.' *Diacritics* 31, no. 4 (2001): 22–40.

Caldeira, Teresa Pires do Rio. *City of Walls: Crime, Segregation, and Citizenship in Sao Paulo.* Berkeley: University of California Press, 2000.

Carr, Edward Hallett. *What Is History?* Basingstoke: Palgrave, 2001.

Certeau, Michel de. *The Practice of Everyday Life.* Translated by Steven Rendall. Berkeley, CA: University of California Press, 1988.

Coaffee, Jon. 'Recasting the "Ring of Steel": Designing out Terrorism in the City of London?' In *Cities, War, and Terrorism: Towards an Urban Geopolitics.* Edited by Stephen Graham. pp. 276–96. Malden, MA: Blackwell, 2004.

Coaffee, Jon. *Terrorism, Risk and the Global City: Towards Urban Resilience.* Farnham: Ashgate, 2009.

Cohen, Stanley and Laurie Taylor. *Escape Attempts: The Theory and Practice of Resistance to Everyday Life.* London: Routledge, 1976.

Comment, Bernard. *The Panorama.* London: Reaktion, 1999.

Connor, Steven. 'Edison's Teeth: Touching Hearing.' In *Hearing Cultures: Essays on Sound, Listening, and Modernity.* Edited by Veit Erlmann. Oxford: Berg, 2004.

Conseil Municipal de la Ville de Beyrout. 'Guide De La Ville De

Beyrouth.' Beirut: AZ Societe d'Edition & Production, 2009-10.

Coward, Martin. 'Community as Heterogeneous Ensemble: Mostar and Multiculturalism.' *Alternatives: Global, Local, Political* 27, no. 1 (2002): 29-66.

Crang, Mike and N. J. Thrift. *Thinking Space*. London: Routledge, 2000.

Cresswell, Tim. 'Mobilities II: Still.' *Progress in Human Geography* 36, no. 5 (2012): 645-53.

Cresswell, Tim and Peter Merriman. *Geographies of Mobilities: Practices, Spaces, Subjects*. Farnham: Ashgate, 2013.

Deleuze, Gilles. *Negotiations, 1972-1990*. New York: Columbia University Press, 1995.

Demos, T. J. *The Migrant Image: The Art and Politics of Documentary During Global Crisis*. Durham: Duke University Press, 2013.

De Witte, Marleen. 'Accra's Sounds and Sacred Spaces.' *International Journal of Urban and Regional Research* 32, no. 3 (2008): 690-709.

Diener, Alexander C., and Joshua Hagen. *Borders: A Very Short Introduction*. New York: Oxford University Press, 2012.

Farocki, Harun. 'Harun Farocki.' In *Ctrl Space: Rhetorics of Surveillance from Bentham to Big Brother*. Edited by Thomas Y. Levin, Ursula Frohne and Peter Weibel. Karlsruhe and London: ZKM and MIT, 2002.

Farocki, Harun. 'Harun Farocki: I Believed to See Prisoners – Eye.' In *Ctrl Space: Rhetorics of Surveillance from Bentham to Big Brother*. Edited by Thomas Y. Levin, Ursula Frohne and Peter Weibel. Karlsruhe and London: ZKM and MIT, 2002.

Fawaz, Mona, Harb, Mona and Ahmad Gharbieh. *Beirut: Mapping Security*. Rotterdam: IBAR, 2009.

Fawaz, Mona and Marwan Ghadour. 'The Reconstruction of Haret Hreik: Design Options for Improving the Livability of the Neighborhood.' Beirut: American University of Beirut – Reconstruction Unit at ARD, 2007.

Fawaz, Mona, Harb, Mona and Ahmad Gharbieh. 'Living Beirut's Security Zones: An Investigation of the Modalities and Practice of Urban Security.' *City & Society* 24, no. 2 (2012): 173-95.

Foster, Hal. *The Return of the*

Real: The Avant-Garde at the End of the Century*. Cambridge, MA: MIT Press, 1996.

Foucault, Michel. *Panopticism*. Harmondsworth: Penguin, 1979.

Friedman, Susan Stanford. 'Mappings: Feminism and the Cultural Geographies of Encounter.' Princeton, NJ: Princeton University Press, 1998.

Gallagher, Michael and Jonathan Prior. 'Sonic Geographies: Exploring Phonographic Methods.' *Progress in Human Geography* 38, no. 2 (1 April 2014): 267-84.

Genberg, Daniel. 'Borders and Boundaries in Post-War Beirut.' In *Urban Ethnic Encounters: The Spatial Consequences*. Edited by Aygen Erdentug and Freek Colombijn. London: Routledge, 2002.

Geuss, Raymond. *The Idea of a Critical Theory: Habermas and the Frankfurt School*. Cambridge: Cambridge University Press, 1981.

Goodman, Steve. *Sonic Warfare: Sound, Affect, and the Ecology of Fear*. Cambridge, MA, and London: MIT, 2009.

Graham, Stephen. ed. *Cities, War, and Terrorism: Towards an Urban Geopolitics*. Malden, MA: Blackwell, 2004.

Graham, Stephen. 'Introduction: Cities, Warfare, and States of Emergency'. In *Cities, War, and Terrorism: Towards an Urban Geopolitics*. Edited by Stephen Graham. Malden, MA: Blackwell, 2004.

Gregory, Derek. *The Colonial Present: Afghanistan, Palestine, and Iraq*. Malden, MA: Blackwell, 2004.

Haggerty, Kevin D. and Richard V. Ericson. 'The Surveillant Assemblage.' *British Journal of Sociology* 51, no. 4 (2000): 605-22.

Hernández, Felipe. *Bhabha for Architects*. Thinkers for Architects. London: Routledge, 2009.

Hirschkind, Charles. *The Ethical Soundscape: Cassette Sermons and Islamic Counterpublics*. New York: Columbia University Press, 2009.

Hind, Dan. *The Return of the Public: Democracy, Power and the Case for Media Reform*. London: Verso, 2012.

Hottinger, Arnold. 'Zu'ama in Historical Perspective.' In *Politics in Lebanon*. Edited by Leonard Binder. New York: Wiley, 1996.

Issa, Rose. *Ayman Baalbaki: Beirut Agian and Again*. London: Beyond Art Production, 2011.

Jenkins, Keith. *Re-Thinking History*. London: Routledge, 2003.

Johnson, Michael. *Class & Client in Beirut: The Sunni Muslim Community and the Lebanese State, 1840-1985*. University of Michigan, Michigan: Ithaca Press, 1986.

Joseph, Suad. 'The Public/Private: The Imagined Boundary in the Imagined Nation/State/Community: The Lebanese Case.' *Feminist Review* 57 (1997): 73-92.

Kaschadt, Katrin. 'Of the Power of the Gaze.' In *Ctrl Space: Rhetorics of Surveillance from Bentham to Big Brother*. Edited by Thomas Y. Levin, Ursula Frohne and Peter Weibel. Karlsruhe and London: ZKM and MIT, 2002.

Kassir, Samir. *The History of Beirut* [in Arabic] [تاريخ بيروت]. Beirut: Dar An-nahar, 2006.

Kerbaj, Mazen and Jana Traboulsi. 'You Here' (2009). In *Beirut: Mapping Security*. Edited by Mona Fawaz, Mona Harb and Ahmad Gharbieh. Rotterdam: IBAR, 2009.

Khalaf, Samir. 'Primordial Ties and Politics in Lebanon.' *Middle Eastern Studies* 4, no. 3 (1968): 243-69.

Khalaf, Samir. 'Urban Design and the Recovery of Beirut.' In *Recovering Beirut: Urban Design and Post-War Reconstruction*. Edited by Samir Khalaf and Philip S. Khouri. 11-62. Leiden: Brill, 1993.

Khalaf, Samir. *Heart of Beirut: Reclaiming the Bourj*. London: Saqi, 2006.

Krayem, Hassan. 'Reading in the Meaning and the Results of Municipal Elections: Representation, Participation, and the Role of Social and Political Powers' [in Arabic] قراءة في معنى الإنتخابات البلدية و نتائجها: التمثيل والمشاركة ودور القوى الأجتماعية والسياسية. In *Municipal Elections in Lebanon in 1998: The Birth of Democracy in Civil Society* [in Arabic] [الانتخابات البلدية في لبنان ١٩٩٨،] [in Arabic] [مخاض الديمقراطية في بنى المجتمعات]. Beirut: Al-Markaz Al-Lobnani Li'Dirasat, 1999.

LaBelle, Brandon. *Acoustic Territories: Sound Culture and Everyday Life*. London: Continuum, 2010.

Latour, Bruno. 'From Realpolitik to Dingopolitik.' In *Making Things Public: Atmospheres of Democracy*. Edited by Bruno Latour and Pete Weibel. Cambridge, MA, and London: MIT, 2005.

Lefebvre, Henri. 'The Everyday and Everydayness.' In *Architecture of the Everyday*. Edited by Steven Harris and Deborah Berke. New York: Princeton Architectural Press, 1997.

Lefebvre, Henri. *The Production of Space*. Translated by Donald Nicholson-Smith. Oxford: Blackwell, 1991.

Lennon, Kathleen and Margaret Whitford. *Knowing the Difference: Feminist Perspectives in Epistemology*. London and New York: Routledge, 1994.

Lévi-Strauss, Claude. *Structural Anthropology*. Trans. Monique Layton. Chicago: University of Chicago Press, 1983.

Lyon, David. 'Technology vs. "Terrorism": Circuits of City Surveillance since September 11, 2001.' In *Cities, War, and Terrorism : Towards an Urban Geopolitics*. Edited by Stephen Graham. Malden, MA: Blackwell, 2004.

Lyon, David. *Theorizing Surveillance: The Panopticon and Beyond*. Cullompton, Devon: Willan Publishing, 2006.

Makdisi, Ussama. 'Reconstructing the Nation-State: The Modernity of Sectarianism in Lebanon.' *Middle East Report*, no. 200 (1996): 23–30.

Makdisi, Ussama Samir. *The Culture of Sectarianism: Community, History, and Violence in Nineteenth-Century Ottoman Lebanon*. Berkeley, CA: University of California Press, 2000.

Maktabi, Rania. 'The Lebanese Census of 1932 Revisited. Who Are the Lebanese?.' *British Journal of Middle Eastern Studies* 26, no. 2 (1999): 219–41.

Mazraani, Dana. 'On Hay El Krad: A Kurdish Sunni Neighborhood in Bourj El Barajneh.' In *Narrating Beirut from Its Borderlines*. Edited by Hiba Bou Akar and Mohamad Hafeda. Lebanon: Heinrich Böll Stiftung Middle East, 2011.

Meier, Daniel. 'Borders, Boundaries and Identity Building in Lebanon: An Introduction.' *Mediterranean Politics* 18, no. 3 (2013): 352–7.

Mermier, Franck. 'The Frontiers of Beirut: Some Anthropological Observations.' *Mediterranean Politics* 18, no. 3 (2013): 376–93.

Miessen, Markus. *The Nightmare of Participation*. Berlin: Sternberg Press, 2010.

Mitchell, Juliet. *Psychoanalysis and Feminism*. London: Penguin, 2000.

Mitchell, W.J.T. *Iconology: Image, Text, Ideology*. Chicago: University of Chicago Press, 1986.

Mitchell, W.J.T. 'Representation.' In *Critical Terms for Literary Study*. Edited by Frank Lentricchia and Thomas McLaughlin. Chicago: University of Chicago Press, 1990.

Monroe, Kristin. 'Being Mobile in Beirut.' *City & Society* 23, no. 1 (June 2011): 91–111.

Moore, Paul. 'Sectarian Sound and Cultural Identity in Northern Ireland.' In *The Auditory Culture Reader*. Edited by Michael Bull and Les Back. Oxford: Berg, 2003.

Mountz, Alison. 'Refugees – Performing Distinction: Paradoxical Positionings of the Displaced.' In *Geographies of Mobilities: Practices, Spaces, Subjects*. Edited by Tim Cresswell and Peter Merriman. Farnham: Ashgate, 2013.

Nasr, Salim. 'New Social Realities and Post-War Lebanon.' In *Recovering Beirut: Urban Design and Post-War Reconstruction*. Edited by Samir Khalaf and Philip S. Khouri. Leiden: Brill, 1993.

Nasr, Salim and Diane James. 'Roots of the Shi'i Movement.' *MERIP Reports*, no. 133 (1985): 10–16.

Parker, Noel and Nick Vaughan-Williams. 'Lines in the Sand? Towards an Agenda for Critical Border Studies.' *Geopolitics* 14, no. 3 (2009): 582–7.

Peteet, Julie. *Landscape of Hope and Dispair: Palestinian Refugee Camps*. Philadelphia: University of Pennsylvania Press, 2005.

Picard, Elizabeth. 'Beyrouth: La Gestion Nationale D'enjeux Locaux.' In *Municipalités et Pouvoirs Locaux au Liban*. Edited by Agnès Favier. Beyrouth: Cermoc, 2001.

Pile, Steve and N. J. Thrift. *Mapping the Subject: Geographies of Cultural Transformation*. London: Routledge, 1995.

Rendell, Jane. *Art and Architecture: A Place Between*. London: I.B. Tauris, 2006.

Rendell, Jane. *Site-Writing: The Architecture of Art Criticism*. London: I.B. Tauris, 2010.

Richardson, Tim. 'Borders and Mobilities: Introduction to the Special Issue.' *Mobilities* 8, no. 1 (2013): 1–6.

Rizk, Hoda. 'Beirut Mukhtar Elections in Light of Its Municipal Elections' [in Arabic] انتخابات بيروت الاختيارية في ضوء انتخاباتهاالبلدية]. In *Municipal Elections in Lebanon in 1998: The Birth of Democracy in Civil Society* [in Arabic] الانتخابات البلدية في لبنان ١٩٩٨، مخاض [الديمقراطية في بنى المجتمعات]. Beirut: Al-Markaz Al-Lobnani Li'Dirasat, 1999.

Rodaway, Paul. *Sensuous Geographies: Body, Sense, and Place*. London: Routledge, 1994.

Said, Edward W. *Orientalism*. London: Penguin, 1995.

Said, Edward W. 'Reflections on Exile.' *Granta* 13, Autumn 1984, 159.

Salloukh, Bassel F. 'The Limits of Electoral Engineering in Divided Societies: Elections in Postwar Lebanon.' *Canadian Journal of Political Science / Revue canadienne de science politique* 39, no. 3 (2006): 635–55.

Samuels, David W., Louise Meintjes, Ana Maria Ochoa and Thomas Porcello. 'Soundscapes: Toward a Sounded Anthropology.' *Annual Review of Anthropology* 39 (2010): 329–45.

Sawalha, Aseel. '"Healing the Wounds of the War": Placing the War-Displaced in Postwar Beirut.' In *Wounded Cities: Destruction and Reconstruction in a Globalized World*. Edited by Jane Schneider. Oxford: Berg, 2003.

Schafer, Murray. *New Soundscape: A Handbook for the Modern Music Teacher*. London: Universal Edition, 1974.

Schafer, Murray. 'Open Ears.' In *The Auditory Culture Reader*. Edited by Michael Bull and Les Back. Oxford: Berg, 2003.

Shedden, Leslie, Don Macgillivray, Allan Sekula, B. H. D. Buchloh, and Robert Wilkie. *Mining Photographs and Other Pictures, 1948-1968: A Selection from the Negative Archives of Shedden Studio, Glace Bay, Cape Breton*. Nova Scotia Series: Source Materials of the Contemporary Arts. (Halifax, NS: Press of the Nova Scotia College of Art and Design/ University College of Cape Breton Press, 1983

Sidaway, James D. 'The Return and Eclipse of Border Studies? Charting Agendas 1.' *Geopolitics* 16, no. 4 (2011): 969–76.

Silverman, Kaja. *The Threshold of the Visible World*. New York: Routledge, 1996.

276   Bibliography

Smithson, Robert. 'The Spiral Jetty (1972).' In *Robert Smithson: The Collected Writings*. Edited by Jack Flam. Berkeley, CA: University of California Press, 1996.

Soja, Edward W. *Postmodern Geographies: The Reassertion of Space in Critical Social Theory*. London: Verso, 1989.

Squires, J. 'Private Lives, Secluded Places: Privacy as Political Possibility.' *Environment and Planning D: Society and Space* 12, no. 4 (1994): 387–401.

Sterne, Jonathan. *The Audible Past: Cultural Origins of Sound Reproduction*. Durham: Duke University Press, 2003.

Theweleit, Klaus. *Lettre International* no. 12 (1991).

Traboulsi, Fawwaz. *A History of Modern Lebanon*. London: Pluto Press, 2007.

Traboulsi, Fawwaz. 'Posters as Weapons.' Foreword to *Off the Wall: Political Posters of the Lebanese Civil War*. Edited by Zeina Maasri. London: I.B. Tauris, 2009.

Vaughan-Williams, N. 'The UK Border Security Continuum: Virtual Biopolitics and the Simulation of the Sovereign Ban.' *Environment and Planning D: Society and Space* 28, no. 6 (2010): 1071–83.

Warner, Michael. *Publics and Counterpublics*. New York: Cambridge, 2002.

Weizman, Eyal. *Hollow Land: Israel's Architecture of Occupation*. London: Verso, 2007.

White, Hayden. *The Content of the Form: Narrative Discourse and Historical Representation*. Baltimore: John Hopkins University Press, 1987.

Wittgenstein, Ludwig. *The Blue and Brown Books*. New York: Harper & Brothers, 1958.

Wood, Denis and John Fels. *The Power of Maps*. New York: Guilford Press, 1992.

Wurzer, Wilhelm S. *Panorama: Philosophies of the Visible*. London: Continuum, 2002.

Yassin, Nasser 'Wp/18 Violent Urbanization and Homogenization of Space and Place: Reconstructing the Story of Sectarian Violence in Beirut.' *UNU-WIDER*, no. 2010/18 (2010).

Zbikowski, Dorte. 'Bruce Nauman.' In *Ctrl Space: Rhetorics of Surveillance*

from Bentham to Big Brother. Edited by Thomas Y. Levin, Ursula Frohne and Peter Weibel. Karlsruhe and London: ZKM and MIT, 2002.

Newspapers, Magazines and Essays (Print/Online)

Al-Husseini, Arwa. 'Lebanon's First Civil Marriage.' *Now* (2013). Accessed 14 July 2014, now.mmedia.me/lb/en/reportsfeatures/lebanons_first_civil_marriage.

An-Nahar. 'Violent Clashes Centred in Corniche Mazraa, Al-Mat'haf Area Bring Back the Memories of Demarcation Lines' [in Arabic] مواجهات دامية محورها كورنيش المزرعة، المتحف استعاد أجواء خطوط التماس] *An-Nahar*, 28 January 2007.

Arasoughly, Alia. 'Haunted Mothers in War in the Video of Mona Hatoum, Measures of Distance.' *The German-French Cultural Centre Ramallah* (2004). Accessed 11 July 2018, virtualgallery.birzeit.edu/media/artical?item=11712

Assabagh, Abass. 'A Fatwa by Imam Shams E'ddine Issued 27 Years Ago Prohibiting Muslims from Selling Muslims' Lands to Non-Muslims Is Revived in Minister Boutrous Harb's Draft Law Aiming for Coexistence' [in Arabic] سبق مشروع الوزير بطرس حرب] وهدفها التعايش فتوى للإمام شمس الدين قبل ٢٧ عاما تحرم بيع الأراضي لغير المسلمين]. *An-Nahar*, 4 January 2011.

Asfour, Lana. 'Lebanon and the Syrian Refugee Crisis.' *Open Democracy* (13 March 2014). Accessed 7 July 2014, opendemocracy.net/opensecurity/lana-asfour/lebanon-and-syrian-refugee-crisis.

As-Safir. 'Beirut after Dahyeh under Shelling and Armed Battles' [in Arabic] بيروت بعد الضاحية تحت القصف والعمليات] الحربية]. *As-Safir*, 7 February 1984.

Atallah, Pierre. 'Harb's Suggestion against Cantonizations and Sectarian Segregation' [in Arabic] اقتراح حرب] للتصدي للكانتونات ومنع الفرز بين الطوائف]. *An-Nahar*, 5 January 2011.

Atallah, Pierre. 'The Maronite Council Expresses Concerns Regarding the Land and Identity' [in Arabic] الرابطة] المارونية قلقة على الأرض والهوية: وزيرا الداخلية والعدل ومصرف لبنان مسؤولون] *An-Nahar*, 13 January 2011.

Chulov, Martin. 'Lebanon Protesters Clash with Army over New Hezbollah-Backed PM.' *Guardian* (25 January 2011). Accessed 7 April 2014, www.theguardian.com/world/2011/jan/25/lebanon-protest-hezbollah-pm.

El-Khazen, Farid. 'Coexistence: The Lebanese Experience.' *Opuslibani*. Accessed 17 March 2014, www.opuslibani.org.lb/Lebanon/coexistence.html.

El-Shoufi, Firas. 'Son of the Beik Is Beik and the Son of the Emir Is Emir' [in Arabic] ابن البيك بيك وابن المير مير]. *Al-Akhbar* (9 July 2013). Accessed 7 July 2014, Al-Akhbar.com/node/186743.

Fahs, Hani. 'Political Inheritance in Lebanon between Muslims and Christians' [in Arabic] من حلو إلى حلو] الوراثة السياسية في لبنان بين المسلمين والمسيحيين] *Al-Mustaqbal* (16 September 2003). Accessed 7 July 2014, www.almustaqbal.com/v4/Article.aspx?Type=np&Articleid=29391.

Guardian editorial. 'Gilad Shalit Exchange for Palestinian Prisoners – as It Happened.' *Guardian* (18 October 2011). Accessed 14 November 2013, www.theguardian.com/world/blog/2011/oct/18/gilad-shalit-release-palestinians-live.

Hadad, Layal. 'Optional Civil Marriage through the Power of Internet' [in Arabic] الزواج المدني الاختياري] بقوة الأنترنت]. *Al-Akhbar*, 27 July 2007.

Harb, Mona. 'Public Spaces and Spatial Practices: Claims from Beirut.' *Jadaliyya* (25 October 2013). Accessed 7 July 2014, www.jadaliyya.com/pages/index/14710/public-spaces-and-spatial-practices_claims-from-be.

Illeik, Hassan 'Hariri Unveils Future's New Slogans Via the Big Screen.' *Al-Akhbar* (15 February 2013). Accessed 15 May 2014, http://english.Al-Akhbar.com/node/14985.

Keiwan, Layal. 'Same Sect Partners:Why Are They Choosing Civil Marriage' [in Arabic] أبناء الطائفة] نفسها... فلماذا يتزوجون مدنيا]. *An-Nahar*, 23 August 2011.

Khbeiz, Bilal. 'The Excitement in Asking for Loss' [in Arabic] الحماسة في طلب الخسارة]. *An-Nahar*, 7 September 2007.

Khoury, Joana. 'Mixed Marriage ... Love Transcends Sectarian Barriers' [in Arabic] الزواج المختلط حب يتخطى قيود] الطوائف]. *An-Nahar*, 5 July 2007.

Krayem, Hassan. 'The Lebanese Civil War and the Taif Agreement.' (Undated). Accessed 15 March 2014, http://ddc.aub.edu.lb/projects/pspa/conflict-resolution.html.

Maktabi, Rima. 'Lebanon's Missing History: Why School Books Ignore the Past.' CNN (June 8, 2012). Accessed 07 July 2014, http://edition.cnn.com/2012/06/08/world/meast/lebanon-civil-war-history/index.html

Mandour, Sahar. '750 Thousand' [in Arabic] [أنفا ٧٥٠]. *As-Safir*, 19 August 2013.

Naoum, Sarkis. 'The Position this Day' [in Arabic] [دققوا جيدا ،الموقف اليوم]. *An-Nahar*, 11 May 2010. في تدني نسبة المقترعين.

Zeineddine, Cornelia 'Transformation and Challenges of the Lebanese Political Parties.' *Middle East Political and Economic Institute* (15 December 2013). Accessed 7 July 2014, mepei.com/in-focus/5419-transformation-and-challenges-of-the-lebanese-political-parties.

Reports

Arsenian Ekmekji, Arda. 'Confessionalism and Electoral Reform in Lebanon.' Aspen Institute (2012). Accessed 15 March 2014, aspeninstitute.org/publications/confessionalism-electoral-reform-lebanon/.

Assaf, Georges and Rana El-Fil. 'Resolving the Issue of War Displacement in Lebanon.' *Forced Migration Review* no. 7 (7 April 2000). Accessed 15 December 2013, fmreview.org/FMRpdfs/FMR07/fmr7.10.pdf.

Bassil, Najwa. 'The Mukhtars' State and their Role in Civil Peace in Lebanon' [in Arabic] واقع المختارين ودورهم. UNDP, 2012. في إرساء السلم الأهلي في لبنان.

Internal Displacement Monitoring Centre. 'Lebanon: No New Displacement but Causes of Past Conflicts Unresolved.' Geneva: Norwegian Refugee Council, 2010.

Salem, Paul. 'Electoral Law Reform in Lebanon: The Experience and Recommendations of the National Commission.' *Arab Reform Initiative* (27 July 2006). Accessed 15 March 2014, arab-reform.net/en/node/343.

Websites

'Conflict in Cities.' Accessed 15 March 2014, www.conflictincities.org.

Kerbaj, Mazen. 'Kerblog.' mazenkerblog.blogspot.co.uk. Accessed 19 March 2014, mazenkerblog.blogspot.co.uk/2006_07_01_archive.html.

Mosireen. 'Mosireen.' mosireen.org. Accessed 19 March 2014, mosireen.org.

Oxford University Press. 'Oxford English Dictionary'. Accessed 19 March 2014, oed.com.

United Nations Relief and Works Agency for Palestine Refugees in the Near East. 'Unrwa.' unrwa.org. Accessed 17 May 2014, unrwa.org/where-we-work/lebanon.

Films

Hadjithomas, Joana and Khalil Joreige. *Je Veux Voir*. 2007.

Hatoum, Mona. *Measures of Distance*. 1988.

Zaatari, Akram. *In This House*. 2005.

Zaatari, Akram. *Letter to a Refusing Pilot*. 2013.

LIST OF FIGURES

All figures © Mohamad Hafeda,
unless otherwise stated.

Introduction: Bordering Practices

Fig. 01
Demarcation line: Mazraa Main Road.

Fig. 02
Photographs taken from residents'
interior spaces, asking them about
the trace left of violent clashes and
physical borders, *The Trace Series*,
2010–present.

Fig. 03
Collage of the gradual intensification
and transformation of bordering
practices, 2005–8.

Fig. 04
Map of the civil war division across
the Green Line.

Fig. 05
Map of the administrative border of
Mazraa district and Municipal Beirut.

Fig. 06
Map of the geographic location
of residents involved in the
research project.

Bordering Practice 01: Hiding

Fig. 07
Map of the geographic location of
S.M. office.

Fig. 08
Text and stills from *The Chosen Two*,
2012–14.

Fig. 09
Diagram of the conceptual planning
of *The Chosen Two*.

Fig. 10
Document 1: Envelope.

Fig. 11
Material Evidence 1: Three booklets
referring to the mukhtar's law by
the Ottoman, French, and
Lebanese authorities.

Fig. 12
Mukhtar Nizar Syoufi office, 2010.

Fig. 13
Mukhtar Salim al-Madhoun
office, 2012.

Fig. 14
Mukhtar Ghareib Hassan office, 2010.

Fig. 15
Mukhtar Nqoula Razzouq office, 2011.

Fig. 16
Document 2: Beirut city guide.

Fig. 17
Material Evidence 2: Map of
municipal Beirut.

Fig. 18
Map of Beirut municipal limit.

Fig. 19
Map of Beirut's 12 districts.

Fig. 20
Map of Beirut Parliamentary
electoral division.

Fig. 21
Document 3: Lebanon 2010, guide
to municipalities and mukhtars.

Fig. 22
Material Evidence 3: no
information used.

Fig. 23
Document 4: personal registry
logbooks.

Fig. 24
Material Evidence 4: written
information on the edges of
the books.

Fig. 25
Document 5: Tarik al-Jdide health
and social guide.

Fig. 26
Material Evidence 5: tramway
photograph.

Fig. 27
Map of Beirut by Julius Loytved,
Danish Vice-Consul, 1876.

Fig. 28
Map of Beirut, Bureau Topographique
de L'Armée Française du Levant
(A.F.L.), 1922.

Fig. 29
Map of Beirut, Bureau Topographique
des Troupes Françaises du Levant
(T.F.L.), 1936.

Fig. 30
Map of Beirut, Annexe de
l'Institut Geographique National
au Levant, 1941.

Fig. 31
Map of Beirut, Service
Geographique, 1959.
© Service Geographique.

Fig. 32
Document 6: Beirut mukhtars'
council guide.

Fig. 33
photograph of Ibrahim al-Kaissi,
the head of the first mukhtars'
council in Beirut.

Fig. 34
Stills from *E'Dinyeh Heik*.
© TV Liban.

Fig. 35
The Chosen Two gallery installation
at Exposure 2012 exhibition,
Beirut Art Center, Beirut, 2012–13.
Photographs: George Haddad.
© Beirut Art Center.

Bordering Practice 02: Crossing

Fig. 36
Map of the geographic location of
S.H. and H.K. residence.

Fig. 37
Photographs taken from H.K. balcony
and from S.H. balcony, *At Her
Balcony*, 2010.

Fig. 38
An-Nahar newspaper article, 2007.
© An-Nahar.

Fig. 39
Photographs taken from H.K. and
S.H. balcony.

Fig. 40
Joana Hadjithomas and Khalil Joreige,
stills from *Je veux voir*, 2007. © Joana
Hadjithomas and Khalil Joreige.

Fig. 41
Mona Fawaz, Mona Harb and Ahmad
Gharbieh, Map of 'Visible security
mechanisms in municipal Beirut',
2009–10. © Mona Fawaz, Mona Harb
and Ahmad Gharbieh.

Fig. 42
H.K. living room, *At Her Balcony*, 2010.

Fig. 43
S.H. living room, *At Her Balcony*,
2010.

Fig. 44
Measuring distances, *At Her Balcony*,
2010.

Fig. 45
Mazen Kerbaj, *You here*, 2009.
© Mazen Kerbaj.

Fig. 46
Jana Traboulsi, *You here*, 2009.
© Jana Traboulsi.

Fig. 47
Mona Hatoum, *Measures of
Distance*, 1988. Colour video with
sound, 15 min 35 s. A Western Front
video production, Vancouver, 1988. ©
Mona Hatoum. Courtesy of the artist.

Fig. 48
At Her Balcony gallery installation
at Cities Methodologies exhibition,
UCL, London, 2010.

Fig. 49
Bruce Nauman, *Live/Taped Video
Corridor*, 1969–1970. © Bruce
Nauman, ARS, Courtesy Sperone
Westwater, New York.

Fig. 50
Mosireen, still from *Don't forget
and keep remembering: the cabinet
battle*, posted on 14 December, 2013.
© Mosireen.

Fig. 51
Map of the route taken when filming
and the location of my cameras in
exercise 1 & 2.

Fig. 52
Stills from 'Crossing', *At Her Balcony*,
2010.

Fig. 53
At Her Balcony gallery installation
at Cities Methodologies exhibition,
UCL, London, 2010.

Bordering Practice 03: Translating

Fig. 54
Map of H.H. vehicle location.

Fig. 55
Detail from *Presence and Absence
01*, 2011.

Fig. 56
Detail from *Presence and Absence
02*, 2011.

Fig. 57
Detail from *Presence and Absence
03*, 2011.

Fig. 58
Presence and Absence part of
*This is How Stories of Conflict
Circulate and Resonate* gallery
installation at Cities Methodologies
exhibition, UCL, London, 2011.

Fig. 59
Map of taxi and walking journey.

Fig. 60
Stills from Look, *Someone is Filming*,
2011.

Fig. 61
Map of the sounds recorded in the
walking journey.

Fig. 62
The Atlas Group in collaboration
with Walid Raad. *Missing Lebanese
Wars*, 1996–2002, plate 134. Archival
inkjet print, 33 × 25cm. Courtesy of
the artist and Sfeir-Semler Gallery
Beirut-Hamburg.

Fig. 63
Akram Zaatari, still from *In This
House*, 2005. © Akram Zaatari.

Fig. 64
*This is How Stories of Conflict
Circulate and Resonate* gallery
installation at Cities Methodologies
exhibition, UCL, London, 2011.

Bordering Practice 04: Matching

Fig. 65
Map of the geographic location of
R.G and L.G. houses.

Fig. 66
Photograph I taken in the lift of the
twin's childhood house, summer
1986, Beirut.

Fig. 67
Photographic survey of the floor and
ceiling plan of R.G and L.G. houses.

Fig. 68
Mazen Kerbaj, *My Life in a Bag*, 2006.
© Mazen Kerbaj.

Fig. 69
Ayman Baalbaki, *Bonjour Wadi
Abu Jamil*, 2006. © Ayman Baalbaki.

Fig. 70
Mona Hatoum, *Mobile Home*, 2005.
Furniture, household objects,
suitcases, galvanised steel barriers,
three electric motors and pulley
system. 119 × 220 × 600 cm (46¾ ×
86½ × 236¼ in.). © Mona Hatoum.
Courtesy Alexander and Bonin, New
York (Photo: Jason Mandella).

Fig. 71
Preparations to swap.

Fig. 72
Escape kits.

Fig. 73
Photographs of political leaders.

Fig. 74
Map of the husband's mobility
on streets.

Fig. 75
Iconic views.

Fig. 76
The route map drawn by R.G.

Fig. 77
The route map drawn by L.G.

Fig. 78
Stills from 'Finding Houses',
*The Twin Sisters are 'About to'
Swap Houses*, 2012.

Fig. 79
*The Twin Sisters are 'About to' Swap
Houses*, gallery installation at Cities
Methodologies exhibition, UCL,
London, 2012.

Fig. 80
Stills from 'Drawing the Route Map',
*The Twin Sisters are 'About to' Swap
Houses*, 2012.

Fig. 81
*The Twin Sisters are 'About to' Swap
Houses*, gallery installation at Cities
Methodologies exhibition, UCL,
London, 2012.

**Epilogue: Temporal Bordering
Practices of Resistance**

Fig. 82
Map of Mazraa and Tarik al-Jdide.

LIST OF INTERVIEWS

A.A.
(Beirut, January 2010)

I.A.
(Beirut, January 2010)

K.A.
(Beirut, January 2010)

W.A.
(Beirut, January 2010)

Amine al-Kurdi
(Beirut, January 2012)

Salim al-Madhoun
(Beirut, January 2012)

Youssef Bazzi
(Beirut, January 2010)

N.F.
(Beirut, January 2010)

L.G.
(Beirut, January 2010–12)

R.G.
(Beirut, January 2010–12)

Abed Ghalayini
(Beirut, January 2012)

Khalil Gebara
(Beirut, January 2012)

H.H.
(Beirut, January 2010)

I.H.
(Beirut, January 2010)

K.H.
(Beirut, January 2010)

S.H.
(Beirut, January 2010)

Ramzi Haidar
(Beirut, January 2010)

Ghareib Hassan
(Beirut, January 2010)

Ahmad Kaabour
(Beirut, January 2010)

F.M.
(Beirut, January 2011)

Nqoula Razzouq
(Beirut, January 2011)

Suleiman Riachi
(Beirut, January 2013)

S.1
(Beirut, January 2010)

S.2
(Beirut, January 2010)

S.3
(Beirut, January 2010)

H.S.
(Beirut, January 2010)

O.S.
(Beirut, January 2010)

Khalid Saghieh
(Beirut, January 2010)

Naji Shamil
(Beirut, December 2013)

Nizar Syoufi
(Beirut, January 2010)

T.1
(Beirut, January 2011)

T.2
(Beirut, January 2011)

T.3
(Beirut, January 2011)

Christine Tohme
(Beirut, January 2011)

Akram Zaatari
(Beirut, January 2011)

D.K.
(Beirut, January 2010)

M.R.
(Beirut, January 2010)

ACKNOWLEDGEMENTS

This book stems from my PhD in Architectural Design that I embarked on at the Bartlett School of Architecture, University College London (UCL), in September 2009. Throughout that long journey, many people became involved in the making of this project, without whom such an ambitious undertaking as a PhD and, later on, a book would have been impossible.

The first person I would like to say thank you to in this journey is my supervisor Jane Rendell. Jane's influence on my personal and intellectual development goes back to when I first read her work in 2003. Her intellectual impact continued after I met her in person, and she has also continued to inspire me on a personal level. Jane lives up to the ideas and the idealism she writes about, the person I met and the writer I read being one and the same. Her excitement about my research project, her encouragement of me, her care in allowing me to develop my own thinking and working method, and her ability to criticize my work without being destructive to the work process are remarkable, and I continue to learn from these academic and humane qualities and to incorporate them into my own work ethics. I am grateful for having worked with her, I hope this project stands up to what she hoped for from me, and I look forward to future collaboration.

Yeoryia Manolopoulou, my second supervisor, was the first person I met at the Bartlett and it was that meeting that encouraged me to take my research to the Bartlett environment. Yeoryia's feedback on the conceptual and material structure of the projects and installations has been incredible. In particular, her enthusiasm and encouragement are infectious, making everything feel possible and attainable. I am grateful for having worked with her too.

The research project would not have been possible without the financial support of several institutions. I would like to thank the Frederick Bonnart-Braunthal Trust for their generous scholarship to study for three years at UCL. Thank you also to the Global Supplementary Grant Program at the Open Society Foundations for their grant. The field trips and the realization of the projects and the gallery installations constituting this book would not have been possible without the support of the Graduate School fund at UCL and the Architecture Research Fund at the Bartlett – I wish to record my thanks for both schemes. A special thank you goes to the Research Unit 32 Art & Design: History, Practice & Theory at the School of Art, Architecture and Design, Leeds Beckett University, and to Simon Morris for supporting the colour printing of the book.

The project series and its associated gallery installations were developed through my engagement with several institutions and individuals. I am grateful to Urban Lab and Ben Campkin for organizing the Cities Methodologies exhibition at UCL, which I used as a platform over three consecutive years (2010–12) to develop and exhibit the first three installations. I am also thankful to the Beirut Art Center where I developed the last installation of the project series as part of the Exposure exhibition 2012. Thank you to the Arab Funds for Arts and Culture for their generous grant that allowed me to expand the ambitions of this research project and to plan further installations. I am grateful to the Heinrich Böll Foundation and for the invitation of my friend and colleague Hiba Bou Akar to contribute with her to the research project that led to the publication *Narrating Beirut from its Borderlines*. Part of the chapters of this book were previously published, I wish to say thank you to the editors of these journals and books who contributed to the development of my argument: M. Gamal Abdelmonem and Ruth Morrow of *Peripheries* (Routledge, 2013); Mona Fawaz, Ahmad Gharbieh, Nadine Bekdache and Abir Saksouk of *Practicing the Public* (As-Safir Daily, 2015); Ore Disu and Monika Umunna of *Open City Lagos* (Heinrich Böll Foundation Nigeria, 2016); Ben Campkin and Ger Duijzings of *Engaged Urbanism* (I.B. Tauris, 2016); and Doreen Bernath and Braden Engel of *This Thing Called Theory: Architecture and Culture* (Taylor & Francis, 2016).

I would like to express my thanks to those who contributed information and material about their work: to artists Akram Zaatari, Rabih Mroué, Ghsaasn Salhab, Joana Hadjithomas and Khalil Joreige, Mona Hatoum, Ayman Baalbaki, Mazen Kerbaj, Jana Traboulsi, Walid Raad, Mona Harb and Ahmad Gharbieh, and to Mona Fawaz and Dana Mazraani for sharing their maps. Thank you to Abigail Wood at SOAS, University of London for providing references on soundscape. Thank you to every person I interviewed/talked to about the political situation in Lebanon: Suleiman Riachi, Abed Ghalayini, Khalil Gebara, Khalid Sagheyeh, and Naji Shamil for his insightful information on his father Mohamad Shamil's work. Thank you to Ruth Morrow and Murray Fraser for their examination of the PhD and the critical comments they provided. Thank you to Rola Riachi for her Arabic translation, and to Virginia Rounding for her incredible editing and proofreading of the early version of the text. Thank you to Stephen Pigney for his thorough and eloquent editing and proofreading of this book.

I am grateful to I.B. Tauris for commissioning the book and to David Stonstreet for believing in it and for his editing and support throughout the process, as well as to David Campbell for managing the production of the book.

I am indebted to Marwan Kaabour, whose graphic design language and thoughts, and his assistance in the production of the artwork and this document, are outstanding and evident in these pages. Much love to Marwan and many thanks.

Friends and family operated as my editors, commentators, tutors, collaborators, and, above all, as providers of emotional support. I am indeed lucky for the new friendships I made at the Bartlett: thank you to Sophie Handler, Pilar Sanchez Beltran, Ricardo Agarez, Popi Iacovou, Tortsen Lange, Tilo Amhoff, Catalina Mejia, and Wesley Aelbrecht. Thank you to Lee Simmons and Dia Batal for the love they provide and for the time we have spent together that has never excluded discussions about the work, and to Samar Maakaroun for her solid and cheerful friendship. Thank you to Rawya Charif for being a family in London. From Beirut (and the Lebanese diaspora), thank you also to Mustafa al-Jundi for his valuable comments on the gallery installations, and to Nada Moumatz for her early comments on the PhD proposal and the writings that followed. Hiba Bou Akar has been a great support throughout the journey, reading and commenting on the text, I am grateful for her friendship and intellectual input. Thank you to Marwan Ghandour for his longstanding influence on my thinking and education, in particular because he introduced me to Mohamad Adra and Ikram Zaatari at Bawader Architects, who for years have acted as mentors and friends.

Thank you to my aunt Iman Bekdache and to Ahmad Kaabour for their love and support of me in pursuing my dream – much love goes to them.

Among the friends who have been a real family to me over many years, I am grateful to my childhood friend Lina Mikdashi: her thorough comments and editing of my text, particularly concerning the history and politics of Lebanon, are notable. Thank you to Reem Mikdashi for her friendship and for her availability to read and comment on my text at any time. Thank you to Rana Mikdashi for the enriching friendship throughout the years, and to Fatima Bashir, Roula Mikdashi, and Denise Kabani, all of whom I miss in my daily life.

I was lucky to have met Reem Charif just after I finished my undergraduate studies and at a time of self-searching. With Reem, friendship and productivity mix, and it is this mixture that led to our work at Febrik. Our lengthy discussions and feedback sessions, as well as her reading and editing of my work, have been of enormous influence on my self and on my work. I am grateful for her and I look forward to the future with her.

Rana, Hiba, and Sahar are sisters and friends, and the best of both are in them. It is their existence in life that gives meaning to my own, and it is through them that I make sense of the world. Their endless support, encouragement, and belief in what I am doing give me strength. Special gratitude goes to Rana who has been the backbone to me in this journey, and without her this document would not exist.

Much love and appreciation goes to my mother, Wafa, for whom I always dreamt of a better life that she is part of. And my deepest love and admiration is for my grandmother, Fayza, the most significant person of all.

I am fortunate that I met Gavin Smith: his engagement with my work and encouragement are motivating, but it is particularly his emotional support that I carry with me every day.

My final thanks go to every person who engaged with me in this research project, and mainly to the residents of Beirut who participated in the four projects making up the book chapters and who mostly remain anonymous in the pages of this document. They let me into their interior spaces and opened their personal lives, and it is from those intimate and concerned spaces that the narrative of this book unfolds in text, images and experiences of bordering.

INDEX

Numbers in **bold** denote figures or graphics

8 March bloc   5, 15, 89, 172, 180
14 March bloc   5, 15, 18, 89, 179

Achrafieh   62, 71, 82
administration, borders of   15, 20, 33–34, 36–101, 262
    see also *Chosen Two, The*
al-Aref, Usama   72
al-Kaissi, Ibrahim   **91**, 92, 94
al-Madhoun, Salim (mukhtar)   39–43, **42–43**, 47–100,
    58, 98–99
    see also *Chosen Two, The*
Amal movement (Shiite)   30, 67, 89, 117, 127
'Arab spring', and communication technology   148–149
arguilé, smoking of (as spatial practice)   22
At Her Balcony (project)   104–157, **106–107, 132–135,
    144–147, 152–155**
Atkinson, Rowland   176
Atlas Group, The (archival project)   200–201, **200**
Attali, Jacques   176

Baalbaki, Ayman   240, **240**
Bærenholdt, Jørgen Ole   230
balcony
    enclosure of 269n34
    as female space   117–118
        see also *At Her Balcony*
Balibar, Etienne   26
Barbour neighbourhood   60, 106, 117
barricades (as bordering practice)   22, **24**
Beirut
    administrative districts   64–66, **66**, 84–89
    elections in   58, 60, 64–67
    maps of   84–89
    1876 map of   84, **84**
    1922 map of   **85**, 85
    1936 map of   **86**
    1941 map of   86–87, **87**
    1959 map of   87–88, **88**
Beirut city guide   **61**, 64
Benjamin, Walter   97, 198–199, 202, 203
Bentham, Jeremy   131
Berri, Nabih   130, **244**, 269n22, 112, 113
Bhabha, Homi   199, 202, 225
binary
    hearing/seeing   181, 190–191
    public–private   138
    thinking as way of dealing with conflict   21, 170
Bissell, David   230
Bonjour Wadi Abu Jamil   240, 240
Borden, Iain   136
border practitioners, Beirut   21, **25**
bordering practices

beyond Lebanon   26–27
definition   21
as a critical method   21, 29–34, 114, 254
list of 24–25
narrating, as form of   27–29
negotiating, as a form of   27–29
overview 4–35
tactical   22–23
temporal aspects of   259–261
strategic   22–23
Borell, Klas   260
Boulevard Mazraa   *see* Mazraa Main Road
Bou Akar, Hiba   237
Bourriaud, Nicholas   28
Braidotti, Rosi   225
Butler, Judith   141

Caldeira, Teresa   28
cars, political speeches in   22
car, playing of music and religious material in   173–174
CCTV as visual surveillance device   114, 119, 122, 125, 148
checkpoint, as surveillance practice   14, **24**, 124
Chosen Two, The (project)   38–101, **50–51, 98–99, 101**
civil war   *see* Lebanese civil war 1975–90
coexistence, Lebanese concept of   226, 234, 238–239
coffee shops, use for surveillance   114, 122, 124
Corniche Mazraa   *see* Mazraa Main Road
confessional system (Lebanon)   57, 79, 235
    see also Taif agreement
Connor, Steven   191
Coward, Martin   238–239
Creswell, Tim   224, 229, 230
critical bordering practice   *see* bordering practices, as
    a critical method
'critical spatial practices' (Rendell)   21, 263
crossing, as bordering practice   *see* surveillance,
    borders of
Crossing Distances (part of *At Her Balcony* installation)
    145, 152–155, 156

de Certeau, Michel   21, 22–23, 28, 169, 178, 229
Deleuze, Gilles   131
Demos, T.J.   248–249
Deneuve, Catherine   120, 122, **123**
    see also *Je veux voir*
Derrida, Jacques   123, 191
dialectic
    of overhearing   198
    of politics and religion   18
    between sonic borders and bordering
        practices   178, 207
    of words and images   191–192
Diener, Alexander C.   26–27
displacement, borders of (project)   208–257

displacement
  in marriage   231–233
  as matching   248–249
  mobility of   228–229
  Norwegian Refugee Council report on (2010)   236
  as subject of art   239–240, 248–249
  short- vs. long-term   239, 241
  key spatial and temporal parameters of   230–231
  post-Syrian withdrawal   236
    see also Lebanese civil war
displacement as swapping   227–228
  see also Twin Sisters are 'about to' Swap Houses, The
distance and difference, negotiation of   140–141
  see also 'Panorama I'; 'Panorama II'; 'Panorama III'
Don't forget and keep remembering: the cabinet battle 149
Druze Progressive Socialist party   89

Edde, Raymond   237–238
E'Dinyeh Heik (TV programme)   39, 47–49, 91–95, **94**
elections, Beirut   58, 60, 64–67
El-Khazen, Farid   234
'enigmatic signifier' (Laplanche)   203
expressive, concept of   122–123

Fawaz, Harb and Gharbieh (on security and gender)
  117–118
    see also Mapping Security project
Febrik   262
fireworks, as bordering practice   22, **24**, 168
flaneur   95, 131
Foucault, Michel   131, 230
Forêt des Pins   see Pine Park
Foster, Hal   32
French mandate for Middle East   57, 81, 84
Friedman, Susan   28

'gaze', concept of (Lacan)   118–119, 136
gender, in balcony project   117–118, 139–140
    see also At Her Balcony
general strike (23 January 2007)   5, 15, 18, 89–90,
  108–109
'governmobility'   see Bærenholdt, Jørgen Ole
Green Line   18, **19**, 236
Gregory, Derek   140
Guide de la Ville de Beyrouth   see Beirut city guide
Gurney, Charles   176

Hadjithomas, Joana   120, **123**
Hagen, Joshua   26–27
Harb, Boutros   237–238
Harb law   see Harb, Boutros
Hariri, Rafic   15, 83, 131, **244, 255**
Hariri, Saad   233
Hassan, Ghareib (mukhtar)   52, **59**, 73
Hatoum, Mona   142, **143**, 240, **241**
hearing/seeing binary   181, 190–191
hearing vs. listening   190, 198
Hezbollah   15, 18, 66, 126, 179
hiding, as bordering practice   see administration,
  borders of

hiding, language of   100
Hirschkind, Charles   174
homogeneity
  of districts in Beirut   78, 224–225, 234, 237
  of politics   238–239
hubble-bubble   see arguilé

'imaginative geographies'   140
'in-between', artist's position of   33, 118, 262
interior/exterior borders   27, 118, 137, 156
In This House   **201**
    see also Zaatari, Akram
Israeli wars   234, 235, 236, 239–240
Israel
  occupation of south Lebanon   73, 89, 235
  use of sound bombs   170

Je veux voir   119, 122, **123**
Jenkins, Keith   29
Johnson, Christopher (on subtitles)   204
Joreige, Khalil   120, **123**
Joseph, Suad   118

Karim, Feryal   94
Khbeiz, Bilal   233
Kerbaj, Mazen   136, **137,** 240, **240**
Khalaf, Samir   58–59, 130
Krayem, Hassan   57, 58, 50, 78
Kurds, Lebanese   232

land sales, restrictions on   237–238
Latour, Bruno   260–261
Lebanese civil war 1975–90   18, 45
  displacement and   235
  demographic changes caused by 71–72, 225, 235
  postwar reconstruction   235, 238
Lefebvre, Henri   21, 23, 47
Letter to a Refusing Pilot 201
    see also Zaatari, Akram
Lévi-Strauss, Claude   231–232
Live/Taped Video Corridor   148, **149**
Look, Someone is Filming   168, 171, **182–189**, 192–193,
  198, 202–205, 207
Loytved, Julius   84

Mandour, Sahar   233
Makdisi, Ussama   18
Mapping Security project   124–126, **125**
marriage, mixed-faith   232–233, 238
matching, as bordering practice   see displacement,
  border of
May 2008 clashes   110, 126, 131, 211, 236
Mazraa district (Beirut)
  early years of   62–63, 86
  administrative borders of   **30**, 44
  Christian/Muslim coexistence in   71
  loose definition of   64
  mukhtars in   58–60
  change in population of   69–70
  as site of research   30–31, **32**
  on 1919 and 1922 maps   85, **85**

on 1941 map   86, **86**
on 1962 map   88, **88**
Mazraa Main Road (Corniche Mazraa)
    in *At Her Balcony* installation **106–107**
        see also *At Her Balcony*
    creation of in 1950s   87, **88**
    dividing line with Tarik
        al-Jdide   82–84
    general strike and   89–90
    sectors of   64
    as site of project   **4**, 5, 30–31
Mazraat el-Arab   85
    see also Mazraa
Measures of Distances   142, **143**
    see also Hatoum, Mona
Measuring distances, *At Her Balcony*   **132–135**,
    144–147, 156
Mermier, Frank   72–73, 78, 237
militias   *see* political party militias
Mitchell, Juliet   228
Mitchell, W.J.T. (on representation)   45–46, 94, 191–192
Mobile Home   240, **241**
    see also Hatoum, Mona
mobility, as spatial practice   229, 230
    see also Bærenholdt, Jørgen Ole
Mohafazat districts   64
Mosireen   149, **149**
motorcycles, use in surveillance and bordering
    114, 126, 130, 168
Mountz, Alison   229
Mourabitoun party   89
muhajar   *see* war-displaced people
mukhtar, definition and role   48–49, 54–57
    as border practitioner   52, 95–100
    council guide   **91**
    offices   **58**, **59**
municipal elections, Beirut   60, 64–65, 265n35
Mustaqbal movement (Sunnis)   15, 30, 59, 66, 89, 176,
    269n23
Mutasarrifiya   59
My Life in a Bag   **240**, 240

narrating, as form of bordering practice   27–29, 47
    see also *Chosen Two, The*
Nauman, Bruce   148, **149**
negotiating, as form of bordering practice   27–29
noise   *see* Atkinson, Rowland; Attali, Jacques; Gurney,
    Charles; songs, as bordering practice; 'sonic crossing';
    'sonic warfare'; sound, borders of; sound recordings

Ottomans
    rule in Lebanon   57, 59
    mukhtar's rule book   53, 54, 57
overhearing   168, 198, 207
'Overhearing' (research exercise)   179–198
    see also *Look, Someone is Filming*

Palestinians, in Lebanon   83, 234–235, 236
panopticon (as space for observation)   114–115, 131
panorama (as space for observation)   114–115, 117
'Panorama I'   116–126, **120–121**

'Panorama II'   126–141, **128–129**
'Panorama III'   142–156, **152–155**
Panorama: Philosophies of the Visible   122
Parker, Noel   26
Peteet, Julie   224–225, 227
photography, use in surveillance   115
    ethical concerns of   148
    see also CCTV
Pile, Steve   27, 32
Pine Park   85, 86
political inheritance (Lebanon)   58–59
political party militias, surveillance practices of   124,
    125–126, 127, 131, 179
political-sectarian
    affiliations, Beirut   140, 168
    conflict, as bordering practice   259, 261
    displays in taxis   192
    sonic practices (songs and speeches)   168, 171,
        173, 180
    structuring of life in Beirut   233
        see also coexistence, Lebanese concept of;
        confessional system (Lebanon); Lebanese
        civil war 1975–90; *Look Someone is Filming*;
        marriage, mixed-faith; sectarianism, in
        Lebanese context; Sunni–Shiite tensions;
posters, as bordering practice   22, **24**
power relationship and spatial practices   21
Presence and Absence   168, 171, **176–177**, 192, 207
Presence and Absence 01   **162–163**
Presence and Absence 02   **164–165**
Presence and Absence 03   **166–167**
    see also *This is How Stories of Conflict Circulate
        and Resonate*
production of space theory   *see* Lefebvre
Pullan, Wendy   79

Raad, Walid   200–201, **200**
Rahbani brothers   95
Razzouq, Nqoula (mukhtar)   52, **59**, 66, 71–72, 76, 94
relational aesthetics   28
Rendell, Jane   21, 203
representation, definition of   45–46
    see also Mitchell, W.J.T.
research ethics in project   32–33
resistance
    art as form of   21, 259, 272n12
    bordering practices as modes of   14, 21
    negotiating as mode of   28
    passive and active modes of   14
    social media and   148–149
    sounds as form of   178
    temporal bordering practices of   258–264
Rizk, Hoda   71
Rue d'Alsace Lorraine   85, 86–87
Rue de l'Orpheline Musulman   86, 87
Rue du Parc   87
Rue Fouad   87
Rue Mazraa   86, 89
Rue Salim Bustani (later Tarik al-Jdide road)   86, 88, **88**
Rue Zraik   87

Said, Edward   140, 248
Salloukh, Bassel   66
Sawalha, Aseel   225, 236
Schafer, Murray   190, 198
'Schizophonia'   190
sectarianism, in Lebanese context   18, 235
        see also *Taifiyya*
security forces, private   124
security measures, Beirut (list)   124–125, **125**
'seeing' as concept   122
Sekula, Allan   115
Shamil, Mohamad   47, 92–93
Shams E'ddine, Mohamad Mahdi   238
Shatila refugee camp   90
Shiites, urbanization of   73
Silverman, Kaja   118
Soja, Edward   23, 26, 171, 207
songs, as bordering practice   20, 22, 168, 170, 173–175
'sonic warfare'   168, 170
        see also sound, borders of
'sonic crossing'   175
sound, in production of borders   *see* sound, borders of
sound, borders of   15, 20, 33, 34, 158–207, 262
sound recordings
        use in project, rationale for   181, 190
        transcription and   187
        temporal and spatial aspect of   204
Soundscapes of the Car   173
space   bordering practices and   22
        see also Lefebvre, Henri
spatial practices
        administrative and political processes as   47, 96
        of artist-researcher   45, 116
        in creation of new spatial reality   205
        overview   22–23
        photography as   156
        of refugees and migrants   224
        self-censoring of   207
        sonic   168
        of surveillance   115–116
        as tactic and strategy   22, 26
        translation as   169, 199
                see also 'critical spatial practices';
                De Certeau, Michel; displacement; mobility,
                as spatial practice; power relationship and
                spatial practices
Squires, Judith   137–136
Sterne, Jonathan   171, 178
stillness, as part of mobility practices   230–231
subjectivity
        of artist in site   32
        of borders 27
        of displacement and mobility   248–249
        in hearing   171, 175, 181
        in visual perception   122
surveillance
        borders of   15, 20, 33–34, 102–157
        domesticated   124–126
        mechanisms of   114
        different kinds of   123

as threat vs. security   139
Sunni–Shiite tensions   15, 71, 73, 89–90, 236–237
Syoufi, Nizar (Muhktar)   52, **58**, 89,
Syria
        civil war   236, 263
        domination of Lebanese politics   65
        tension along border   236
        withdrawal of troops from Lebanon   15, 236

Taaif agreement   66, 78–79
Taifiyya (sectarianism)   18 (definition)
Tarik al-Jdide, Beirut
        administrative borders of   44
        early development   81, 86, 87–88
        Al-Aref work on   72
        Christians vs Muslims in   72
        health and social guide   **80**
        imprecision of definition   64
        mukhtars in   59
        on 1876 map   86, **85**
        on 1962 map   88
        as site of research   30, **32**
taxi drivers, bordering practices and   *see This is
        How Stories of Conflict Circulate and Resonate*
        (project); translating, as bordering practice
Temporal bordering practices of resistance   258–264
temporality
        of language   204
        of mobility and borders   230
        of sound   169–170
        of sound recordings   204
        see also Temporal bordering practices of resistance
This is How Stories of Conflict Circulate and Resonate
        (project)   158–207, **162–167, 206**
        see also sound, borders of
Thrift, Nigel   27, 32
Traboulsi, Jana   136–137, **137**
tramway (train), Beirut   **80**, 81, 85–86
'translatability'   203
translating, as bordering practice 169, 199, 202–203
        see also sound, borders of
translation of language   97, 100, 199–203
'triple dialectic'   23, 26
        see also Soja, Edward
Twin Sisters are 'About to' Swap Houses, The (research
        project)   208–257, **210, 212–223, 250–253, 255,
        256–257**

untranslatability between languages   98, 199
'urbicide'   238–239

Vaughan-Williams, Nick   26
war-displaced people *muhajar* (Lebanon) 226
Wittgenstein, Ludwig   192
Wurzer, Wilhelm S.   122–123

Yahya, Maha   52

Zaatari, Akram   201–202, **201**
zawaj al-mukhtalat   see marriage, mixed-faith

Published in 2019 by
I.B.Tauris & Co. Ltd
London · New York
www.ibtauris.com

Book design by Marwan Kaabour
Cover design by Adriana Brioso
Cover image © Mohamad Hafeda, still from *The Chosen Two*, 2012–14.

References to websites were correct at the time of writing.

HB ISBN: 978-1-7883-1253-0
PB ISBN: 978-1-8386-0377-9
eISBN: 978-1-78831-984-3
ePDF: 978-1-78831-985-0

A full CIP record for this book is available from the British Library

A full CIP record is available from the Library of Congress

Library of Congress Catalog Card Number: available